Nume...

Tests

FOR

DUMMIES®

Numeracy Tests FOR DUMMIES®

by Colin Beveridge

A John Wiley and Sons, Ltd, Publication

Numeracy Tests For Dummies®

Published by
John Wiley & Sons, Ltd
The Atrium
Southern Gate
Chichester
West Sussex
PO19 8SQ
England

Email (for orders and customer service enquires): cs-books@wiley.co.uk

Visit our home page on www.wiley.com

For general information on our other products and services, please contact our Customer Care Department within the U.S. at 877-762-2974, outside the U.S. at 317-572-3993, or fax 317-572-4002.

For technical support, please visit www.wiley.com/techsupport.

Wiley also publishes its books in a variety of electronic formats and by print-on-demand. Some content that appears in standard print versions of this book may not be available in other formats. For more information about Wiley products, visit us at www.wiley.com.

British Library Cataloguing in Publication Data: A catalogue record for this book is available from the British Library

ISBN: 978-1-119-95318-0 (paperback), 978-1-119-95402-6 (ebook), 978-1-119-95403-3 (ebook), 978-1-119-95404-0 (ebook)

Printed and bound in Great Britain by TJ International, Padstow, Cornwall

10 9 8 7 6 5 4 3 2 1

About the Author

Colin Beveridge is a maths confidence coach for Flying Colours Maths, author of *Basic Maths For Dummies* and co-author of the *Little Algebra Book*.

He holds a PhD in Mathematics from the University of St Andrews and worked for several years on NASA's Living With A Star project at Montana State University, where he came up with an equation which is named after him. It's used to help save the world from being destroyed by solar flares. So far so good.

He became tired of the glamour of academia and returned to the UK to concentrate on helping students come to terms with maths and show that not all mathematicians are boring nerds; some are exciting, relatively well-adjusted nerds.

Colin lives in Poole, Dorset with an espresso pot, several guitars and nothing to prove. Feel free to visit his website at www.flyingcoloursmaths.co.uk or follow him on Twitter at www.twitter.com/icecolbeveridge.

Dedication

For my students and teachers, past and present.

Author's Acknowledgements

I'm very grateful to the team at Dummies Towers for their help and guidance, especially my editors Rachael Chilvers and Mike Baker.

The Little Red Roaster coffee shop in Parkstone provided the enormous quantities of excellent coffee needed to turn half-baked ideas into a fully-formed book; without Martin Stellar's hospitality and flakey internet connection, it would have taken twice as long to write. I'm thankful to the students who helped me to shape this book, especially Julie Carter, Phil Jewell and Rebecca Murray.

And as always, I thank my parents – Linda Hendren and Ken Beveridge – for their endless support and encouragement.

Publisher's Acknowledgements

We're proud of this book; please send us your comments through our Dummies online registration form located at www.dummies.com/register/.

Some of the people who helped bring this book to market include the following:

Commissioning, Editorial, and Media Development

Project Editor: Rachael Chilvers

Commissioning Editor: Mike Baker

Assistant Editor: Ben Kemble

Technical Editors: Sam Harrison and Giles Webberley

Proofreader: James Harrison

Production Manager: Daniel Mersey

Publisher: David Palmer

Cover Photo: © iStock / CTR design LLC

Cartoons: Ed McLachlan

Composition Services

Project Coordinator: Kristie Rees

Layout and Graphics: Sennett Vaughan Johnson, Lavonne Roberts, Erin Zeltner

Proofreader: Lindsay Amones

Indexer: BIM Indexing & Proofreading Services

Publishing and Editorial for Consumer Dummies

Kathleen Nebenhaus, Vice President and Executive Publisher

Kristin Ferguson-Wagstaffe, Product Development Director

Ensley Eikenburg, Associate Publisher, Travel

Kelly Regan, Editorial Director, Travel

Publishing for Technology Dummies

Andy Cummings, Vice President and Publisher

Composition Services

Debbie Stailey, Director of Composition Services

Contents at a Glance

Table of Contents

Introduction

*H*i, I'm Colin, and I want maths to be easy for you.

I don't want to turn you into a geek like me – I couldn't if I tried. I don't want to cram maths down your throat, either – that would be pretty rude.

All I want to do is help you learn enough maths to do well in your numeracy test and to feel confident tackling the kinds of maths problems that will come up in your future career and/or studies.

As you work through this book, answering the questions will get quicker and easier with time and practice, and you'll be in great shape for your numeracy test. Once you have that, you may never have to do another maths test again! Here's hoping!

I'd love to hear how you get on. The best way to catch me is on Twitter (I'm `http://twitter.com/icecolbeveridge`) – I'll read your news and get back to you if I can!

About This Book

This book is for you if you have to take a numeracy test in order to follow your chosen career path or to qualify for further study.

I take you through the maths you need to know to do well in these tests and try to help you understand how it all fits together.

Maths might sometimes look like a chaotic system of funny symbols and bizarre rules, but it's actually a very neat and concise way to communicate information.

I break down maths into smaller, simpler parts that I hope you'll understand.

Among other things, I cover the following in this book:

- ✔ **Preparing for your test** – both for studying and for keeping yourself calm while you sit it.
- ✔ **Working with whole numbers** – the 'big four' of adding, subtracting, multiplying and dividing are pretty much the key to doing well in numeracy tests.
- ✔ **Handling maths on paper** – the dreaded 'mental arithmetic' questions don't have to be dreadful!
- ✔ **Dealing with decimals and fractions** – these are easier than they seem, honestly! You already use decimals every time you do anything with money, and you only need to know a few fraction rules.
- ✔ **Making sense of measurements** – you may have a head start here! If you've ever used a scale, a clock or a ruler, you have some idea of how measurements work.
- ✔ **Getting on top of graphs and tables** – reading data in a neat table or graph is normally easier than from a raw, disorganised list. Once you figure out the rules, you're off to the races!

That sounds like fun, doesn't it?

Conventions Used in This Book

I keep the conventions to a minimum in this book. Here are the ones I use:

- ✔ I use *italics* for emphasis or to highlight new words or phrases.
- ✔ **Boldfaced text** indicates key words in bulleted lists or the key steps of action lists.
- ✔ `Monotype font` is used for Internet and email addresses.

Foolish Assumptions

Making assumptions is always a risky business, but knowing where I'm coming from may put you at ease. So, in writing this book, I assume that:

- ✔ You know how to count and are familiar with the basic maths symbols.
- ✔ You understand the idea of money and changing a banknote for an equivalent value of coins or smaller notes.
- ✔ You know what the basic shapes look like.
- ✔ You're prepared to think fairly hard about maths and want either to pass a numeracy qualification or to simply brush up on your maths skills.

How this Book is Organised

Like all *For Dummies* books, *Numeracy Tests For Dummies* is a reference book, and each topic is allotted its own part in the book. Within each part are individual chapters relating specifically to the topic in question.

Part 1: Preparing for Your Numeracy Test

Part I is all about setting yourself up so that when you sit your exam you'll find it relatively easy to stay calm and show what you can do.

You'll learn about the various types of numeracy tests, what's in them and why you need to sit one, as well as how to prepare properly and what you need to do on test day.

Part II: A Whistle-Stop Tour of the Maths You Need

This part is a quick but thorough guide to all the maths you need to know for your numeracy test. I cover:

- **Working with whole numbers** – the building blocks of maths and really, the key to doing well in any numeracy test.

- **Dealing with decimals, fractions and percentages** – a traditional stumbling block, but I show you how to deal with them quickly and confidently.

- **Making sense of measures** – nothing is particularly difficult about working with measurements (such as kilograms, miles and litres) compared to working with real numbers: all you need to remember is how to convert between units and you're most of the way there.

- **Getting to grips with graphs and statistics** – once you nail the vocabulary and remember how to work out the different types of average, you'll know pretty much all you need to.

- **Handling sums in your head** – many numeracy tests have a non-calculator component, in which you have to work out the sums on paper or a whiteboard. I take you through some of the tricks of the trade for doing well in this type of test.

Part III: Practice Tests

Part III is all about checking what you know! In this part, I give you a whole range of tests on the various levels and topics so you can figure out what you can do already, and what you need to spend a bit more time studying.

The tests are followed by worked answers, where I explain how I reached the solution I came up with.

Part IV: The Part of Tens

All *For Dummies* books finish with 'The Part of Tens', a bunch of lists full of practical tips to help you manage the material in the rest of the book.

I run you through ways of calming down and some ideas for remembering your number facts. I show you how to deal with some of the tougher questions examiners may set, and I offer some exam-technique tips so you can get in there and ace it.

Icons Used in This Book

Here are the icons I use to draw your attention to particularly noteworthy paragraphs:

Theories are fine, but anything marked with a Tip icon in this book tells you something practical to help you get to the right answer. These are the tricks of the mathematical trade.

Paragraphs marked with the Remember icon contain the key takeaways from the book and the essence of each subject.

The Warning icon highlights errors and mistakes that can cost you marks or your sanity, or both.

You can skip anything marked with the Technical Stuff icon without missing out on the main message, but you may find the information useful for a deeper understanding of the subject.

Where to Go from Here

Now, no two numeracy exams are the same, and the different tests range over quite different types of content. Before you start studying a section, it's a good idea to make sure it's part of the test you're working towards! Head to Chapter 1 for an explanation of what you're likely to find in each test. If you're in a hurry to see where you are, you may want to jump straight into the tests in Chapters 9–13. On the other hand, if you have plenty of time before you start the exam, you may prefer to start with Chapter 2 and set yourself up with a detailed study plan.

You can also use the index and Table of Contents to find the areas you want to study. This book is a reference – keep it with your maths kit and turn to it whenever you have something you want to look up!

I wish you the very best in your numeracy exam, and hope this book helps you to get the best mark you can. Good luck!

Part I
Preparing for Your Numeracy Test

'Before we start on the numeracy
tests, I hope you're not feeling too nervous.'

In this part . . .

Whatever kind of numeracy test you're taking, you need a solid plan of action for studying and for doing well in the exam. These chapters give you an idea of what each type of numeracy test involves, ways you can organise yourself to give yourself the best chance, and suggestions for how to handle exam day so you can make the most of your time in the test.

Chapter 1

Getting Started

*B*efore you really get stuck into this book, I want to ask you a favour, especially if you're someone who often says 'I'm no good at maths' or 'Maths scares the beejeezus out of me'.

I'd like you to start talking positively about maths. I don't mean you have to say 'I'm a super-genius and I'm going to win the next series of *Countdown!*' (although that's not a bad ambition). Whenever you're next tempted to say 'I'm no good at maths,' say something different. Here are some ideas:

✔ 'I used to struggle with maths, but I'm putting that right.'

✔ 'I'm much better at maths than I thought.'

✔ 'I'm working on my maths skills.'

It sounds crazy, but it makes a big difference to the way you approach studying. I'm convinced that the reason people tend to have a bad day on Mondays is that they've decided that Monday is going to be a bad day – and the same thing happens with maths.

This book can help you make those positive statements true. I help you build your maths confidence and skills so that you can sail through any numeracy test that gets thrown at you.

In this chapter, I run you through what numeracy is, which organisations ask you to take numeracy tests and how the tests are structured.

Covering the Basics

You may have a mental image of a mathematician – enormous forehead, crazy hair, thick glasses, tweed jacket over a tasteless shirt with pens neatly arranged in the breast pocket, gibbering manically away at a blackboard covered in crazy equations.

Actually, I *do* know mathematicians like that – but we're not all so poorly adjusted. Being good at maths doesn't automatically turn you into a socially awkward egghead.

That's not the only good news: you're also excused from having to understand all those crazy equations. There's virtually no algebra in the numeracy curriculum (just a few simple formulas). All you need to be able to do is:

✔ **Add, take away, divide and multiply confidently.** If you can do all of these, you're going to rock. If not, you're still going to rock, but you may want to spend some time getting a solid foundation in place.

✔ **Figure out the right sum to do.** This can be tricky, but if you can keep a clear head and think through what the question is asking, it will make sense in the end. Promise.

✔ **Make sense of measures.** 'Measure' doesn't just mean being able to use a ruler, although that's a good starting point. It's also about weighing, taking temperatures, telling the time and working with shapes. There are a few simple formulas you may need to know for area and volume.

✔ **Read and understand graphs and basic statistics.** Once you 'get' graphs, the answers start to jump off the page at you – there are only a handful of types of graph you need to care about, and you just need to figure out where each of them is hiding the information. Until you know that, graphs can be a bit confusing – but don't worry, I take you through them as gently as I can!

Defining numeracy

The UK Numeracy Standards define numeracy like this:

> *Numeracy is a proficiency which is developed mainly in mathematics, but also in other subjects. It is more than an ability to do basic arithmetic. It involves developing*

confidence and competence with numbers and measures. It requires understanding of the number system, a repertoire of mathematical techniques, and an inclination and ability to solve quantitative or spatial problems in a range of contexts. Numeracy also demands understanding of the ways in which data are gathered by counting and measuring, and presented in graphs, diagrams, charts and tables.

This definition makes me want to cry. A repertoire of mathematical techniques? You're not a performing seal.

Here's my less technical, more useful definition. Numeracy is *the maths the average person needs to stay out of trouble.* Unless you're doing something pretty technical, you probably don't have much need for algebra, trigonometry or calculus in your daily life – but you may well need to be able to work out lengths and volumes, percentages, or to interpret graphs.

So, numeracy is about *useful* maths skills that you could conceivably need to use at work, at home or anywhere else, and those skills are usually the ones that numeracy tests cover.

What numeracy tests typically cover

Numeracy test questions tend to break down into four broad categories (although sometimes the questions bleed across the boundaries):

- ✔ **Whole number arithmetic** is about being able to deal with adding, taking away, multiplying and dividing. This is really the basis for all of the other categories, so knowing your number facts and methods really pays off.

- ✔ **Fractions, decimals, percentages and friends** are about working with the slightly more awkward but still useful sums.

- ✔ **Measures, space and shape** are used to talk about the world, whether you're describing how long a journey should take or how warm it is.

- ✔ **Graphs and statistics** come up all the time: at work, in the news, in adverts and so on. You only need to know a few basic types of graph and statistic for a numeracy test.

Opening Up Your Options with Numeracy Tests

Many employers ask for some level of maths skill when recruiting – more often than not, a good GCSE grade 'or equivalent'. Some of them – particularly the armed forces, emergency services and recruitment agencies – ask you to take a specific numeracy test to show that you have a good grounding in maths.

If you don't have a maths qualification, a lot of these doors are currently closed to you, so taking and passing a numeracy test is a good step towards qualifying for a job (or, of course, a better job) – and also makes it possible for you to take more advanced qualifications that open even more doors for you.

Improving your chances

You may need a maths qualification if you want to begin training or studying for certain professions and degrees. If you want to be a teacher or start any kind of medical study, you need to pass a numeracy test covering the kinds of situations you may need to deal with in practice.

Numeracy skills are generally a good thing to have – making it easier for you to follow presentations, understand the news and work out the best deals on anything you might want to buy.

Examining Common Numeracy Tests

Different qualifications (and different jobs) have different ideas about exactly what numeracy skills you need to have. This makes sense – if you're going to be a teacher, you're probably going to need more maths in a day-to-day setting than if you're going to be a soldier. (I say 'probably' – plenty of jobs in the armed forces need excellent maths skills, and plenty of teachers manage to avoid anything to do with maths – but they're missing out on all the fun.)

In this section, I tell you about the contents of the main types of numeracy test you may have to take.

Acing ALAN

The ALAN qualifications (Adult Literacy and Adult Numeracy) are sometimes called Adult Basic Skills, and are the exams you usually take if you're doing classes in numeracy or basic maths.

The numeracy qualifications are divided into five levels – Entry Levels 1-3 and Levels 1 and 2, which cover material from counting through to GCSE-level maths. The ALAN numeracy test isn't quite as broad-ranging as a GCSE, but some jobs and colleges accept it as an equivalent. If things go wrong, you're allowed to retake the test at a later date.

The qualifications themselves are assessed either by an on-screen or paper multiple-choice exam, which generally contains 40 questions you need to answer in an hour and 15 minutes (so you have a little less than two minutes per question). You can't use a calculator in the ALAN numeracy test.

Find out more on the ALAN website: www.edexcel.com/ quals/skillsforlife/alan/.

Training to be a teacher

At the time of writing, the Government is making sweeping changes to the way teachers train. The details in this section are based on the current proposals, but it's not possible to be 100 per cent sure of what the future will hold. It's always a good idea to check out the TDA website at www.tda.gov.uk to see the most up-to-date information.

You currently have two numeracy hurdles to jump if you want to be a teacher: you need to pass a GCSE-equivalent test in maths before you start teacher training, and you need to pass a second numeracy test to reach Qualified Teacher Status (or QTS). These tests are quite different in scope, and I talk about them in more detail in the following sections.

Starting in late 2012, the two hurdles are likely to be replaced with one: if you want to become a teacher, you'll have to pass a test, probably similar to the QTS, *before* you begin teacher training.

Initial Teacher Training (ITT) prerequisite

Before you even begin teacher training, you need to have qualifications in English and maths equivalent to a C grade or above at GCSE. If you already have those qualifications, congratulations, there's no problem – assuming you meet the other entry requirements, you can start training.

If you don't have those qualifications, you'll almost certainly need to sit a maths test of roughly the same difficulty and breadth as the GCSE before you can begin training. Unfortunately, the details of these tests are rather vague and vary between training institutions. Some colleges offer a 'brush up on your maths' type of course to help you get up to speed – they may offer this as part of your teacher training or ask you to take it beforehand. The best way to find out what you're meant to know for your course is to call up the institution you want to study at and ask what their requirements are.

Some institutions may even ask you to take a GCSE in maths. This book isn't a Maths GCSE textbook, but it can help you get to grips with the basics. There are some topics in the GCSE – particularly algebra and trigonometry – that are beyond the scope of this book, but if you understand everything I present here, you'll have a good foundation for success in your test.

Qualified Teacher Status

Even if you do have a good Maths GCSE, you have to pass tests in numeracy, literacy and using computers (ICT) before you can achieve Qualified Teacher Status (QTS).

Fortunately, the scope of the QTS numeracy test is much narrower than the GCSE, and you're currently allowed several attempts to pass it. It consists of two parts: mental arithmetic, which is a quickfire non-calculator test, and on-screen questions, which involve statistical information (such as graphs and tables) and real-world maths.

> ✓ **Mental arithmetic:** This section of the test stands alone, and you have twelve minutes to answer twelve questions given to you through headphones. The name isn't completely accurate – you're allowed to write things down rather than do everything in your head. You're not allowed to use a calculator, though. You hear each question twice but that's it – you're not able to go back and listen to questions again. In this part of the test, you need to be able to

deal with questions on basic arithmetic, fractions and percentages, as well as time and conversion problems.

✔ **On-screen questions:** In the on-screen section of the test, you need to be able to read, understand and answer questions involving graphs and tables, and to apply general arithmetic to situations that might come up in your teaching career. You're allowed to move back and forth between the questions, and you have access to the computer's calculator.

Most of the QTS questions involve you typing your answer as a number into the computer, although some involve selecting the correct answer with a mouse.

You can find details of the QTS tests, including practice papers, at `www.tda.gov.uk/trainee-teacher/qts-skills-tests/numeracy.aspx`.

Fighting your way into the armed forces

All the branches of the British Armed Forces require numeracy skills before you're allowed to enroll. In most cases, your score in the test is used to work out what jobs within the service you're a good fit for, so the better you do, the more technical the jobs you qualify for.

You can find an example of each of the army recruitment tests by visiting `www.army.mod.uk/join/` and following links from there.

Army numeracy test

If you want to join the British Army, you need to go through a series of recruitment tests, including numeracy, literacy, teamwork, memory and the *BARB* (British Army Recruitment Battery), which is about reasoning and understanding information. The good news is that the numeracy test doesn't require many of the more difficult sections of this book, and you're provided with a calculator.

For some of the questions, you need to type in a number as your answer, while some are multiple-choice questions where you simply select the right answer. You're allowed to retake the test if you feel you could get a better result.

Army Technical Selection Test (TST)

If you're looking for a more technical job in the army, you also need to do well in the Technical Selection Test (or TST). This involves some more advanced maths, roughly up to GCSE standard. One or two topics are slightly beyond the scope of this book (particularly transposing formulas, powers, standard form and factorising), but I cover everything else that's in the test.

You have 45 minutes to answer 55 questions, so there's not much time for hanging around. You're provided with a calculator, but need to bring your own pen! (Damn those budget cuts. . . .) You may be allowed to retake the test if you're disappointed with your result.

Royal Navy Recruit Test (RT)

To join the Royal Navy, you need to pass the Recruit Test (or RT), which tests your literacy, numeracy, problem-solving and mechanical skills. As with the army numeracy test, you're unlikely to need all of the material in this book. Don't worry too much if you don't pass first time – you're allowed to take the test again.

You can find a booklet of a sample Recruit Test at www. royalnavy.mod.uk/careers/how-to-join.

Royal Air Force Airman/Airwoman Selection Test (AST)

If you want to join the Royal Air Force as an airman or airwoman, you need to take seven aptitude tests:

- ✔ **Verbal Reasoning,** which assesses how well you can interpret information from written text.

- ✔ **Numerical Reasoning,** which tests your ability to work with fractions, decimals and formulas, as well as interpreting graphs and tables.

- ✔ **Work Rate,** in which you show how accurately and quickly you work through routine tasks.

- ✔ **Spatial Reasoning,** which examines how well you deal with shapes.

- ✔ **Electrical Comprehension,** which looks at your ability to work with electrical concepts, including vocabulary and circuit diagrams.

- ✔ **Mechanical Comprehension,** which tests how well you work with mechanical concepts and diagrams.

- ✔ **Memory,** which tests your ability to remember sequences of letters and patterns.

This book helps you with the Numerical Reasoning part of the test, in which you have four minutes to answer 12 questions on fractions, decimals and formulas, followed by 11 minutes to answer 15 questions on graphs and tables.

You need to pass all seven tests and reach an overall points total to qualify. After taking the exam, your results are valid for a year; if you fail, you have to wait a year before you reapply.

You can find some sample questions at www.raf.mod.uk/careers/applicationzone/aptitudetests.cfm.

Helping out with the emergency services

If you're beginning a career in the emergency services, you need to pass stringent qualification tests, including role-plays, interviews, fitness, written communication and – of course – numeracy. Here are the details for each of the branches.

Police Numerical Reasoning Tests

When I was growing up, I was told that if I wanted to know the time, I should ask a policeman. It makes sense, then, that police officers need a decent level of maths skills – although, obviously, this isn't the only reason you need to be passable at maths for a career in the police.

As part of your initial recruitment, you need to sit a short non-calculator exam, in which you have 12 minutes to answer 25 multiple-choice questions. The test covers topics such as working with money, speed and distance, averages, and shape. Chapters 4, 6 and 9 should cover almost everything you need to know.

You can find more details of the tests at www.police-recruitment.co.uk/police_test.html.

UK Fire and Rescue Service Working with Numbers test

To become a firefighter, you need to pass a whole battery of tests covering your physical and mental aptitude for the job. Listed sneakily under Psychological Tests is the Working with Numbers test.

The test contains 32 questions covering six scenarios you're likely to encounter as a firefighter. They involve combinations of adding, subtracting, multiplying and dividing, as well as estimating quantities. Chapters 4, 6 and 9 cover pretty much everything you need to know for this test.

The fire service psychological test website is at www.fire service.co.uk/recruitment/psychological-tests.

Ambulance service

Because the ambulance service has such a wide variety of roles, there isn't a specific numeracy test that applicants have to pass. However, the jobs within the service do require you to have a good all-round level of education, generally including a GCSE grade C or better in maths and some roles require you to pass an appropriate numeracy test.

You can learn about all manner of NHS careers at www.nhs careers.nhs.uk/.

Maritime and Coastguard Agency

You don't need to take a particular numeracy qualification to become a volunteer coastguard rescue officer. However, you are expected to be able to understand and exchange complex information by phone or radio, which requires at least basic maths skills.

You can find out more about the MCA at www.dft.gov.uk/mca/.

UK Clinical Aptitude Test (UKCAT)

To qualify for a university course in medicine or dentistry, you usually need to pass the UK Clinical Aptitude Test (or UKCAT) – a series of papers that determine how suitable you are to become a medical or dental professional. UKCAT consists of four tests:

- ✔ **Verbal Reasoning,** which tests your ability to take in and analyse information in written form.

- ✔ **Quantitative Reasoning,** which is about interpreting numerical and graphical information and doing calculations from it.

- ✔ **Abstract Reasoning,** which is about finding patterns using odd shapes.

- ✔ **Decision Analysis,** which tests how well you interpret codes.

This book helps you with the Quantitative Reasoning test. Pay particular attention to the chapters on statistics and graphs (Chapters 8, 11 and 12), but you may well be asked about anything in this book. You can learn more about the UKCAT at www.ukcat.ac.uk, and check out *UKCAT For Dummies* by Chris Chopdar (Wiley).

And the rest . . .

While the tests explained in the previous section are the most common, they're not the only ones. Big companies may have aptitude tests they ask candidates to take as part of their application procedure, and I've had to take numeracy tests at employment agencies. (I have a PhD in maths, but they still asked me to do a numeracy test. I almost refused, but I needed the money.)

I can't tell you what is likely to come up in these tests, simply because they're too varied and too numerous. In general, though, unless you're applying for a job or course that requires specialised mathematical knowledge, the content in this book should be more than enough to steer you through.

Good luck!

Reviewing Common Test Types

Most numeracy tests are made up of two or three different topics to find out how well you understand various techniques in maths. You're usually allowed a calculator for some parts of the test – depending on the exam, you may be able to bring your own or (in computer exams) use a calculator program, but you may also have a strict non-calculator section where you have to work things out on paper or in your head.

The topics of the test are usually chosen from the following three: mental arithmetic (working things out in your head or on paper), general maths (normally using a calculator) and handling data (interpreting graphs, charts and so on).

Mental arithmetic

The mental arithmetic portion of a numeracy test isn't as accurately named as it could be. You're not normally expected to work everything out in your head without writing anything down, which is good: working sums out on paper is usually much easier than trying to do them in your head, especially if the sum is rather complicated.

What it does mean, though, is that you're not allowed to use a calculator in this part of the test. You need to be pretty sharp with your arithmetic skills to do well here – particularly adding, taking away, multiplying and dividing.

The different flavours of test ask you questions on widely varying topics – some tests only want you to be able to do basic arithmetic without a calculator, but it's more common to be tested on fractions, percentages, time and money problems.

Real-world maths

Real-world maths questions do exactly what they say on the tin! It's a wide-ranging review of all of the everyday maths you may have to deal with.

That may sound a little frightening, but don't worry – they're not going to throw advanced calculus or quantum physics at you. Instead, the questions are likely to cover topics such as weights and measures, understanding time, and dealing with money. Depending on the exact type of test, there may even be topics here you don't need to worry about; on the other hand, there may be a few gaps if you're doing a specialised maths test (the other topics most likely to come up are algebra and trigonometry).

Find out as much as you can about the test you're taking as early as possible, including whether you're allowed to use a calculator – check out the website or call them up and ask for information. The more you know about what you're facing, the more efficiently you can prepare.

Handling data

Any numeracy test you sit will probably involve at least one graph or table. Handling data is one of the areas most likely to require some maths of you in a real-life professional situation, and it's important to be able to pick out the relevant information quickly and efficiently.

The types of graph you need to deal with and the kinds of sums you're asked to do really depend on the test. Particularly in the UKCAT and the QTS exams, you need a fairly deep understanding of reading graphs and tables and of interpreting and analysing the data. Some of the other numeracy tests just need you to be able to look at a bar chart and draw a sensible conclusion or make a decision based on a bus timetable.

Again, forewarned is forearmed: have a good look at your test's website and see what kinds of questions it asks. Don't waste time learning the ins and outs of working out averages from scatter graphs if you only need to read values from less complicated graphs!

Taking the Test

Not many people like exams. You don't want to fall apart under the pressure, so here are a few tips to help you keep your head in the exam.

Chapters 2 and 3 give you a lot more detail on preparing for an exam in terms of covering the material, staying calm and working under pressure. The Part of Tens chapters near the end of the book are helpful, too!

Depending on the kind of exam you take, and where you live, you may need to travel for your numeracy test. If your test is for a specific job in a specific location, you'll probably need to go there for an interview and do the test while you're there. Alternatively, your exam may take place in a test or recruitment centre in your nearest big town or city.

You can normally find out where the test is likely to be from the organisation's website, from their promotional material or by calling up and asking. Don't be afraid to ask for details! The more you know, the less you have to worry about.

The experience of sitting the exam also depends on the type of test you take. It's almost certainly not like the olden days where you file silently into the sports hall with two hundred other stressed-out students.

Instead, you're likely to be in an office or a classroom. You may be the only student there, or there may be a few others. If it's a computer test, you sit in front of a PC and fill out your answers using a mouse and keyboard; if not, you sit at a desk and answer on paper, either writing out your answers or filling in multiple-choice boxes. In either case, you receive clear instructions about what you need to do.

Computerised tests are far more common for numeracy exams than for exams at school and university. Normally, you're also given scrap paper to do your working out on – this is very useful, especially for spoken questions where you need to write down the information as you hear it so you can figure out what sums you need to do.

In a written exam, you may or may not have access to scrap paper, but you never lose marks for showing your working in the margins of the paper!

Find out what type of test you'll be taking and practise appropriately. Many websites have sample tests you can do on your own computer.

Knowing what to expect

The more practice you have with the exam you're going to be sitting, the less likely it is to throw up unpleasant surprises when you sit down to take it. I strongly encourage you to get hold of past papers or sample tests wherever you can (check out the websites listed in the 'Examining Common Numeracy Tests' section earlier in this chapter and the tests in Part II of this book).

Preparing from past papers has all kinds of benefits, such as:

✔ **Confidence.** The more familiar you are with something, the less fear you have of it. You can build your confidence by working through sample papers and (hopefully) seeing your scores increase each time.

✔ **Focus.** If you often slip up on a particular type of problem, that's priceless information – it tells you that you may want to revisit your notes on that topic and focus your practice on that kind of question until you find it comes a bit more naturally.

✔ **Timing.** Working against the clock is something I recommend once you've built up some confidence – but make sure you can get questions right before you try to do them fast! It also gives you a sense of how much of a paper you can get done in a given time and whether you'll have time at the end to go back to check your answers and fix any mistakes.

✔ **Topics.** When you work through a paper, you can see which topics you definitely need to know about and get a grip on how deeply you need to cover them. For example, if you notice one type of graph comes up in every paper, you may want to make sure you understand it inside out!

✔ **Wording.** All examiners phrase questions slightly differently – and they can sometimes be a bit cryptic. By working on past papers beforehand, you can get a feel for the kind of wording examiners in your field use.

Calming yourself down

Dreading exams is quite normal. It can feel as if everything is at stake, and it's easy to work yourself up into a serious fluster about them.

If you're the kind of person who stresses out about tests, I want you to do two things right now. First, take a great big deep breath, and then head over to Chapter 14 to learn some techniques for keeping your head.

Meanwhile, remember that doing poorly in a test isn't the end of the world – I won't tell you how many attempts it took me to pass my driving test! Just as with driving tests, you can usually retake your numeracy test until you get a score you're happy with.

Check the details of your particular test – although many tests allow you to try several times, yours may be different.

Obviously it's easier, cheaper and less time-consuming to do well first time, but it's not the end of the world if things go a bit pear-shaped.

Chapter 2

Putting a Practice Plan Together

I know of two broad ways to approach studying for a numeracy test. I like to think of the first one as the mud-flinging technique: you throw as much information as possible at your brain in no particular order and hope that some of it sticks. The second way is to have a plan of some sort and stick to it as well as you can.

Now, your plan can be as detailed or as vague as you like. Some people do well by getting quite specific and saying things like, 'I'll do these three exercises and call it a day', and having a huge colour-coded wall-planner. I find that's a bit *too* organised for most people, but if it works for you, brilliant, do that! Just don't take too long over the planning, make sure you leave some time to study!

I prefer a plan along the lines of, 'This week, I want to do some work on fractions, long division and pie charts.' This approach is enough that you know which parts of your notes and textbook you need to look at, but not so specific that you feel like you can't deviate from the plan in any way.

The other huge benefit of a plan is that it gives you an idea of where you are. By seeing what you've covered, you can get an idea of whether you're ahead of the game or slightly behind and adjust your study patterns appropriately – by giving yourself an evening off or trying to find an extra hour or two to squeeze some work into.

Working Out What to Learn

The first step to making a study plan for passing a numeracy test is to figure out what you need to learn. This can be a big, scary step: I sometimes put off planning projects because I'm frightened of how much I'll have on my list. But doing so is like not opening a bill because you're afraid of how much you owe – opening the envelope doesn't change anything, it just gives you information about where you are.

And that's the idea of having a plan: it's to tell you where you are and where you're going, like a road map. Any journey is easier with a map, right? In this section, I help you figure out how to make a learning map of your own.

Finding out what's in your test

Now, if you could find out exactly what questions were going to come up in the numeracy test, you wouldn't need a book like this: you could just learn all the answers and rattle them off.

That's not a maths test. That's a memory test.

However, you *can* figure out what topics are likely to come up in the exam by looking at the test's website, if it has one. (You can check out Chapter 1 for links to some of the more common numeracy tests, or – failing that – Google is your friend.) You may also be able to talk to people who have taken the test in the past, or the people who administer the test. In any event, the more you can figure out about the content of your numeracy test, the more efficient your study plan can be – you can focus your attention on just the things you need to learn.

You can also work out what kinds of questions are likely to come up by the clever tactic of finding papers to practise on. Again, start by looking at the website for the exam you're planning to take.

Make a big list of all the topics you think are likely to come up in the numeracy test. You can use this as a checklist to see where your strengths and weaknesses lie as you get closer to the exam.

Working out what you already know

Once you have a list of topics you need to know for the exam, the next step is to work out how comfortable you are with each of them.

This can be a bit daunting, especially if you're just starting to get to grips with maths. Don't worry, even if you don't understand what any of the topics mean, you're just finding out what you have to learn so you can plan how to learn it – you're not taking the test right now.

One thing I get my students to do with their list of topics is to draw a face beside each topic – a smile for the ones they're pretty comfortable with, a down-turned mouth for ones they don't get at all and a straight-line mouth for the topics they know a bit about but aren't completely happy with.

If you do this, it's totally okay if your list is covered with frowns – this is just to find out where you are and what you need to work on. If you need to work on everything, that's good information.

Filling in the gaps

Perhaps you're someone who likes to have everything planned out to the minute, or maybe you prefer to make a decision as you go along. Personally, I'm somewhere in between the two: I have a short list of things I plan to cover, but on any given day I pick the one I like best.

If you're the kind of person who plans everything in great detail, great! Get your diary out, put the topics you need to learn in a sensible order (start with the stuff that seems easier but that you're not sure of, and end up with things that seem difficult), and map things out – pencil in a topic for each day you plan to work, and stick to it.

I suggest leaving a few sessions – maybe one in every four – blank, to give yourself space to catch up if you fall behind, or in case there's something you want to go over again.

If, on the other hand, you like to fly by the seat of your pants, you can just keep the list somewhere handy and pick whichever topic takes your fancy whenever you sit down to study.

If you prefer something in between, make a selection of, say, half a dozen topics and put little tick boxes beside them. Each time you start a session, pick one of the topics with a box by it; when you finish, put a tick in the box.

When you've ticked all your boxes you get to choose your next selection. You can go back over topics you've already covered or pick new ones – it's entirely up to you.

If you're not sure which topic to look at next, do the smiley face exercise from the previous section – it's a good way to figure out what you need to focus on.

Finding Time to Study

Studying for a test is like driving hundreds of miles to park the car: in a sense, that's the end of the journey, but it's really not why you put all the effort in.

Managing your time

Here are some tips that can help to keep you productive:

- ✔ **Plan your day.** Keep track of exactly what you do and when. Within a few days, you're almost certain to find some wasted time you can put to better use.

- ✔ **Turn off the TV.** It's not going to kill you to miss Corrie for a few weeks – and it frees up several hours for you to hit the books.

- ✔ **Work at your best time.** Find a time when you're alert and receptive to information – it's no

good trying to study when you're tired or distracted. Experiment! Does the information sink in better first thing in the morning, during the day or in the evening?

For heaps more tips, read *Time Management For Dummies* by Clare Evans (Wiley). I'm also a big fan of the productivity blog run by Charlie Gilkey at http://productive flourishing.com.

You can also check out some of the tips in Chapter 16 about motivating yourself to study.

You're not studying to do well in the numeracy test. You're studying so you can qualify to be a teacher, or a soldier, or a medic, or a student, or whatever a numeracy qualification opens up for your future.

The test is just a hoop you have to jump through on your way to where you're going. It might be the hardest hoop you're facing, but making time to practise is much easier if you focus on what you'll be able to do when you've qualified.

Find a picture of someone doing the thing you want to do after the test and put it near where you study.

If you find it difficult to make time for studying, have a look at the 'Managing Your Time' sidebar to see where you can squeeze a few extra hours a week into your busy schedule.

Making a habit of it

It's much easier to get into bad habits than good ones, probably because the rewards are more immediate.

You might read that and think there's no hope. But wait! That's actually a clue about how to build a good habit. The trick is to reward yourself immediately after you've done the thing you're trying to establish – perhaps you treat yourself to a chocolate biscuit after your day's studying. This connects the behaviour with the reward in your mind and makes you want to do the thing that earns you the reward.

You wouldn't go to work if you weren't getting paid, now, would you?

The other key to building a habit is repetition. It's surprising how quickly small, concentrated bursts can reinforce each other and leave you enjoying your studies. In Chapter 16, I tell you about Jerry Seinfeld's calendar of crosses, which is a great way to motivate yourself to work at least a little bit on maths (or any habit) every day.

Finding a space for yourself

Finding the time to revise for your numeracy test is important, but you need to work in an environment that supports you as well.

You can work anywhere you're comfortable. That could be at a desk, on your bed, at the library, at a cafe, pub, in the park – anywhere you like. The important things are:

- ✔ **Comfort.** Don't put your body under undue strain – make sure you're set up to sit up straight, and not contorted into unnatural shapes.

- ✔ **Good lighting.** Don't strain your eyes – find somewhere bright and pleasant.

- ✔ **No distractions.** You may like to wear headphones – either to listen to music that drowns out background noise, or to signal to everyone else nearby that you're not interested in small talk right now. It's fine to tell your family and friends to leave you alone while you're studying.

- ✔ **Refreshment.** I like to make sure I've got a glass of water and a bowl of fruit nearby when I'm working at home – and usually a cup of coffee if it's the morning. That way, I'm much less tempted to get up and grab a drink or a snack, breaking up my flow.

Catching Up if You Fall Behind

It's perfectly natural to sometimes fall behind with your studies – life gets in the way sometimes, or you get sick, or you simply fall out of the habit of studying. It happens to everyone and the worst thing you can possibly do is beat yourself up about it.

When you fall out of the saddle, the right thing to do is to get back on.

Being realistic

If you suddenly realise that the exam is three days away and you haven't even looked at one of the sections, trying to cram everything into your poor, exhausted brain in the short time you have left is a recipe for burnout. You need to be sensible about what you can realistically learn in a short space of time.

So, rather than cover everything, pick two or three topics you think are within your grasp and see how much you can pick up on those. It's usually better to know three topics well than six topics very superficially.

Meeting yourself where you are

Most people, when they find their studies aren't as far along as they'd like, immediately start bullying themselves by wishing they'd done more, or had more time, or were smarter, or any number of other impossible things.

This is an absurd waste of energy. Don't do it. You can't change the past, all you can change is what you do right now – so rather than fret about all the things you would have done differently if you had only realised, say 'Okay – I'm in this situation, all I can do is work to get myself out of it. What's one thing I can do to improve what I know?'

Doing what you can

It may be that you don't have time to cover everything in the depth you'd like. It may be that you don't have time to cover everything, full stop. That's okay – again, don't beat yourself up.

Just do what you can. There's no point in pulling an all-nighter before the exam, because you'll be exhausted when you take it, and even if you can stay awake long enough to finish the paper, you'll be far less alert and coherent than you would be if you had had enough sleep.

Make sure you get a good night's sleep the night before the exam. If you're going to show up feeling like a zombie, you won't perform at your best.

If the worst comes to the worst and you make a mess of the exam, don't panic! In most cases, you're allowed to take the test again another time. Next time, you'll be better prepared!

Revising What You Know

One of the reasons I hear most often from my students when they can't start a sum is, 'But we did that so long ago!' Recall, especially if you have a long list of topics to cover, can be a real problem.

Fortunately, there's a solution: review as you go along. If you make a point of testing yourself once in a while on topics from the last week or the last month, you find they stick more readily in your mind.

Boosting your confidence with the easy bits

One good reason to review topics you've already looked at is that it can provide you with a confidence boost: when you remember how to do a sum, it reminds you that your hard work is paying off.

Each time you reinforce the topics that you know are going to come up over and over again, you get a little bit more accurate and a little bit quicker – which adds up to a little bit better at maths, and a little bit more likely to shine in your numeracy test.

Stretching a little further each time

When I was in the Live Music Society at university, the unwritten rule was that whenever you performed, at least one of your songs had to be new. The idea was to avoid getting into the rut of doing the same pieces over and over again, so that you'd continually develop as an artist (and not bore the long-suffering audience).

Do the same with your revision: don't just go over the same old stuff every time, make sure you add in something you haven't tested yourself on before.

Doing so helps you to extend the topics you're confident with and, hopefully, avoids boring your long-suffering self.

Working on practice tests

One of the best ways to revise what you've learnt and to see how you're getting on is to work on practice papers or exams from previous tests.

You can work through them under exam conditions when you're ready to discover how you'd get on if you sat the exam today, but before then, treat them as open-ended, open-book tests. You don't have to set a timer, and you can look at your notes if you get stuck. That way, you have help available when you're struggling, and you don't feel so stressed about getting everything done in a set time-frame.

You can leave a test unfinished and come back to it another time when you're revising. This is good practice because it gives your mind a chance to mull over the questions before you go back to them – and that's when genius strikes!

Here are some of the many advantages to getting hold of, and working through, past papers or sample exams for the test you're planning to take:

✔ You learn what topics tend to come up.

✔ You familiarise yourself with the language that examiners use in questions.

✔ You find out where your strong points are and where you need to do some more studying.

✔ You discover how you're doing time-wise, and whether you need to do some speed work.

✔ You go into the final exam knowing roughly what you're going to see.

Getting rid of as many nasty surprises as possible helps to build your confidence and convince yourself you're going to do well – which is half the battle.

Depending on the test, you can normally get hold of exam papers from the particular exam's website (check out Chapter 1 for links to the more popular exam sites). You may also be able to get hold of them from a further education college if you call up and ask nicely. And, of course, you can find practice tests in Chapters 9-13 of this book (remember, these are based on the various numeracy tests, but they're certainly not official past papers).

Picking up the Pace

One of the most common struggles I hear from my numeracy students is that they don't have time to finish the test.

The good news is, with a bit of practice, you can pick up your speed dramatically. The important things are to:

- ✔ Keep track of your improvement.
- ✔ Concentrate on getting things right, fast!

In this section I give you several training methods to build your speed and improve your recall.

Tackling timing

You need to find time to practise answering questions quickly for several reasons:

- ✔ The quicker you are with your number facts, the easier you find other topics.
- ✔ Being able to work quickly gives you breathing space in the exam.
- ✔ If you're fast and accurate with your numbers, your maths confidence increases exponentially.

Take a few minutes at the start or end of each study session to work on your speed and accuracy – you'll probably get more value from this than from any topic you care to pick.

Flashing cards

One of the best ways to learn any facts is to use *flash cards*. These are normally postcard-sized bits of card with a question on one side and the answer on the back. You can buy them ready-made, or you can make your own – making your own is better because by writing down the question and correct answer, you're helping your brain remember the information.

Here are the steps to making your own flash cards:

1. Decide on the facts you want to learn! If you're just starting out, you may like to work on your times tables, or if you're confident with those, pick some different questions that you struggle with.

2. Get hold of some cards or make your own. Fold a sheet of A4 paper in half, in half again and in half once more. Unfold and cut along the creases.

3. On each card, write a question from your list of things to learn on one side and the answer on the back.

4. Repeat Step 3 until you run out of things you want to learn!

Once you've made your flash cards, it's time to train yourself:

1. Shuffle your cards. This is important so that you don't just remember the answers in order.

2. Look at the question on top of your stack of cards, answer it, and check your answer.

3. If you get it right, put it to one side. If not, put it to the back of the pack.

4. Repeat steps 2 and 3 until you've answered all of the questions correctly.

5. If you've gone through the whole pack without making a mistake, give yourself a treat! You've earned it.

Some variations of learning from flash cards include:

✔ **Taping them up.** I've always been a fan of putting cards and post-it notes around my flat when I'm studying, and one of my students sticks the things she wants to learn on the doors in her house. Every time she wants to go through a door, she has to answer the question on it first!

✔ **Playing games.** You can replace the questions in any quiz board game you like with your flash cards. Try playing *Trivial Pursuit* with maths questions. You don't even need board games – you can get a friend to be Chris Tarrant and play *Who Wants To Be A Millionaire?* or even sit in a big black chair if *Mastermind* is more your cup of tea.

✔ **Getting your friends and family to help.** Another student of mine asked her mum to ask the questions so she wouldn't be tempted to cheat. Your partner doesn't need to know the answers herself, just be able to check if you got them right.

Once you've learned a fact so well you can answer the question in your sleep, you can file that card away. As you come across new things you want to learn, add a card for each of them.

You'll find yourself improving in both speed and accuracy in a really short space of time.

Speeding up a little at a time

If you're the competitive sort, like me (only, I'm way more competitive than you), then you thrive on breaking your own records.

You can use this to your advantage, especially if you're using flash cards. A great variation on the steps in the previous section is to add a timer into the equation – start it when you read the first question and stop it when you answer the last one correctly. Keep track of your times and reward yourself when you break your record!

Even if you're not as competitive as I am, you can still find ways of speeding up a little at a time. A good exercise is to work through past papers (or the exercises in Chapters 9-13) and time yourself as you go – challenge yourself to finish the questions in gradually shorter times.

As with everything else, making regular small improvements to your speed and accuracy begin to add up very quickly – before long, you're be blazing through your numeracy test!

Keeping on target

In the exam, you're going to be under time pressure, but there's no point in rushing through the exam in a world record time if you get all the questions wrong. On the other hand, the quicker you can work, the more time you have at the end of the exam to check over your answers and make sure you got them right. Trying to do maths fast can lead you to make mistakes. Finding the balance between being speedy and getting the right answer can be tricky.

The answer is to practise with an eye on accuracy as well as speed – give yourself an extra treat every time you improve how many questions you got right first time.

Slow and right is much better than fast but wrong.

Chapter 3

Tackling Test Day

I'd like you to go into a numeracy test feeling calm, relaxed and confident, knowing that you're smart, well prepared and ready for anything. I'd like you to have a plan of action for how you're going to make mincemeat of the test. And I'd like you to know how to respond if you trip up and things go slightly wrong. I'm sure you want the same!

This chapter is all about the specifics of how to do well in a numeracy test from a mental point of view (keeping calm and believing in yourself), a preparation point of view (what to bring and where to go) and a practical point of view (how to get as good a mark as you possibly can).

Preparing for Exam Day

Imagine two students. The first has never seen the kind of test he's going to be sitting, has only a vague idea of how to find the test centre, didn't think about whether he'd need to bring pens, pencils and/or a calculator and works pretty much on the 'I'll wing it' philosophy. The other student has got hold of some past papers, has checked out the parking situation at the test centre, knows exactly what to bring and has a specific plan about what he'll do once he starts the exam.

Which of the two is going to be less anxious about the exam? Which of the two would you expect to do better?

The more you know about the practical side of sitting your exam, the less stressed you are. The less stressed you are, the easier it is to think clearly. And the more clearly you can think, the more marks you get in the exam.

Knowing where the exam is

Funnily enough, sitting an exam is really hard if you don't know where it is. Find out where you'll be sitting the paper – what room, in what building – and, if it's at all possible, go there to check it out.

If you can't see any signs to tell you where you need to go for your numeracy test, ask a member of staff for help.

If you're planning to travel by car, check that you can park there. Do you need to bring change for the car park machine? If you're planning to use public transport, give yourself plenty of time.

Always plan to arrive early. You don't want to be panicking about arriving on time – giving yourself an extra half-hour can save you from some of the stress of getting caught in traffic or having your train delayed.

Bringing what you need

Different numeracy tests have different requirements for the items you need in the exam. In some cases the test centre provides all you need; in other exams you might need to bring everything. Err on the side of caution and bring a bag with the following things:

- ✔ **At least two pens and pencils.** Just in case you run out of ink or break the pencil lead mid-exam.

- ✔ **A calculator.** Unless you know for sure you're not allowed one, it's a good idea to have a calculator handy in case you need it.

- ✔ **A mathematical drawing set.** You know the type: the silvery tin with a protractor, a ruler, compasses, a stencil and some set squares in. The ruler is likely to be the most useful of these things, but again, you never know when the others might come in handy.

I was once reduced to drawing circles freehand because I'd forgotten my drawing set. It's much better to have the things and not need them than the other way around!

Getting in the right frame of mind

Feeling nervous or anxious before an exam is completely normal – it's just a sign that you care about doing well.

Within limits, the adrenaline rush that comes with doing something scary can be helpful – you can come up with some great ideas when you're under pressure – but you do need to keep it under control so you're not in a complete panic! Thinking straight is very hard when you're in full-blown panic mode.

I recommend three things if you find yourself in a bit of a fluster about an exam (or even studying), and you can remember them with the acronym POPS, which stands for *posture*, *oxygen* and *positive self-talk*:

- ✔ **Posture.** Have you ever noticed that confident people tend to sit up straight? It's not just about looking confident, but sitting up straight with good posture actually helps you feel positive and ready for anything, while slouching over the desk can make you feel negative and unsure of yourself.

- ✔ **Oxygen.** If you find yourself getting nervous or distressed, practise *diaphragmatic breathing* – breathing slowly and deeply into the bottom of your lungs while counting – to calm you down. Chapter 14 gives more detailed instructions. This kind of breathing is really good for calming you down and getting oxygen to your brain.

- ✔ **Positive self-talk.** Brains are funny things: they quite often do what you tell them. If you tell yourself you're smart and you're going to rock your exam, it's much more likely to come true than if you tell yourself something poisonous like 'I can't do maths' or 'I'm going to fail'. As Homer Simpson once said, 'Yes! I *am* highly suggestible.'

When I feel the onset of panic – which still happens, even though I'm largely anxiety-free these days – I go through a quick routine of doing all of these things. I sit up straight, take a few deep breaths and I tell myself I'm going to be ok. It's amazing how well it works!

If you're prone to panic attacks or serious anxiety, see a doctor or a counsellor. I wish I could tell you that these things go away on their own, but they don't. The doctor may be able to prescribe exercises or medication to help you overcome anxiety on test day.

Connecting with a Computer Test

In most cases, you do your numeracy test on a computer, which has many advantages, the main one being that you should get your results as soon as the test is over.

Sitting a computerised test also makes it easier for you to go back and change your answers if you make a mistake, and means that people with horrible handwriting (like me) can give legible answers.

In this section, I explain what to expect from a computerised test and how to use the on-screen calculator.

You don't need to be a computer geek to work the computers in a numeracy test. You need to be able to move a mouse and click a button, and possibly type in some of the answers. Computers don't bite! If you're a bit wary of them, and don't have one of your own, try visiting your local library and asking the staff for help.

What to expect

The short version of what to expect is that the questions come up on your screen, and you answer them.

You're likely to be given scrap paper or a small whiteboard so you can do your working by hand when you need to. You're also given instructions on how and when to start the test.

When you start the test, questions appear on the screen one at a time. The two types of question are:

- **Multiple choice,** where you're given a selection of possible answers. You click your mouse on whichever one of the given answers you think is the right one.

✔ **Fill-in,** where you type your answer in a box on screen.
Read the instructions carefully in case you have to
answer in a particular way.

If you're not sure of any answer, you can normally flag the
question to come back to later. When you've finished answering the questions, you can usually review all of your answers
to check that you're happy with them.

The only computer test I know of that doesn't allow you to
go back and spend more time on a question or check your
answer is the mental arithmetic section of the teacher training
tests. To learn more about this test, look at Chapter 6.

Magic numbers: Using the on-screen calculator

In some computerised numeracy tests, you're allowed to use
the computer's built-in calculator. Most of the time, the calculator is part of the testing software, and you just need to click
on the 'calculator' button to make it appear.

Depending on the test, you may be able to download a program
that shows you exactly what the test will look like on your
screen, including the calculator. Check out your test's website
and see!

If you do have access to a calculator, it's likely to be similar to
the basic calculator on your own computer. Here's how you
do a sum on it:

1. Enter the first number in the sum, either by typing it
   on your keyboard or by clicking on the numbers with
   your mouse.

2. Click or press the appropriate operation button
   (+, −, ÷ or ×).

3. Enter the second number in the sum.

4. Type in or press the equals (=) button. Your answer
   appears on the screen.

Calculators can be very powerful tools, but it's very easy to make a mistake when you're typing in a sum. Always check your work if you possibly can.

Previewing a Paper-and-Pencil Test

Although many numeracy tests are now completely computerised, with some tests you still work on paper.

Getting your results for pencil and paper tests takes longer than for computer tests, but they aren't any harder. Some people even find answering questions quicker and easier on paper than on the computer. In a sense, it's academic whether you prefer a computerised or pen-and-paper test – you probably don't get a choice about which method you use, so there's not much point in worrying about it!

Exam halls look pretty much the same wherever you go. You may remember them from your secondary school exams – row upon row of uncomfortable chairs and identical, graffiti-covered desks. Luckily, most exam rooms for adult numeracy tests are a bit more welcoming, although it's very hard to make an exam room anything other than intimidating.

Once you're in and have found your seat, you can have a look at your paper – read the front page to check you're in the right exam and when you're allowed to start. Normally, you need to wait until you're told to begin before you can turn the paper over and start working.

Answering the exam questions

I recommend taking a deep breath and skimming through the *whole* paper before you begin, to reassure yourself that you don't have too many monster questions lying in wait and so you can get a rough idea of the questions you can answer quickly and those you need to spend more time on.

Usually, the questions you have to answer in a paper-and-pencil test are multiple choice. You're given several possible answers and need to choose which one is correct. Depending on the exam, you may need to write down the letter of the correct answer or fill in the appropriate bubble on a sheet.

If you're filling in answers on a bubble sheet, be extra careful to check the number of the question each time you give an answer – you don't want to miss one and find all of your answers are off by one space.

Making sense of multiple choice

I quite like multiple-choice questions. They take a bit of the uncertainly out of how you're expected to give your answer, and there's no ambiguity in marking (either you get the answer right or you don't).

Multiple-choice questions also give you a one-in-four or one-in-five chance of getting the right answer even if you guess – which should be a last resort, of course (see the section 'Guessing When You Need To' later in this chapter for more advice).

Answering multiple-choice questions

A multiple-choice question consists of three parts:

- ✔ The information you need to answer the question.
- ✔ The question itself.
- ✔ Several possible answers (usually four or five).

Here's how I recommend answering multiple-choice questions:

1. Read the information and the question carefully. Think about how you may be able to estimate the answer.

2. Figure out what sum you need to do, and work out the answer.

3. Check your answer is among the answers you have to choose from. If not, think about where things might have gone wrong, and try step 2 again.

4. If you're on a computer, click on the answer you've come up with.

5. If you're doing a paper-and-pencil test, find the question number on your answer sheet and fill in the circle or box corresponding to your answer.

Checking your answer is there

I find it reassuring to work through a calculation and find that the answer I've come to is among the options listed. Watch out, though – examiners can be sneaky, and sometimes put in answers that result from common mistakes to lull people into a false sense of security.

One thing's for sure, though: if the answer you reach isn't among the four or five options you have to pick from, you've made a mistake somewhere. It's not a disaster – it may be that you need to tweak your answer a little to get it into the form they want, or you may need to start from scratch and try again.

 If you can't see where you've gone wrong straight away, go on to the next question and come back to it later – quite often your brain figures out where you went wrong even while you're thinking about something else. Don't spend too long on one question, or else you may miss out on easy marks elsewhere in the paper.

Eliminating the impossible

Another thing that's great about multiple-choice questions is that you can quite often figure out before you begin your own calculations which answers simply can't be correct. For example, if you know a temperature has dropped, you know the final temperature can't be higher than where it started – so you can immediately throw out any answers higher than the original value.

You can also use common sense to reject answers that are ridiculous – if the question is talking about the distance between two towns and gives an option of 5 metres, you can see straight away that that's far too small a distance to be sensible. In the same way, I've seen questions that suggested a car park might be 45 kilometres from the road – I've certainly been to airports that feel that way, but 45 kilometres (about 30 miles) is much too far.

Working backwards

My last pro tip for answering multiple-choice questions is especially useful if you're better at one kind of sum than its opposite – for example, if you just can't get division, but you find multiplying not too bad. The trick is to start from each of the answers you're given and work backwards to get to the original number.

This can be a little time-consuming, especially if you have five answers to check – remember to eliminate any impossible or unlikely answers as quickly as possible!

Working backwards is also a good way to check your answer makes sense – if you work through the sum backwards and find you get back to the start, you can be pretty sure you have it right.

This technique is very useful if you're working on a 'which formula gives this answer?' problem. All you need to do is work out each of the formulas in the answer and see which one gives you the correct answer.

Approaching Tricky Questions

This section gives you some good strategies for how to set about solving a problem when you're stuck and simply don't know where to start. For me, this is one of the most important topics in this book – maths is all about solving problems and finding ways to come up with sensible answers, even if you don't recognise the question.

Explaining the problem to the bear

Are you sitting comfortably? I'm going to tell you a story about Teddy Bear Theory. Bear with me.

A genius computer programmer kept being interrupted by his colleagues – because he was a genius, everyone went to him with their problems. Nearly every time, the conversation went the same way: the colleague would explain her problem, and before the genius could say anything, she would figure out the solution.

The genius got a bit fed up of this, as it wasted his time. So he bought a giant teddy bear, put it in the middle of the room and whenever someone came to him with a problem, he'd stop them short and tell them to ask the bear first. Nine times out of ten, they'd figure out the solution, just by explaining what was wrong.

Here's the thinking: when you explain a problem to someone who's not familiar with it, you look at it from a completely different angle. You make connections you don't make when you're just staring at it, and you jog your memory.

Now, you're not really allowed take a giant teddy bear into the exam hall, and you certainly couldn't talk to it even if you were allowed. You might get away with a small cuddly mascot though. I have a toy koala named Impala who helps me with the *really* tricky problems. Alternatively, you can simply use your imagination!

Here are some things you might choose to explain to the teddy bear, whether he's real or imaginary:

- **What information do I have?** The teddy bear can't help you solve the question if he doesn't have all the facts! What numbers are in the question, and what do they represent?

- **What am I trying to find out?** What kind of answer is the question asking for? For example, does the answer need to be a distance? A number? Something else?

- **What would I *like* to know?** Maybe you can see a way of doing the question, if only you knew this one other thing. Sometimes working like this gives you a clue about what to look for.

- **Can I break down the problem into smaller parts?** For example, you may have a speed-distance-time question that uses miles per hour, but is set in a country that uses kilometres. In this case, you can work out your answer in miles and then convert it to kilometres at the end.

Considering what you'd do with the information

Not knowing where to start is a horrible feeling, but in most cases, you need to work with at least one of the 'big four' operations (adding, taking away, multiplying or dividing) – the trick is just deciding which ones, and the order to do them in.

Tell yourself (or the teddy bear) a story about what you'd do in the situation – if the question is asking about the cost of hiring a venue, imagine you're in that situation. Think about what money you'd pay out at each stage of the process. Picture yourself handing over the cash as you work out the sum – it's much easier to work through a sum if you can picture it.

Keeping it tidy

If your work is hard to read, it's hard to follow. If your work is hard to follow, it's easy to miss things out and make avoidable mistakes. The end result is that you lose marks you would have got if you'd laid everything out neatly.

Here are some tips on how to keep your sums neat and tidy:

- ✔ **Give yourself room.** Don't try to fit too much into too small a space. Just start a new page if you're worried about running out of room to work and don't worry about wasting paper.

- ✔ **Line up your columns.** If you're doing any kind of sum, you don't want to mix your tens up with your units. Use a ruler if necessary to set up neat columns to write your numbers in.

- ✔ **Check your numbers.** One of my biggest failings is to write down a different number to the one I'm thinking. There's no problem harder to find than the one where you think '50' but write down '70' – it's hard to find it even when you realise what you've done! Take your time.

- ✔ **Keep your crossings out neat.** If you do write something down wrongly, the immediate temptation is to scribble it all out and obliterate it in a great big inky mess. While this is therapeutic, it's not all that good for getting the right answer, which is what you want. If you make an error while you're working, just cross it out neatly and continue on the next line. You can go back and scribble at the end if you feel like it!

Neat work is easier to read and understand – so it's easier to find any mistakes you might have made. I don't mean to sound like your mum, but sometimes keeping things tidy really is a good idea.

Managing Your Time

All exams are a race against time. You have a certain number of minutes to answer as many questions as you possibly can. Some questions may be quick and easy, while others take a bit more thought, effort and time.

This section gives you a few ways to use the time you have in the exam effectively, so you can milk the paper for every mark.

The three keys to good exam technique are making sure you:

- ✔ **Don't spend too long on any one question.** If you don't move along at a steady pace through the exam, you may miss out on easy marks. If you struggle with one, move on to the next and come back to the hard one later.

- ✔ **Give a good answer to the easy questions.** I call this the 'picking low-hanging fruit' strategy – pick up the easy marks as quickly as you can and you have longer to work on the hard stuff. But still answer the question carefully even if it is an easy one.

- ✔ **Give an answer to every question.** A blank answer is always wrong – so, if you don't know the answer, give a sensible guess rather than leaving it blank. The rare exception to this advice is: if your exam takes off marks for wrong answers, you may prefer to leave answers blank.

Starting off gently

A big part of exam day nerves is the fear of the unknown, as you don't know what questions are going to come up (or else you could just memorise the answers!). In order to get over that fear as quickly as possible, have a plan for what you'll do when you get into the exam.

Your plan might be to sit down, have a stretch, and take a big, deep breath while mentally running through the things you need to remember – stay calm, work steadily, read the questions. When the invigilator says 'start', turn over the paper and quickly skim through to see what questions you need to answer.

One of the many benefits of reading through the paper as soon as possible is that it gives you an idea of where the easier questions are. That means, when you start answering the exam in earnest, you can skip straight to those questions and pick up several points without having to think too hard. (In some cases, you can practically pass the exam before your brain has even got going properly. That's a great position to be in!)

Moving swiftly along

If you get hit with a tricky question, and you're not getting to an answer quickly, flag it as one to come back to later and move on. One of the phrases I dread hearing from students after an exam is 'There was this really hard question and I spent a lot of time on that.' This approach will lose you time and marks!

The thing is, exam questions aren't necessarily in order of difficulty – the time you're spending cranking your brain gears on a hard question is usually time you can spend picking up comparatively easy marks later in the paper.

As a bonus, while you're consciously working your way through those other questions, your subconscious is still mulling over the difficult one you've temporarily abandoned. Quite often you'll come up with an amazing insight while you're in the middle of something else.

In most exams, you can come back to time-consuming questions later on.

Guessing when you need to

Generally in maths, you're better giving reasoned, correct answers than wild guesses – if you want to get lots of credit for guesswork, you might want to look at a career as an economics correspondent.

That said, in some situations it makes sense to guess your answer. Have a guess if:

  ✔ **You're running out of time.** If the clock is counting down fast and you're not going to have time to work out the problem fully, have a guess rather than leaving your answer blank.

✔ **You really don't have a clue how to do the question.** If you've spent a little while thinking about it, and you've tried all the tricks from the earlier section 'Approaching Tricky Questions', and you still don't know what to do, just pick an answer. Don't throw good time after bad.

Guess smart. You can often throw out one or two obviously wrong answers before you pick between the others.

If your paper isn't multiple choice, eyeball the question and have a go anyway – it's still worth writing down a guess.

The other day, I came across the first exam I've seen in ages where you could lose a mark for a wrong answer. This type of marking is rare, but not entirely extinct! It still may be worth guessing if you can eliminate a wrong answer or two, but be a bit more wary about it.

Checking your work

If your preparation has gone really well and you've figured out how to do questions quickly, congratulations! That's great. You have a chance to do even better, though: if you have time left at the end of the exam, go back and check some or all of your answers.

If you're less sure of some answers than others, make a note of them (put a pencil asterisk next to them) – check these ones first. The way I check my answers is to come up with a rough guess of what the answer ought to be – if I rounded off all of the numbers very roughly and did the sum again, would I get an acceptably close answer? If not, it's worth working through the original sum again.

Working through whole sums again is also a good (if time-consuming) way to check your work. If you get a different solution second time around, you might want to consider changing your answer.

Part II
A Whistle-Stop Tour of the Maths You Need

THE FOUR HORSEMEN OF THE ARITHMETICS

In this part . . .

This book wouldn't be much use if it didn't tell you how to do the maths you need for your test! In Part II, I take you through the basic maths techniques you need, the more advanced stuff you may use in certain tests, and the tips of the trade for dealing with mental arithmetic tests, real-world maths and graphs.

Chapter 4

Refreshing Your Basic Maths

1 had a football coach whose mantra was 'good players do the simple things well'. To be a good footballer, you need to be able to do the basics easily and reliably.

Exactly the same thing is true of maths – if you have the fundamentals under your belt, you're well on your way to success in your numeracy test.

In this chapter, I show you how to deal with the basics. I start with whole numbers, which are the building blocks of maths, before going on to trickier decimals and fractions.

Perhaps you know some of the content in this chapter already – or perhaps you know some things inside out, and some aspects may be a bit rusty. Maybe it's all a bit of a struggle. Either way is okay – just concentrate on the topics you need to concentrate on to pass your numeracy test with flying colours.

Handling Whole Numbers

If you can do whole number arithmetic well – the big four of adding, taking away, multiplying and dividing – you have most of the tools to do well in a numeracy test. This knowledge certainly makes the other topics much easier.

You may remember spending endless hours at school slogging your way through worksheets that didn't make any sense, blindly following recipes for the kind of sum they decided to torture you with that week. Here at Dummies Towers, things are a bit more enlightened, so in this section I explain what's going on when you work through the recipes, thinking about how you use money.

Adding and subtracting

Once you can add up and take away whole numbers, you've got a really solid foundation for the rest of the maths you may need in real life. The most common examples of everyday maths are adding up your shopping bill and working out change.

Of course, if that was all there was to maths, this would be a very short book! The other topics are also important, but adding and taking away are fundamental skills that everything else builds on.

Adding up

You *add* things whenever you end up with a specific amount more than you started with – for instance, if you earn some money, or pack more weight into your suitcase, or combine two groups of people.

Obviously, if you have a calculator, all you need to worry about is making sure you enter the sum correctly.

On the other hand, if you're in a non-calculator (mental arithmetic) test, you need to know how to add up quickly on paper. Here's what you need to do:

1. Line up the numbers you want to add so their ends are in line, just like in Figure 4-1.

2. Add up the right-most column.

3. If your total is less than ten, write the total under the column. If the total is ten or more, write the second digit under the column and put the first digit under the next column to the left. (In the middle column of the first example in Figure 4-1, 7 + 6 = 13, so you write a 3 under the 7 and 6 and a 1 below the next column to the right.)

4. Go to the next column to the left and add up the numbers – and add any numbers you've written below this column. (In the left-hand column of the first example in Figure 4-1, 4 + 3 = 7, but there's a 1 below the column as well so you write down 8.)

5. Repeat Steps 3 and 4 until you run out of numbers.

```
    4   7   5              9   4   3
+   3   6   2          +       1   7
========              ========
    8   3   7              9   6   0
1                          1
```

Figure 4-1: Adding up.

The method for adding decimal numbers is almost identical to this – see the section 'Dealing with Decimals' later in this chapter.

Taking away

You _subtract_ or _take away_ whenever you end up with a specific amount less than you started with – for example, if you spend money, or pour away some drink, or remove some people from a group.

As with most things in maths, several ways exist to do take-away sums and get the right answer. Here, I show you how to take away the traditional way using the _column method_, and then an alternative, the _do the same thing_ method, which some people find easier.

If either of the numbers in the sum is negative, you have to use a different method from the two described here – see the section 'Negative numbers' later in this chapter.

The _column method_ mirrors what you do when you get change in a shop – you can imagine it as spending a certain amount and seeing how much money you have left over.

Here's how it works:

1. If the second number is bigger than the first, swap them around and write a big minus sign somewhere you won't miss it. Your answer is going to be less than

zero, or a *negative number*. (Luckily, this is quite rare in numeracy tests.)

2. Write down your numbers with the bigger one above the smaller one. If they're different lengths, make sure they're *right-justified* – that they end in the same column, as in Figure 4-2. Underline the lower number. Give yourself plenty of space!

3. Starting from the left, compare the lower digit with the upper one.

4. If the lower digit is bigger, then you've got a problem. You need to *borrow* one from the next column to the left. Reduce the upper number of the next column by one and write a little one above and to the left of the upper number – for instance, in the right-hand column of the second example in Figure 4-2, 3 has become 13.

5. Now take away the lower number from the upper number and write the answer below the underline in that column.

6. Repeat steps 2 to 4 until you run out of digits.

7. If you didn't write down a big minus sign in Step 1, your answer is the number beneath the underline. If you did write down a big minus sign, put a minus in front of the number beneath the underline and that's your answer.

I glossed over a problem there: what happens if you want to borrow from a zero? You can't really reduce nothing by one! In that case, what you have to do is borrow one from the *next* column to the left, turning the zero into a ten, so you can borrow one from it. The third example in Figure 4-2 shows this.

$$
\begin{array}{ccc}
4 \ 7 \ 5 \\
-\ 3 \ 6 \ 2 \\
\hline
1 \ 1 \ 3
\end{array}
\qquad
\begin{array}{ccc}
9 \ \ ^{}4^3 \ \ ^13 \\
- \ 1 \ \ 7 \\
\hline
9 \ \ 2 \ \ 6
\end{array}
\qquad
\begin{array}{ccc}
^{}4^3 \ \ ^4 0^9 \ \ ^13 \\
-\ 2 \ \ 8 \ \ 4 \\
\hline
1 \ \ 1 \ \ 9
\end{array}
$$

Figure 4-2: Take away sums (column method).

All of this borrowing is very dangerous, as any economist can tell you – you can get into all kinds of mess. I much prefer the *do the same thing* method, which involves – surprise, surprise – doing the same thing to both numbers, and trying to make the small one easier to deal with. You're allowed to add the same thing to both numbers, or take away the same thing from both numbers – and if you do that, the difference remains the same.

Here's why it works: imagine you're playing a game – if you score some points and your opponent scores the same number, you're just as far ahead or behind as you were before. By the same token, if you both lose the same number of points, the margin still doesn't change. Also, most people find it easier to work out 179 – 40 rather than 173 – 34.

Here are the steps you follow:

1. Write down the sum.

2. First, you want to make the second number into a multiple of 10. Look at its last digit and work out how many you need to add to make it end in 0. Add this number on to *both* numbers and write down the new sum. If you had 435 – 79, you'd add 1 to both numbers to get 436 – 80.

3. If you can do the sum easily, do the sum. If not, you make the second number into a multiple of 100. Look at the last two digits and see what you need to add to make it end in 00. Add this number onto both numbers and write down the new sum. In this example, you'd add 20 to both numbers and get 456 – 100 (which gives you 356).

4. If your sum still isn't easy, keep going – make the second number into a multiple of 1,000, then 10,000, then 100,000 and so on until you can easily take away the second number. (You'd be really unlucky to need to do this!)

Figure 4-3 shows two take-away sums done with the *do the same thing* method. This involves a little more writing than the column method, but a lot less thinking.

```
403 – 284
+6    +6
---------
409 – 290        943 – 17
+10   +10         +3   +3
---------        ---------
419 – 300 = 119   946 – 20 = 926
```

Figure 4-3: Take-away sums (do the same thing method).

Negative numbers

You may have to deal with small negative numbers in a numeracy test. They're not hard if you take a deep breath and think about them carefully!

You may need to:

✔ Add something on to, or take something away from, a negative number.

✔ Find the difference between two negative numbers.

✔ Find the difference between a positive and a negative number.

✔ Take away a bigger number from a smaller number.

The only places in real life where negative numbers often come up are in cold temperatures and goal or point differences in a league table. You can use your understanding of temperatures to help work these sums out.

To add or take away from a negative number, think about the first number as your original temperature, and then getting warmer or colder by the second. To work out –12 + 5, imagine it being –12°C and getting 5°C warmer: you'd end up at –7°C. To work out –8 – 3, imagine a temperature of –8°C getting 3°C colder: you'd end up at –11°C.

The bigger the number after the minus sign, the colder it is!

Finding the difference between two negative numbers is also easy: it's the same as the difference between the two numbers ignoring the minus signs. The difference between –3 and –7 is 4, the same as the difference between 3 and 7.

The easy way to find the difference between a positive and a negative number is to drop the minus sign and add the numbers together. The difference between 5 and –5 is the same as 5 + 5 = 10.

Lastly, taking a bigger number away from a smaller number is something you can do using the recipes for taking away from earlier: you do the sum the wrong way around (for example, if you had to do 15 – 20, you'd work out 20 – 15), and then put a minus sign in front of your answer. For that question, the answer is –5.

Multiplying and dividing

Multiplying and dividing are really just repeated adding and subtracting. If you work out 4 + 4 + 4 + 4 + 4, you get 20, which is 5×4 – you even say 'five times four', meaning you add four to itself five times. With dividing, you're just finding out how many times you can take away one number from another before you get to zero: 20 – 5 – 5 – 5 – 5 = 0; you can take away five from 20 four times, so $20 \div 5 = 4$.

It would be pretty irritating to have to work with those methods, though – imagine doing $1,000 \div 2$ by taking away two at a time: you'd be there all day! Here I walk you through more efficient ways of doing times and divide sums.

Piling things up: Multiplication

Multiplying numbers is the same as repeatedly adding – it's also the same as making piles of the same size – for example, 3×6 just means 'how many things do you get if you make three piles of six things each?' (or six piles of three, it doesn't matter).

The quick way to multiply is to *chunk* one of your numbers into smaller numbers – for example, if you have to multiply a number by 12, you can easily work out ten times the number and two times the number and add the answers together.

Here's how you multiply two numbers together – for example, 45×17 (and look at Figure 4-4 to see how to lay it out).

1. Split the smaller number into tens and units (and hundreds if you need to – but that would be a pretty involved sum!) So, you'd split 17 up into 10 and 7.

2. Split each of these into smaller chunks if you need to – ones, twos and fives work best. In the example 10 is already a nice number; 7 would become 5 and 2.

3. Work out the big number multiplied by each of the chunks – in the example, you'd need $45 \times 10 = 450$, $45 \times 5 = 225$ and $45 \times 2 = 90$.

4. Add these numbers together to get your final answer.

You can chunk numbers however you like – pick chunks that you find easy to multiply, though, there's no sense in making your life any harder than it needs to be!

$17 = 10 + 5 + 2$

$45 \times 2 = \mathbf{90}$
$45 \times 5 = \mathbf{225}$
$45 \times 10 = \mathbf{450}$

$45 \times 17 = \mathbf{450 + 225 + 90} = 765$

```
    4  5  0          6  7  5
 +  2  2  5       +     9  0
   ========         ========
    6  7  5          7  6  5
                     1
```

Figure 4-4: Multiplication sum.

Splitting the piles: Dividing

Division is where some people start to lose confidence in maths – so I want to make it as easy as possible for you. In this section, I show you how to divide numbers using the *chunking* method.

This may or may not be the way you've learned division before. If you know how to do it another way, don't be afraid to use that! Anything that gives you the right answers is A-OK in my book.

The chunking method comprises three stages, which I go through in more detail in a moment:

1. **Writing out highlights of one of your times tables.**
   Don't worry – you only have to do fairly easy multiply-ing here.

2. **Taking away numbers in groups until you get to
    zero.** This bit is fairly easy, but can take some time.

3. **Adding up how many groups you took away.** That's
    your answer.

In the rest of this section, you're going to see how to solve
$1098 \div 9$.

Writing out the highlights

The first thing to do is write out the highlights of your times
table – in fact, just the ones that are fairly easy to work out.
Follow along with Figure 4-5 as I walk you through the steps:

1. Work out two times the number you're dividing by.
    Write down $2 \times$ (your number) = (your answer) in the
    top left of your paper. In this example, you'd write
    down $2 \times 9 = 18$.

2. Leave a gap below that, then work out ten times the
    number you're dividing by and write down $10 \times$
    (your number) = (your answer). Here, you'd write
    down $10 \times 9 = 90$.

3. Halve your answer from step 2 and write down $5 \times$
    (your number) = (your answer) between your answers
    for steps 1 and 2. For this case, you'd write $5 \times 9 = 45$.

4. Now comes the clever bit! You know $2 \times$, $5 \times$ and $10 \times$
    your number, so you can easily work out $20 \times$, $50 \times$
    and $100 \times$ your number by simply adding a zero to the
    end of each. In the next column, you'd write down $20 \times$
    $9 = 180$, $50 \times 9 = 450$ and $100 \times 9 = 900$.

5. You can carry this on for $200 \times$, $500 \times$ and $1000 \times$
    your number, and even higher numbers if you need
    to (don't bother with numbers that are higher than
    the number you're trying to divide!). I've done this in
    Figure 4-5 so you can see the pattern, but you wouldn't
    need to work them out in this example.

$9 \times 2 = \mathbf{18}$	$9 \times 20 = \mathbf{180}$	$9 \times 200 = \mathbf{1800}$
$9 \times 5 = \mathbf{45}$	$9 \times 50 = \mathbf{450}$	$9 \times 500 = \mathbf{4500}$
$9 \times 10 = \mathbf{90}$	$9 \times 100 = \mathbf{900}$	$9 \times 1000 = \mathbf{9000}$

Figure 4-5: Highlights of your nine times table.

Taking away the groups

This middle step is the most time-consuming part of long division – the quicker you can do take-away sums, the more quickly you'll be able to divide!

Here are the steps you need to take – follow along with Figure 4-6 to see how to lay it out:

1. Write down the number you're trying to divide, 1098 in this case. Leave yourself plenty of space below and to the right.

2. Find the biggest answer in your times table highlights that's smaller or the same as your last answer; write the sum down to the right as well.

3. Draw a line beneath your number from Step 2 and take the number away from the number above it.

4. Repeat Steps 2 and 3 until your answer is zero!

 You may end up with your answer being the number you're dividing by instead of zero. That's okay: in that case, you just write the number and 1 × (the number) = (the number).

```
1098
 900  = 100 × 9
====
 198
 180  =  20 × 9
====
  18
  18  =   2 × 9
====
   0
```

Figure 4-6: Taking away the groups.

In the example in Figure 4-6, I started by saying $100 \times 9 = 900$ is less than 1098, and taking it away – that gives 198. Then $20 \times 9 = 180$ is the biggest number in the highlights smaller than 198, so I took that away to leave 18. That's 2×9, so I write down that sum and end up with zero. Job done!

 It doesn't matter if you don't pick the biggest available number – it's just generally quicker if you pick the biggest one.

Working out word problems

This translation from English into maths takes a lot of practice, but once you get it, you'll wonder what you found so hard!

Here are some tips for how to translate:

- Write down any values you're given and what they represent. Something like 'Height = 15cm' is good.

- Think about what you might have to do with your values once you know them. Are you adding them up? Multiplying?

- Ask what kind of answer you're expecting. Is it a number? A measurement?

For example, you may be told about a party where Malcolm ordered 20 pork pies from the caterers and cut each pie in half. After the party, he notices that 28 halves are left and wants to know how many halves the partygoers ate.

I would write down something like:

- 20 pies cut in half – I'll have to double 20 to get the number of halves.

- 28 halves left afterwards – I'll have to take that away to find how many were eaten.

In this case, the sums are $20 \times 2 = 40$ and $40 - 28 = 12$. Maybe everyone preferred the sausage rolls!

Adding up the groups

The last part is the easy bit! You simply pick out the first number in each of the times sums you wrote down (in this case, 100, 20 and 2), and add them up! So in this case, you get 122, which is $1098 \div 9$.

Roughly Speaking: Finding Approximate Answers

Once in a while, you may get a question that looks absolutely impossible – a complicated sum with insanely detailed numbers, for example, almost as if it's designed to make you panic.

Don't let the evil numeracy test wizards catch you in their clever trap! Make sure you read the question carefully: almost always, they ask you to give an *approximate* answer, which is a much, much easier thing to do.

An approximate answer is one that's very close to the exact answer – if you buy six pens that cost £1.99 each, you could say that that would cost roughly 6 × £2 = £12 and be pretty close to the correct answer. That's really all approximation is – rounding off your numbers to the nearest thing that's easy to work with and doing the sum with those rough numbers.

Rounding off with decimal places

A *decimal point* is a dot somewhere in a number. You use one almost every time you write down an amount of money, such as £19.50. The dot tells you where the whole pounds (or whole numbers) end and the pennies (or parts of a whole number) begin.

Decimal places are simply how many numbers there are after the dot. Money is normally limited to two decimal places, but in other contexts you may get more decimal places.

A very common question in numeracy tests is to *round* a number to a certain number of decimal places, which means to find the number of the right size that's the nearest to the exact answer. Here's how:

1. Find the dot in the number and count that many spaces to the right of it. Draw a vertical line here.

2. If the number to the right of the line is small (from 0 to 4), just cross out everything to the right of the line.

3. If the number to the right of the line is big (5 to 9), you have to *round up*. Replace the last number to the *left* of the line with one number higher.

If the number to the left of the bar is a nine and you have to round up, you have to add one to the next digit to the left as well. If that happened to be a nine as well, you'd have to add one to that and so on. So if you had to round 37.997 to two decimal places, the answer would be 38.00.

If you have to round 43.254 to two decimal places, you count two spaces to the right of the dot and draw a line: 43.25 | 4.

The next number is small, so you just chop off everything after the line to get 43.25.

To round 84.05 to one decimal place, you count one space to the right and draw in a line: 84.0|5; the next number is large, so you replace the 0 with a 1 to get 84.1.

If you have to round a number to the nearest whole number, you use a very similar method – you just put the line where the dot is. For example to round 45.34 to the nearest whole number, it would become 45|34; the three is small, so you would round it down to 45.

To round to the nearest ten, you put the line one space to the left of the dot, just after the 'ten' part of the number. After you've rounded, you add a zero at the end so the number is about the same size as it was before – to round 248 to the nearest ten, it would become 24|8 which rounds up to 25, but 25 isn't anywhere near 248, so you add a zero to make it 250.

The same kinds of rules apply for rounding to the nearest hundred (you put the line after the 'hundreds' digit and add two zeros at the end) or the nearest thousand (the line goes after the 'thousands' digit and you add three zeros when you've rounded).

Working roughly

Getting an approximate answer to a complicated sum is as easy as this two-step recipe:

1. Round all of the numbers involved as roughly as the question tells you to (for example, it might say 'to the nearest 10p' or 'to the nearest whole number'). If it doesn't tell you, round it after the first digit.

2. Do the sum with your nice round numbers. Your answer won't be as precise, but it'll be in the right ballpark – which is what they want when they ask for a rough answer.

Dealing with Fractions

It's ok, I know: nobody (apart from me) likes fractions. Even the examiners don't like them; they just put them in the exam to be mean. Fractions can be hard to get your head around, but in this section I try to make as convincing a case as possible for why the rules are what they are.

A fraction is a pair of numbers, one on top of the other, and I like to think of it as representing a number of slices of cake or pizza. The *bottom* (or *denominator*) tells you how big each slice is; the *top* (or *numerator*) tells you how many of the slices there are. So, ¾ represents the pizza in Figure 4-7: the pizza was split into four slices (so the number on the bottom is four), and three of the slices are still there (so the number on the top is three). Simple enough?

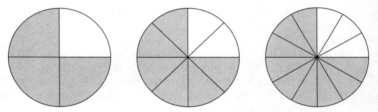

Figure 4-7: Fractions of a pizza. Three quarters can be written as ¾, ⅝ or ⁹⁄₁₂ (among many other ways).

Figure 4-7 shows other ways of representing the same fraction. You could have split up the pizza into eight slices and be left with six, or into twelve and have nine slices left (so three-quarters is the same thing as ⅝ or ⁹⁄₁₂). It's also the same as ⁷⁵⁄₁₀₀, or ³⁰⁄₄₀, or ²⁷⁰⁄₃₆₀ (trust me).

Equivalent fractions and cancelling down

This bit is important, so pay attention:

Two fractions are equivalent if you can get from one to the other by multiplying or dividing the top and bottom by the same number.

So, ¾ is equivalent to ⁶⁄₈ because you can get from one to the other by multiplying both the top and bottom by two. In the same way, ⁵⁰⁄₁₀₀ is the same as ½ because you can get from one to the other by dividing both the top and bottom by fifty. This process – dividing top and bottom by the same number – is known as *cancelling down* or *simplifying* a fraction.

The idea of equivalent fractions is really important for adding and taking away fractions – which I talk about in the next section.

Adding and taking away fractions

The most common fraction sums, both in real life and in numeracy tests, involve adding and taking away fractions.

The big trick to doing adding and take-away sums is to make sure the number on the bottom of both fractions is the same. This is just like making sure your units are the same when you're adding up measurements – you wouldn't add miles to kilometres; you'd make sure to put both distances into the same units first.

So, here's the recipe for adding or taking away fractions; you can work through the example in Figure 4-8 (⅔ + ¼) as you read:

1. Find an equivalent fraction for the first fraction by multiplying the top and bottom by the *bottom* of the second fraction. If you multiply the top and bottom of ⅔ by 4, you get ⁸⁄₁₂.

2. Find an equivalent fraction for the second fraction by multiplying top and bottom by the original *bottom* of the first fraction. The bottoms of the two new fractions should now be the same. If you multiply the top and bottom of ¼ by 3, you get ³⁄₁₂.

3. Add the tops of the new fractions, and write the answer over the new bottom you found in step 2. Adding ⁸⁄₁₂ to ³⁄₁₂ gives you ¹¹⁄₁₂.

4. Cancel down if you can – if you see a number you can divide the top and bottom by, divide by it! There's nothing you can evenly divide both 11 and 12 by (except 1, which doesn't help), so your answer is $\frac{11}{12}$.

5. Repeat Step 4 until you can't see any more numbers to cancel. Once you've done this, the fraction is in its *simplest form*.

$\frac{2}{3} + \frac{1}{4}$

Step 1: multiply first fraction top and bottom by 4	$\frac{8}{12}$
Step 2: multiply second fraction top and bottom by 3	$\frac{3}{12}$
Step 3: add the tops	$\frac{11}{12}$

$\frac{1}{2} - \frac{3}{10}$

Step 1: multiply first fraction top and bottom by 10	$\frac{10}{20}$
Step 2: multiply second fraction top and bottom by 2	$\frac{6}{20}$
Step 3: take away the tops	$\frac{4}{20}$
Step 4: cancel down	$\frac{1}{5}$

Figure 4-8: Adding and taking away fractions.

Fractions of a number

Working out a fraction of a number is a simple, two-step process. Once you've done a few sums like this, the process becomes almost automatic. Here are the steps:

1. Divide the number by the bottom of the fraction. If you have to find ⁷⁄₁₀ of 300, you divide 300 by 10 to get 30.

2. Multiply the answer by the top of the fraction. Multiply 30 by 7 to get 210.

That's it!

Multiplying and dividing fractions

In some numeracy tests, you may be asked to multiply two fractions together or to divide one fraction by another. This falls into the 'straightforward but pointless' category, but if it's in your test, you need to know how to do it.

Here's how you multiply two fractions:

1. Multiply the top of the first fraction by the top of the second. Write this number down.

2. Multiply the bottom of the first fraction by the bottom of the second fraction. Write this number down underneath your answer to step 1. Draw a line between the two answers you just wrote down. This is your answer.

3. Cancel it down if you see an obvious number you can divide the top and the bottom by.

To divide fractions, it's only one step more complicated:

1. Flip the second fraction upside down. If the second fraction was ¾, it would become ⁴⁄₃.

2. Multiply the first fraction by the flipped second fraction using the fraction multiplication recipe.

Figure 4-9 shows a fraction multiplication and a fraction division sum.

$$\frac{3}{4} \times \frac{2}{3}$$

Step 1: multiply the tops	6
Step 2: multiply the bottoms	—— 12
Step 3: cancel down	$\frac{1}{2}$

$$\frac{2}{3} \div \frac{4}{5}$$

Step 1: flip the second:	$\frac{2}{3} \times \frac{5}{4}$
Step 2: multiply as before:	$\frac{10}{12}$
Step 3: cancel down	$\frac{5}{6}$

Figure 4-9: Fraction multiplication and division.

Converting between decimals and fractions

Fractions and decimals are two sides of the same coin – they both give you a way of talking about numbers that aren't whole. In fact, they're literally two sides of the same coin – you can see a 50p piece as either half of a pound or £0.50.

Converting from a decimal to a fraction is quite easy. Here's what you do to convert 0.54 into a fraction:

1. Rewrite the original number without a dot in it. If it starts with zeros, you can ignore them. In this case, it'd be 54.

2. Count how many digits are after the dot in the original number. Write down 1 followed by this many zeros underneath the number you wrote down in Step 1. You'd now have $^{54}/_{100}$.

3. Cancel down this fraction as far as you can. The top and bottom of the fraction in Step 2 are both even, so you can halve them both to get $^{27}/_{50}$, which is as far as it goes.

When you're cancelling down fractions that came from decimals, 2 and 5 are especially good numbers to try to divide by.

Dealing with Decimals

When you're adding or taking away decimals, the way you lay out your working becomes even more important than normal. If you get your dots in the wrong place, you'll end up adding the wrong things together and get a wildly wrong answer!

Adding and taking away decimals

Adding and taking away decimal numbers works just the same as adding and taking away normal numbers. The one thing to take care of first is if you have different numbers of digits after the decimal point, add in enough zeros at the end of the shorter number to make them the same length. After that, you can just use the same methods as you normally use for adding and taking away numbers (see earlier in this chapter). Figure 4-10 shows how to work out 15.32 + 7.9 and 15.32 − 7.9 (in two different ways).

```
                                                      15.32 −  7.9
                                                      +0.1   +0.1
                                                      ==========
                                                      15.42 −  8.0
    1  5 . 3  2                                        +2       +2
 +     7 . 9  0          ₁0  ₁5 .₄  ₁3  2              ==========
    ============       −        7 . 9  0              17.42 − 10.0
    2  3 . 2  2                 ============             = 7.42
    1  1 .                           7 . 4   2
```

Figure 4-10: Adding up and taking away decimals.

Multiplying and dividing decimal numbers

I have two more bits of happy news when it comes to multiplying and dividing decimal numbers:

✔ In a numeracy test, it's really unlikely that you'd be asked to do anything trickier than multiplying or dividing a decimal number by a whole number. (The one exception is dividing by a simple decimal – see Chapter 6.)

✔ The same methods you use for multiplying and dividing normal numbers work just the same as for decimals.

As with adding and taking away, you need to be a bit careful about where the dots go, but follow these steps, and you'll be fine to work out sums such as 5.67×3 and $7.413 \div 7$:

1. Count how many spaces from the end of the decimal number the dot is. Write this down and put a circle around it, you'll need it later. For the first example, that would be 2; for the second, it would be 3.

2. Forget about the dot and do the sum as normal. $567 \times 3 = 1702$ and $7413 \div 7 = 159$.

3. Put a dot at the end of it.

4. Move the dot *left* by the number of spaces you wrote down in Step 1. If you go off before the start of the number, it's ok – just put as many extra zeros at the beginning as you need. In the first example, you need to move the dot back two spaces to make it 17.02; in the second, you move it back three spaces to make 0.159.

Chapter 5

Blitzing Beyond the Basics

*M*any people think of maths as 'doing really complicated arithmetic', but for me, maths is about *using* sums or processes to understand the world or to make decisions in real life. Being able to do complicated sums helps, of course, but it's only a part of the story.

In this chapter I take you through some of the maths you need if you want to make sense of measuring the world, and take you a little further into the details of working with more complicated arithmetic, such as BIDMAS and number sequences.

Percentages, proportions and ratio are all really the same thing, and you can do all of them easily with a simple technique called the *Table of Joy*. It's a versatile and memorable grid that helps you figure out exactly what sum you need to do – and once you get the hang of it, you'll never have any problem with percentages again.

Last up, I take a look at some of the details of *statistics*, which is all about describing lists of numbers in ways you can compare, so you can answer questions such as 'Does this washing up liquid really cut through grease better than the leading competitor?' or 'How long can I expect these batteries to last?'

Perfecting Percentages and Parts of the Whole

Percentages are one of those topics that some students fear and dread – usually because the topic was taught poorly at school and everyone got confused.

Per cent just means 'out of every hundred' – so if you have to pay 20% income tax, that means for every £100 you earn you pay the taxman £20. It's all about the relative size of the two amounts: if you earn twice as much under that tax regime, you have to pay twice as much tax.

Proportion and ratio involve the same kind of idea – they express the relative size of two numbers: how many times bigger one number is than the other. Because proportion and ratio are similar to percentages, some students are just as confused by them.

Happily, I have a cure for the confusion, and it's called the Table of Joy.

Doing basic percentages with the Table of Joy

The *Table of Joy* is a technique for figuring out what sum you need to do when you have two amounts you know to be *proportional* – that is, if you double the size of one, you double the size of the other. This includes things like percentages and ratios, as well as dozens of other topics, from currency conversion to cake recipes and beyond.

There are four steps to follow when you're doing a Table of Joy sum:

1. **Drawing a table**, so you have a framework to work in.

2. **Labelling the rows and columns**, so you know what goes where.

3. **Filling in the gaps** with the information you've been given.

4. **Working out the sum**, which is normally the easy bit.

To show you how it's done, I take you through how to work out 20% of £340. Follow along with Figure 5-1 to see how it works.

Drawing the table

The Table of Joy looks like an oversized noughts and crosses grid. Make sure you have space to fit labels in the rows and columns.

The top row and the first column are for labels, so that you know which number to put where; the four squares in the bottom right are for writing the numbers in the sum.

Labelling the rows and columns

You may be tempted to skip this step, but it's actually quite important. By labelling your rows and columns, you make it a piece of cake to figure out which number has to go where.

I like to put the *quantities* I'm measuring in the top middle and top right spaces – in this case, that would be 'pounds' and 'per cent'. In the middle left and bottom left spaces, I put the *situations* I'm looking at – in this example, I'm interested in the whole thing and 20% of it, which I label 'whole thing' and 'part'.

Filling in the gaps

Now it's time to fill in the numbers. The whole of anything is always 100% – in almost every percentage sum you do, you'll need to put 100% in one of the boxes. Here, it goes in the middle right – in the 'per cent' column and the 'whole thing' row.

The 100% always represents either 'the whole thing' or 'where you started'.

The question also states that the 'whole thing' is £340, so that has to go in the 'whole thing' row and the 'pounds' column – the middle.

The last number I know about is that my answer has to be 20% of the whole thing, so I have to put 20 in the 'per cent' column and the 'part' row, which is the bottom right square.

Working out the sum

Now, it's time to work out what sum I need to do, and to find the answer. Any time you work through a Table of Joy problem, this is the sum you need to do! Here's the recipe:

1. Shade in the grid like a chessboard, so the squares alternate between dark and light, with the shaded squares making an 'X'.

2. Find the two numbers that are in the same coloured squares and write them down with a × between them (in this case, I get 340 × 20).

3. After this, write down a divide sign (÷) and the remaining number. For this example, my Table of Joy sum is 340 × 20 ÷ 100.

4. Do the sum 340 × 20 = 6,800; divide this by 100 to get 68 – which means £68 is 20% of £340.

				£	%
			whole thing		
			part		

	£	%		£	%
whole thing	340	100	whole thing	340	100
part		20	part		20

$$340 \times 20 \div 100 = 6800 \div 100 = 68$$

Figure 5-1: The four stages of a Table of Joy percentage sum.

Percentage increase and decrease

In the news, you often hear items that begin 'the price of train tickets is set to rise by 5%' or 'house prices have fallen by 2% across the country'. In better news, you might hear that your favourite clothes shop has a 10% off sale this weekend.

The chances are that in your numeracy test, you'll need to be able to work out exactly how good or bad the news is in a particular case – for example, how many more pounds will a train ticket cost, or how many pounds less will that shirt be?

The Table of Joy makes this kind of sum easy. Working with the train ticket example: say a day return from Brighton to London currently costs £30, and prices are to go up by 5%. How much will the new ticket cost? Here are the steps to work through, and you can follow along in Figure 5-2.

1. **Draw out the Table of Joy.** Draw a big noughts-and-crosses grid.

2. **Label the columns and rows.** The columns are the quantities you're measuring – in this example, pounds and per cent. The rows are the different situations – which would be 'now' and 'later' in this case.

3. **Fill in the numbers you know**. You know that the ticket currently costs £30, so put that in the 'now/pounds' cell, which is the middle square. You also know that you always start from 100%, so that goes in the 'now/per cent' cell (middle-right). Lastly, 5% more than 100% is 105%, so you put 105 in the 'later/per cent' cell (bottom-right).

4. **Shade in the squares and write down the sum**. When you shade the squares like a chessboard (in the shape of a cross), you notice that 30 and 105 are shaded, and that 100 is unshaded. You write down the sum $30 \times 105 \div 100$.

5. **Work out the sum!** Thirty times 105 is 3,150, and $3{,}150 \div 100 = 31.50$. This is the new price of the ticket.

To work out a percentage decrease, you follow the same steps – only instead of adding on the percentage in step 3, you take it away. In the '10% off sale' example, you'd write '90' in the 'later/per cent' cell.

	£	%
now	30	100
later		105

$30 \times 105 \div 100 = 3150 \div 100 = 31.50$

Figure 5-2: Percentage increase and decrease with the Table of Joy.

You can also use the Table of Joy to calculate the percentage change in a price or measurement. If a season ticket increases from £500 to £520, what percentage increase is that? You do the same process of drawing the table, filling in the squares, writing down the sum (this time from the non-shaded squares) and solving it. In the last step, though, you need to find the difference between your answer and 100 to see how many per cent your value has changed. Figure 5-3 shows an example of this.

If your answer is less than 100, you take your answer away from 100 to get the decrease. If your answer is bigger than 100, you take 100 away from your answer to get the increase. Normally, if you get a minus sign in your answer, you've done it the wrong way round – but it's okay, you can just throw out the minus sign and pretend nothing went wrong!

	£	%
start	500	100
end	520	

$520 \times 100 \div 500 = 52,000 \div 500 = 104$

$104 - 100 = 4\%$ increase

Figure 5-3: How many per cent has a price changed?

Rattling Off Ratios

A ratio is usually a pair of numbers with a colon between them, such as 2:1. It describes the *relative size* of two things – if you imagine two people splitting up a pile of sweets (or equal-valued banknotes, or anything else) and saying 'two for me, one for you', you're imagining them dividing the loot in a 2:1 ratio – the first person gets two sweets for every one the other person gets.

Ratios are very similar to percentages, and you can solve them in exactly the same way, using the Table of Joy.

The only tricky thing with ratio problems is making sure you pick the right numbers to go into the table. You have to decide whether the ratio is simply talking about the numbers given, or if it involves a total.

If the question uses words such as 'all together' or 'in total', it's almost certainly a total question – if not, then it's most likely a normal ratio (see the next sections).

Normal ratio sums

A typical normal ratio question would ask something like 'In a drink, juice and water are mixed in the ratio of 1:7. If you use 20 millilitres of juice, how much water do you need?' Notice that there's no mention of 'all together' or 'total'.

To solve a regular ratio problem with the Table of Joy, here's what you do:

1. Draw out your Table of Joy grid.

2. Label the top with what you're measuring – in this example, juice and water.

3. Label the side with 'ratio' and 'answer'.

4. Fill in the ratio row. Here, you'd put 1 underneath 'juice' and 7 underneath 'water'.

5. Fill in the last row. In this case, 20 goes in the 'juice' column.

6. Shade the grid like a chessboard, and write down the Table of Joy sum: multiply the two numbers on the same colour squares and divide by the other number. For this example, the sum is $7 \times 20 \div 1$.

7. Do the sum. The answer here is 140 millilitres.

Total ratio sums

When your sum involves a total, there's bad news and good news. The bad news is you need to think a little bit harder about setting up the sum; the good news is that the Table of Joy works just as well.

A question of this form might say, 'Chris and Steve agree to split their lottery winnings in the ratio of 2:3. If they won £1,500 all together, how much would Chris get?'

Notice the key phrase 'all together' – that means you have to think about the *total* rather than just the numbers you're given.

In this situation, you need to know the total of the ratio: $2 + 3 = 5$. When it comes to writing your Table of Joy, remember that you need to include the *total* in the table, as well as the relevant part of the ratio – here, that's Chris's share, which is 2. You don't care about Steve's share at all, so you can safely ignore him.

To solve a total ratio problem with the Table of Joy, here's what you do:

1. Draw out your Table of Joy grid.

2. Label the top with what you're interested in – in this case, Chris's share and the total.

3. Label the side with 'ratio' and 'answer'.

4. Fill in the ratio row. Because Chris gets two shares out of a total of five, you put 2 under Chris and 5 under total.

5. Fill in the last row. In this case, 1,500 goes in the 'total' column.

6. Shade the grid like a chessboard, and write down the Table of Joy sum: multiply the two numbers on the

same colour squares and divide by the other number. For this example, the sum is $1500 \times 2 \div 5$.

7. Do the sum. The answer here is £600.

Three-part ratios

In some tests, you may see a ratio that looks like 2:3:4. This looks harder than a two-number ratio, but it really isn't: you can do the sums in exactly the same way, by picking out the two interesting numbers in the ratio (or one number and the total, depending on the question) and putting them in the Table of Joy. See Chapter 9 (Test D) for a couple of test questions about a three-part ratio.

Simplifying ratios

Simplifying ratios is very similar to simplifying fractions (if you need a refresher on that, check out Chapter 4). Just as you can write fractions in many different ways (you can write a half as ½ or ¾ or ⁵⁰⁄₁₀₀, among others), you can write ratios in many different ways. The ratio 3:2 is the same as 6:4, or 15:10, or 60:40.

Just like with fractions, ratios have a *simplest form*, which just means a form where the two numbers have no *factors* (apart from 1) in common – there's no number you can evenly divide both parts of the ratio by. For instance, 3:2 is in its simplest form, because 3 and 2 have no factors other than 1 in common. 60:40 isn't in its simplest form because you can divide both of the numbers by 20.

To simplify a ratio, here are the steps you take:

1. Look for a number that divides evenly into both (or all) of the numbers in the ratio.

2. If you can't find one, you're finished! The ratio is in its simplest form.

3. If you found a suitable number in step 1, divide all of the numbers in the ratio by it.

4. Go back to step 1 until you're finished.

Further fractions

You can also use the Table of Joy to find a fraction of a number. A typical question may ask, 'What is ⅔ of 360?'

The thing to remember is that the bottom of the fraction represents the whole thing – three in this case, because three thirds make a whole. Once you remember that, the Table of Joy almost fills itself in for you! Here are the steps, and you can follow along with Figure 5-4:

1. Draw out the Table of Joy grid.

2. Label the top with 'number' and 'fraction', and the side with 'part' and 'whole'.

3. Fill in the fraction column as you'd expect, with the top on the top and the bottom on the bottom. Here, two goes above three in the right column.

4. Put the number in the 'whole/number' cell. In this example, 360 goes in the middle-bottom square.

5. Shade the grid like a chessboard and write down the Table of Joy sum – multiply the two numbers on the same colour squares and divide by the other one. Here, that's 360 × 2 ÷ 3.

6. Work out the sum: 360 × 2 = 720, and 720 ÷ 3 = 240, which is the answer.

	number	fraction
part		2
whole	360	3

360 × 2 ÷ 3 = 720 ÷ 3 = 240

Figure 5-4: Finding a fraction of a number with the Table of Joy.

The Number Knowledge You Need

In this section I explain a few advanced arithmetic (or, if you prefer, basic algebra) topics that you need to be aware of for your numeracy test:

✔ The order of operations (also known as BIDMAS).

✔ Working with formulas, where you replace letters with numbers and work out a sum.

✔ Number sequences, which involve spotting patterns in lists of numbers.

Not so bad, is it?

Bracing yourself for BIDMAS

BIDMAS stands for 'brackets, indices, divide, multiply, add, subtract' and tells you the order in which to do a complicated sum. (*Indices*, by the way, are little numbers above and to the right of a number, like this: 14^2. What it means is 'times the number by itself that many times', so 14^2 is $14 \times 14 = 196$, and 4^3 is $4 \times 4 \times 4 = 64$).

Here's how it works:

✔ If your expression has any brackets in, work out the value of each of the brackets.

✔ If your expression has any indices in, figure out what they are next.

✔ Multiplying and dividing are just as important as each other – you work these out from left to right through the sum.

✔ Lastly, you work out any adds or take aways you have left over at the end, again working from left to right.

Here's a fairly nasty example:

$$((6 + 13) \times 7 + 5 \times 3) \div 2^2 \times 100$$

The first thing to do is to take a deep breath and say 'I can do this if I break it down'.

Now, work out the sums one step at a time. First, look for brackets – there are two pairs. Work out the inner one first: $6 + 13 = 19$. Easy – you can replace that bracket with the number now, to give the following:

$$(19 \times 7 + 5 \times 3) \div 2^2 \times 100$$

Next up, do the remaining bracket, which contains $19 \times 7 + 5 \times 3$. There aren't any brackets or squares in there, so you do the times-and-divide step, working from left to right. The first times you come to is 19×7 – which you can work out to be 133. The next one is $5 \times 3 = 15$.

You don't do $133 + 5 = 138$ and then times that by 3. Remember BIDMAS! The adding and subtracting comes after dividing and multiplying.

The second bracket works out to be $133 + 15 = 148$. So now you have $148 \div 2^2 \times 100$.

Now, you don't have any brackets, so the next thing to work out is the index: 2^2 is the same as 'two multiplied by itself', which makes $2 \times 2 = 4$. The sum now becomes $148 \div 4 \times 100$.

You have just times and divide to do, and you do these sums from left to right: $148 \div 4 = 37$. Then $37 \times 100 = 3,700$, which is your final answer. Phew!

When you see brackets, they mean 'do this bit first'.

Finding the magic formula

A *formula* is a very concisely written recipe for working out a value. They look a bit funny at first because they're sums with letters in instead of numbers – but don't panic! All you have to do is replace the letters with the right numbers and work out the sum.

The main difference between 'normal' sums and formulas is that you don't write times signs in formulas. Whenever you have two things with no sign between them, you have to times them together.

Here's a sample formula you may be given in a numeracy test:

$S = 2wl + 2wh + 2lh$, where S is the surface area, w is the width, h is the height and l is the length.

If you wanted to write that formula in English, you'd say 'The surface area equals two times the width times the length, plus two times the width times the height, plus two times the length times the height.' – which may be slightly easier to understand, but it takes up a lot more space. With a bit of practice, you'll soon be able to 'translate' between formulas and English with no problems at all.

A typical question with this kind of formula would ask, 'if the width is 20cm, the length 40cm and the height 50cm, what is the surface area?'

Here's how you'd work it out:

1. Put a times sign everywhere one belongs, to get $S = 2 \times w \times l + 2 \times w \times h + 2 \times l \times h$.

2. Replace all of the letters with the numbers you're given – so all of the *w*s become 20, all of the *l*s become 40 and all of the *h*s turn into 50.

3. Work out the sum following BIDMAS. There are no brackets or indices, so you do the multiplications first:

   $2 \times 20 \times 40$ and $2 \times 20 \times 50$ and $2 \times 40 \times 50$.

4. You're left with the adds to get your answer: 1600 + 2000 + 4000. So $S = 7600\text{cm}^2$.

Number sequences

A *number* sequence is exactly what it sounds like – a list of numbers that follow some kind of pattern. Here's an example of a number sequence:

1, 2, 3, 4, 5 . . .

You recognise that one, right? The pattern is a very simple one – you add one each time, and you can immediately see that the next three numbers (also called the next three *terms*) in the sequence are 6, 7 and 8.

Sadly, you're not going to get anything quite as easy as that. That said, this type, where you add on the same number each time, is one of only three types of sequence you may have to think about for a numeracy test:

✔ **Add-on series** (like the previous example), in which you add the same number each time.

✔ **Take away series,** in which you take away the same number each time. An example of this would be something like 12, 10, 8, 6 because you take away two each time. The next three terms are 4, 2 and 0.

✔ **Multiplying series**, in which you multiply by the same number each time. You'll only have very simple examples of this, such as 1, 3, 9 – in this case, you times by 3 each time, and the next three terms are 27, 81 and 243.

Adding on and taking away series are sometimes called *arithmetic series*. A multiplying or dividing series is a *geometric* sequence.

Sorting Out Statistics

A *statistic* is just a number that tells you something about a set of values. If I say, 'On average, I take four long-haul flights a year', that's a statistic describing my travel habits. If I say 'My longest-ever flight was 18 hours', that's another statistic.

In this section, I go through some particular types of statistics that come up in numeracy tests: the mean, median and mode, all of which are types of *average*. I cover some more types of statistic (cumulative frequency and the interquartile range) in Chapter 8.

Mean, median and mode

The three main kinds of average you may need to know about are:

✔ The *mean* – what an equal share for everyone would be.

✔ The *median* – the value in the middle.

✔ The *mode* – the most common value.

Mean

The *mean* is probably the first thing you think of when you think of the word 'average' - it's the one you work out by adding up all of the numbers in a list and dividing by how many there are. It's the most complicated of the three to work out (you can remember which one it is by thinking 'It's the *meanest* thing they can ask'), but if you have a calculator and a bit of patience, you can work it out easily enough. Here's what you do:

1. Add up the numbers on your calculator (or on paper).

2. Count how many numbers were in the list.

3. Divide your total from Step 1 by your count from Step 2. Your answer is the mean.

4. Check the number makes sense! It has to be between the highest and lowest number in the list, and is usually somewhere near the middle.

Grouped frequency mean

Finding the mean of a grouped frequency table is about the meanest of the mean questions. Even though it's a more involved topic than the normal mean questions, if you break it down into logical steps, it's not all that difficult.

The starting point for these questions is always a table that looks like the one in Figure 5-5. You need to find the mean – in this case, the mean number of bedrooms per house.

The trick is to think about what the table tells you: 7 houses have 1 bedroom each, 9 houses have 2 bedrooms each, 7 houses have 3 bedrooms each and 1 house has four bedrooms. Just like before, you need to know the *total* (how many rooms there are all together) and the *count* (how many houses there are).

Here are the steps you take:

1. In each house-bedroom group, times the two numbers together and write them down next to the row.

2. Add up the numbers at the end of each row.

3. Count up the frequency column – in this case, the houses. When the question asks you for the mean number of 'somethings' per 'something else', the frequency is the 'something else' column; the one that comes after 'per'.

4. Divide your answer from Step 2 by your answer from Step 3. The answer is the mean.

Don't be tempted to divide your total number (your answer from Step 2) by the number of groups.

So the first group has 7 bedrooms for 7 houses. The next group has 18 bedrooms for 9 houses: 2 apiece. The third group has 21 bedrooms for 7 houses. The last group has 4 bedrooms in 1 house. That makes a total of 7 + 18 + 21 + 4 = 48 bedrooms, split between a count of 7 + 9 + 7 +1 = 24 houses: you divide 48 by 24 to get the mean of 2 bedrooms per household. Phew!

Bedrooms	Frequency
1	7
2	9
3	7
4	1

$1 \times 7 = 7$
$2 \times 9 = 18$
$3 \times 7 = 21$
$4 \times 1 = 4$

7 + 18 + 21 + 4 = 48 (total rooms)
7 + 9 + 7 + 1 = 24 (number of houses)
48 ÷ 24 = 2

Figure 5-5: Finding a grouped frequency mean.

Median

The *median* value in a list of numbers is the one in the middle. Median is another word for the central reservation of a road, which also goes in the middle.

To work out the median value of a list, here's what you do:

1. Check whether your list is in order. If not, you need to put it in order. It doesn't really matter which way around you sort them, but I prefer lowest to highest.

2. Circle the first number and the last number in the list - have a look at Figure 5-6 to follow along.

3. Find the first and last numbers in the list that aren't already circled, and draw circles around them.

4. Repeat Step 3 until you have only one or two numbers left uncircled.

5. If you've only got one number left, that's your median and you're done.

6. If you have two numbers left, add them together and divide by two – that's your median.

Raw scores	In order	Circle first and last...		
84	80	80	80	80
89	84	84	84	84
93	84	84	84	84
80	87	87	87	87 ← median
84	89	89	89	89
87	93	93	93	93
104	104	104	104	104

Figure 5-6: Finding the median.

To find the median of a frequency table, here's what you do:

1. Add up the 'frequency' column to find out how many items there would be in the list.

2. Add one to this number and divide it by two. (You might not end up with a whole number but that's okay.)

3. Go through the groups one at a time, adding up the frequencies until your total is bigger than your answer from step 2.

4. Find the label attached to that group – this is the median group!

If you wanted to find the median group in Figure 5-5, you would find that the total frequency is 24. If you add one and divide by two, you get $25 \div 2 = 12.5$.

Adding up the frequencies one at a time, you get 7 (which is below 12.5) and then $7 + 9 = 16$ (which is above 12.5). The label of the group that took you over 12.5 is 2, so the median number of bedrooms is two.

Mode

The *mode* is the most common number in a list. You can remember that 'mode' is a fancy word for 'fashion' and the mode is the most fashionable number in the list, or you can really draw out the 'o' sound: the moooooooode is the mooooooost common. I recommend doing that in your head, or else someone will tell you that you sound like a cow. I speak from experience.

The mode is probably the easiest of the three main averages to find. Here's all you need to do:

1. Put the list in order if it isn't already. Be careful not to change the size of the list – if there are,say, three 7s in the original list, you need three 7s in the sorted list.

2. Count how many of each value there are.

3. The one with the highest count is the mode.

It's even easier if you have a table: you simply find the group with the highest frequency – in the table in Figure 5-5, the '2' group has 9 houses in, more than the others, so the mode is 2.

In Figure 5-5, the mean, mode and median all happen to be 2 – however, there's no guarantee that the three averages will be the same. Unfortunately, you have to work each of them out separately!

Chapter 6

Mastering Mental Arithmetic

*M*ental arithmetic – or, more strictly, non-calculator maths – comes up in many numeracy tests. Some people find this way of doing maths quite stressful, and answering questions both accurately and quickly can take a lot of practice.

In some tests, such as the ALAN, the whole exam is non-calculator; in others, such as teacher training exams, a mental arithmetic section counts for a significant part of your final mark. In others, you may be able to use a calculator throughout – check the website for the test you're taking or ask for the precise details.

In this chapter, I show you some of the tricks and shortcuts you need to get up to speed with answering questions quickly when you don't have a calculator. I don't show you the recipes again (check out Chapter 4 for that), but I do give you some worked examples.

Like anything else, the more you practise working without a calculator, the better you get at it.

Breaking Down the Big Four

The vast bulk of what you have to do in a mental arithmetic test involves picking the right sum to do, and working it out. Most of the time, it's either a whole number sum or a decimal sum, both of which I talk about in this section. Otherwise, it's likely to be something to do with fractions, percentages or time and money – in which case, see the sections later in this chapter.

Adding and subtracting

Adding and subtracting quickly on paper are two skills you're definitely going to need when you sit a mental arithmetic test.

Building up speed

A good way to improve your speed and accuracy in adding and taking away numbers is to learn all of your adding and subtracting facts up to 10 + 10 and 20 – 10. Figure 6-1 shows them in a handy, easy-to-use table.

To find the answer to an addition sum, here's what you do:

1. Hold a ruler sideways across the grid and move it downwards, looking at the first column.

2. When you find the first number in the sum, stop and leave the ruler there.

3. Look across the top row to find the first number in the sum.

4. Read down the column until you get to the ruler.

5. The number in that column above the ruler is your answer.

To use the table for taking away, here are the steps:

1. Find the second number (the one after the minus sign) in the top row.

2. Read down the column until you find the first number (the one before the minus sign).

3. The number at the left end of that row is your answer.

This method only works if the second number is smaller than the first! Otherwise, do the sum the other way around and put a minus sign in front of your answer.

+	1	2	3	4	5	6	7	8	9	10
1	2	3	4	5	6	7	8	9	10	11
2	3	4	5	6	7	8	9	10	11	12
3	4	5	6	7	8	9	10	11	12	13
4	5	6	7	8	9	10	11	12	13	14
5	6	7	8	9	10	11	12	13	14	15
6	7	8	9	10	11	12	13	14	15	16
7	8	9	10	11	12	13	14	15	16	17
8	9	10	11	12	13	14	15	16	17	18
9	10	11	12	13	14	15	16	17	18	19
10	11	12	13	14	15	16	17	18	19	20

Figure 6-1: Addition and subtraction facts up to 10 + 10 and 20 – 10.

Avoiding mistakes

The most common mistakes in mental arithmetic come from untidy layout. I'm as guilty of this as anyone (my work usually looks like a cross between alphabetti spaghetti and chaos theory), but you really don't want to make your sums any harder than they have to be. Here's how you keep your layout neat:

- ✔ Give yourself plenty of space, and make sure your columns are clearly separated.

- ✔ If it's a decimal sum, make sure your dots are all between the same two columns, and fill in any missing zeros if you like to.

- ✔ If it's not a decimal sum, make sure all your numbers end in the last column.

The more neatly you lay out your work, the fewer mistakes you'll make – and the easier it is to put right any mistakes.

Multiplying and dividing

Practising multiplying and dividing is a two-stage process: first, you have to learn how to do the sums correctly, and then how to do them quickly. You may feel that you can do this type of sum when you're not under time pressure, but as soon as the clock is ticking, it seems to become impossibly hard.

Getting faster

Like most things, the more you practise multiplying and dividing, the quicker you get. Here are a few ways you can focus your practice on speeding up:

- ✔ **Practise your times tables.** I know, it's boring and you have bad memories of this in primary school, but the better you know your tables, the quicker you'll be in your numeracy test. On the plus side, once you know them off by heart, you never have to learn them again! Figure 6-2 shows the times tables up to 10×10.

- ✔ **Do easy sums against the clock.** If you struggle to complete the hard questions in a short time, try doing less complicated questions. This hopefully gets you used to working under time constraints and helps build your confidence.

- ✔ **Give yourself longer.** If you find the psychological ticktock factor to be a problem, try giving yourself much, much longer than you'd get in a test to answer a question. If you'd expect to have a minute, give yourself ten. Gradually reduce the time and aim to get a little quicker each time.

×	1	2	3	4	5	6	7	8	9	10
1	1	2	3	4	5	6	7	8	9	10
2	2	4	6	8	10	12	14	16	18	20
3	3	6	9	12	15	18	21	24	27	30
4	4	8	12	16	20	24	28	32	36	40
5	5	10	15	20	25	30	35	40	45	50
6	6	12	18	24	30	36	42	48	54	60
7	7	14	21	28	35	42	49	56	63	70
8	8	16	24	32	40	48	56	64	72	80
9	9	18	27	36	45	54	63	72	81	90
10	10	20	30	40	50	60	70	80	90	100

Figure 6-2: Times tables up to 10×10.

Keeping it neat and getting it right

With multiplying and dividing sums (just like with adding and taking away), keeping things neat and tidy makes things a lot easier. Here are some tips:

- ✔ **Lay it out the same way each time**. The more consistently you set your work out, the easier it is to go back and see what you did before; also, when things go wrong, it's easier to find the mistake if your working out is tidy.

- ✔ **Give yourself room and keep sums separate.** Draw a line under every sum before you start the next one – it stops you from getting muddled up between what you're working on now and what was on your mind before.

Taking stock of tens

Ten is an incredibly important number in maths, for all manner of reasons. Here are some of them:

- ✔ There are ten digits in the number system, and ten digits on most people's hands. Coincidence? I think not. The number system is called the *decimal* system, and decimal means 'to do with tens'.

- ✔ Ten is a really easy number to multiply and divide by (of which more in a moment).

- ✔ The money system used everywhere in the world is based on tens and hundreds.

- ✔ The whole metric system used for measuring things is based on tens, hundreds and thousands.

Multiplying and dividing by ten

When you do your numeracy test, I can *guarantee* that you'll have to multiply or divide something by a power of ten, whether it's to work out a percentage, convert a unit, or any one of a dozen other possibilities.

You may be relieved to hear that it's really easy to multiply any number by ten – and, in fact, by any *power* of ten, such as 100 or 1,000. Here's how you do it:

1. If your number doesn't have a decimal point (a dot) in it, put one after the last digit.

2. Count how many zeros are in the power of ten you're multiplying by – so, if you're multiplying by 10, your count is 1; if it's 1,000, your count is 3.

3. Move the dot that many spaces to the **right**. If you go off the end of the number, it's okay – just keep track of how many spaces you have left over and add that many zeros to the end. You're left with the answer.

Figure 6-3 shows you an example of multiplying a number by a power of ten. It also shows you an example of dividing a number by a power of ten, using the following steps:

1. If your number doesn't have a decimal point in it, put one after the last digit.

2. Count how many zeros are in the power of ten you're dividing by – if you're dividing by 10, your count is 1; if it's 1,000, your count is 3.

3. Move the dot that many spaces to the **left**. If you go off the start of the number, it's ok – note how many spaces you have left over and add that many zeros to the front of the number.

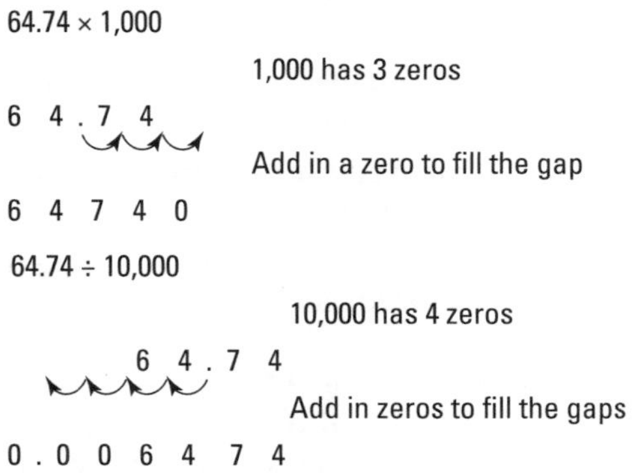

64.74 × 1,000

    1,000 has 3 zeros

6 4 . 7 4
                    Add in a zero to fill the gap

6 4 7 4 0

64.74 ÷ 10,000

    10,000 has 4 zeros

        6 4 . 7 4
                    Add in zeros to fill the gaps

0 . 0 0 6 4 7 4

Figure 6-3: Multiplying and dividing by powers of ten.

Dividing by a decimal

Sometimes you get asked something that looks utterly impossible, like 464 ÷ 0.02. Dividing by a decimal? Surely no mortal being could be expected to know how to do that!

However, if you know how to multiply and divide by ten (which, if you've read the previous section, you do), you can make this kind of sum simple:

1. If the second number is a decimal, multiply **both** numbers by ten. Yep, you read that right, *multiply*. In this example, you'd get 4640 ÷ 0.2.

2. Repeat step 1 until the second number is a whole number. After another step, you'd get 46400 ÷ 2.

3. Do the divide sum as normal (see Chapter 4). In this case, you end up with 23200.

That's a bit strange – you just divided by a number and got a bigger number as the answer! Don't worry: this only happens when you divide by a number that's smaller than one. You could see this question as 'how many 2p coins would you need to make £464', if you like.

Finding factors

Finding factors is a process that comes in really useful when you're trying to cancel down fractions or ratios. (I cover cancelling fractions in Chapter 4 and ratios in Chapter 5, in case you need a reminder of how they work). A *factor* is any number that divides exactly into the number you're interested in. For example, because 6 = 2 × 3, two and three are both factors of 6; however, 6 ÷ 4 doesn't give a whole number, so 4 is not a factor of 6.

Every number bigger than one has at least two factors – because 1 × the number makes the number, 1 and the number are both factors.

A number whose only factors are one and itself, such as 3 and 5, is known as a *prime number*. These are the building blocks of quite a lot of maths, and have all manner of interesting properties, if you're into that kind of thing.

Being able to spot a few factors is really useful if you're trying to simplify a fraction. Here are a few you can find easily:

✔ If a number ends in 2, 4, 6, 8 or 0, it has two as a factor.

✔ If a number ends in 5 or 0, it has five as a factor.

✔ If a number ends in a zero, it has ten as a factor (as well as 2 and 5).

✔ If the digits in a number add up to a multiple of three, it has three as a factor. So 201 and 111 have 3 as a factor.

✔ If the digits in a number add up to a multiple of nine, it has nine as a factor. So 72 and 153 have 9 as a factor.

The 'adding up' method from those last two bullets only works for three and nine!

Chapter 9 includes questions on simplifying fractions.

Putting Percentages in their Place

As with most things in this book, you have several ways of dealing with percentages. In Chapter 5, I show you how to do them with the Table of Joy, which is a quick and useful way to remember what sum you need to do, but the actual sum is normally easier on a calculator. What about when a percentage question crops up in a non-calculator test?

This section walks you through some other techniques for quickly dealing with percentage questions when you're reduced to working on paper.

Converting percentages into other forms

Converting a percentage into a decimal is as easy as converting pennies into pounds – in fact, it's the same sum!

If you have a two-digit percentage (such as 25%), all you need to do is put a zero and a dot in front of the first number. For this example, 25% is the same as 0.25.

If you have a one-digit percentage, you have to put a zero, a dot and another zero in front of your number – so 9% is the same as 0.09.

The reason 9% isn't the same as 0.9 is that 0.9 is the same as 90%, nearly a whole one rather than a little less than a tenth. Imagine it as 9p rather than 90p. Technically, what you're doing here is dividing by 100, but don't let that scare you. If it does scare you, check out the section on Powers of Ten earlier in this chapter.

Finding a percentage

Percentage questions in non-calculator tests tend to work with comparatively easy percentages, and here are the steps you take to work out a number as a percentage of another, for example, 45 as a percentage of 180:

1. **Label the smaller number as the 'part' and the larger number the 'whole thing.'**

2. **Divide the 'whole thing' number by 10.** This gives you 10%. If you're looking for 45 as a percentage of 180, you can work out that 18 is 10%.

3. **Double your answer from step 1.** This gives you 20% of the number. In this example, you have 36.

4. **Repeatedly add your 10% number until you go past your part number.** Be sure to write down which percentage you've figured out at each stage. If you reach your number exactly, the percentage you got to is your answer!

5. **If the 'part' number is halfway between two of your answers, split the difference.** For example, you know that 20% is 36 and 30% is 54. 45 is halfway between 36 and 54, so the percentage is halfway between 20 and 30: 25%. This is your answer.

This method works in almost all non-calculator percentage questions. If it doesn't work, you can find one number as a percentage of another using the Table of Joy followed by a fairly tedious divide sum.

If you need to find a percentage of a number, here's what you do – for example, to find 35% of 240:

1. Divide the number by 10 to find 10%. In this case, 10% is 24.

2. Multiply this number by how many tens are in the percentage you're looking for – in this case, that's 3, so you work out 30% to be $24 \times 3 = 72$. If your percentage number was a multiple of ten, this is your answer!

3. If your percentage number isn't a multiple of ten, you need to find 1%. You do this by dividing your answer from Step 1 by 10 again. In this case, 1% is 2.4.

4. Multiply this number by the number of units in your answer – here, that's 5, and you get $5\% = 5 \times 2.4 = 12$.

5. Add your answers from Steps 2 and 4 to get your answer. Here, it's $72 + 12 = 84$.

Percentage increase and decrease

Percentage increase and decrease aren't any more difficult than simply finding percentages, except that there's an extra step involved. Here are some situations where you might need to work out a percentage increase or decrease:

✔ A price has gone up or down by a given percentage.

✔ You want to give a certain percentage of a meal price as a tip.

✔ You're given a price without tax and need to add the tax rate.

✔ You're given an investment or a loan and an interest rate.

✔ You're told that a value has gone up or down by a given percentage since the previous year.

This type of question is fairly common in numeracy tests, and as long as you keep your head it's quite straightforward. In this recipe, you can work out what happens if the price of a £180 bike goes up or down by 15%. Here are the steps you take if you want to find the value after an increase or decrease:

1. Work out the given percentage of the full price, using either the Table of Joy or the method in the previous section. Fifteen per cent of £180 is £27.

2. If it's an 'increase' question, add this on to the original value; this is your answer. If the price of the bike went up 15%, it would now cost £207.

3. If it's a 'decrease' question, take this away from the original value. If the price of the bike had dropped by 15%, it would now be £153. Bargain!

 Be very careful to read the question and give the value it asks for – if it only wants the interest, or the tax, or the increase, or the saving (rather than the amount *after* the increase or decrease) you have to give the answer from Step 1!

Making Sense of Money and Time

I'm willing to bet that your mental arithmetic test will include something about money and something about time, and possibly both at once.

Money sums tend to be a little bit easier than time sums. With time sums, you have to be careful about there being 60 minutes in an hour rather than 100 (personally, I can't wait until time is decimalised, it'll make everyone's life easier).

Counting your cash

Doing sums with money is just like doing sums with normal numbers. You add, take away, multiply and divide just like you do with normal numbers. However, you need to watch out for a couple of things:

 ✔ When you're doing any kind of money sum, make sure your dots are lined up – you don't want to add pennies when you meant to add pounds!

 ✔ Some examiners like to throw in tricks in money questions just to be mean. Especially if you're working out a bill for several items, make sure you've worked out the price for right number of items.

> ✔ As always, lay out your work neatly. If you're doing a sum with many parts to it, write down the answer to each part somewhere you can easily find it.
>
> ✔ Read the question carefully! Don't give the total if the question asks for the change from a certain amount, and vice versa.

Converting your currency

Currency conversion is about as difficult as money sums get in mental arithmetic tests – and luckily they're not all that difficult.

Figure 6-4 shows how to convert £150 into dollars if you know that £1 = $1.60. Here are the steps you take:

1. Draw out a noughts and crosses grid, leaving plenty of space for labels. Oh yes, this is a Table of Joy sum (see Chapter 5).

2. Label the top row with the names of the currencies and the left hand side with 'exchange rate' and 'amount'.

3. Fill in the exchange rate in the middle row. In the example, you'd put 1 underneath 'pounds' and 1.60 underneath 'dollars'.

4. Put the amount you're given in the correct column of the bottom row – in this case, you'd put '150' in the 'pounds' columns.

5. Shade in the grid like a chessboard.

6. Write out the Table of Joy sum – multiply the two numbers on the same colour squares together, and divide by the other. In this case, it's $150 \times 1.6 \div 1$.

7. Work out the sum! Here, the answer is $150 \times 1.6 = \$240$.

To multiply by a decimal, count how many spaces from the right end the dot is (in 150×1.6, that's one space), then ignore the dot. Work out the sum without the dot: $150 \times 16 = 2400$, and then put the dot back in the right number of spaces from the end (one space) – so your answer is 240. See Chapter 4 for more details!

	Pounds	Dollars
Rate		
Money		

	Pounds	Dollars
Rate	1	1.60
Money		

	Pounds	Dollars
Rate	1	1.60
Money	150	

$$\frac{150 \times 1.60}{1} = 240$$

Figure 6-4: Currency conversion with the Table of Joy. _____

Currency conversions always involve multiplying or dividing by the rate you're given – if you can use your common sense to figure out whether your answer should be bigger or smaller than the number you're given, you may be able to work out the right sum to do without the Table of Joy.

Time for the 24-hour clock

The 24-hour clock – also known as military time – is the way times are usually displayed on timetables, as well as digital alarm clocks, digital watches and mobile phones.

Traditionally when you tell the time, you use a 12-hour clock – you say 'ten past nine' whether it's 9.10 in the morning or 9.10 in the evening. You can show which one you mean by writing 'a.m.' after the time if it's in the morning, or 'p.m.' after the time if it's after midday.

By convention, midnight is 12 a.m. and midday is 12 p.m.

Military time gets rid of the ambiguity – if you're giving a time that's 1 p.m. or later, you add 12 to the number of hours – so 1.00 p.m. is 1300 in military time, and 8.30 p.m. is 2030.

You may notice that military time doesn't look like a normal clock time – with no colon or dot in the middle of it, and no a.m. or p.m. That's normal – you always give military time as a four-digit number (morning times before 10 a.m. have a nought in front of them when you use the 24-hour clock – so 9 a.m. is 0900).

Converting military time to normal time

Here's a recipe for converting military time to normal time:

1. Split the time into two halves – the first two digits are the hours and the last two digits are the minutes.

2. If the hours number is less than 12, it's a morning time – write down 'a.m.' somewhere. Otherwise, it's after noon, so you write down 'p.m.'.

3. If it's an afternoon time, take away 12 from the 'hours' number; otherwise, leave it alone.

4. If your hours number is zero, make it 12.

5. Write down your hours number, a dot, then the minutes from Step 1, then either 'a.m.' or 'p.m.' as you decided in step 2.

Converting normal time to military time

Going the other way isn't much more difficult. Here's what you do:

1. Split your time into hours and minutes.

2. If your time is 'a.m.' and the 'hours' number is 12, make it zero.

3. If your time is a 'p.m.' time, add 12 to the 'hours' number.

4. Write down the 'hours' number followed by the 'minutes' number.

How long things last

Numeracy tests often ask you to find how long things last given the start and the end time. Easy-peasy, you may think – but a trap is lying in wait for you. Finding the difference between two times isn't just a matter of taking one time away from the other, because there are sixty minutes in an hour rather than 100.

Finding the difference between two times in the same hour is very simple: you just take away the minutes of the earlier time from the minutes of the later time – that's your answer in minutes. For example, 10.15 to 10.50 is 50 – 15 = 35 minutes.

When you're in different hours, you need to be a bit more careful. Here's the way I recommend doing it, working out how long it is between 11.15 a.m. and 3.45 p.m.:

1. Work out how many minutes it is to the next 'o'clock' after the earlier time. After 11.15, the next o'clock would be 12 o'clock, in 45 minutes' time.

2. Work out how many hours it is from that o'clock to the o'clock immediately before the later time – in this case, 3 o'clock is right before 3.45, and that's three hours after 12 o'clock.

3. Work out how many minutes it is from the o'clock in Step 2 to the later time – in this case, another 45 minutes.

4. Add up the hours and the minutes – in this case, you have 3 hours and 90 minutes.

5. If your minutes are more than 60, add 1 to the number of hours and take 60 away from the number of minutes. In this example, you'd get 4 hours and 30 minutes.

Finding start and end times

You use a very similar technique to this to find a start or end time, if you know the other time and how long the event took. You know it takes 1 hour and 50 minutes to drive to your nan's house, and you need to be there by 4 p.m. – when must you set off? Here's what you do:

1. Figure out whether you're going backwards or forwards in time. If you have the end time of the event, you need to go back in time; if you have the start time, you need to go forward. In the example, you're travelling backwards in time (you're looking for an answer before 4 p.m.).

2. Reverse the flux capacitor. Okay, not really.

3. If you're going backwards in time, take away the hours and minutes the event lasts from the hours and minutes of the end time (it's ok if you get a minus number for the minutes). In the example, you get 3 hours, –50 minutes.

4. If you're going forwards, add the hours and minutes the event lasts to the hours and minutes of the start time (it's ok if the number of minutes goes over 60).

5. If your number of minutes is between 0 and 60, you have your answer.

6. If your number of minutes is more than 60, take 60 away from it and add 1 to the hours in your answer. You're done!

7. If your number of minutes is less than 0, add 60 to it and take 1 away from the hours in your answer. Finished! In the example, 3 hours and –10 minutes becomes 2 hours and 10 minutes, or 2.10 p.m.

If you need to do something like –15 + 60, you can turn it around to get 60 – 15. This gives you the same answer (45).

Chapter 7

Reaching Into
Real-World Maths

. . . .

In This Chapter

▶ Making sense of metric measurements

▶ Dealing with degrees (and other conversions)

▶ Spotting patterns with shapes

. . . .

*P*robably 90 per cent of the maths you do at work or in study involves *real-world applications*, by which I mean things like:

✔ Measuring distance, area, volume and capacity.

✔ Describing shapes.

✔ Weighing things.

✔ Taking temperatures.

✔ Summarising your measurements.

This chapter is all about this kind of real-world maths.

The main thing to remember in real-world maths is to check you're using the right units. It's very easy to mix up your grams and kilograms, or your miles and kilometres, and end up with the wrong answer despite doing everything else right.

Measuring Up with the Metric System

Once upon a time, literally dozens of measurement systems were in use around the world. A pound in London was a different weight to a pound in Paris – and, in fact, a pint in the US is still 20% smaller than a pint in the UK. Each system of weights and measures was divided into a different number of smaller units – a foot is 12 inches, and a pound is 16 ounces – and it was all a bit of a mess.

At some point in the 19th century, scientists said, 'Enough! We can't *possibly* work under these conditions!' and came up with a different, altogether simpler way of measuring things. They took a lump of metal and said 'that's a kilogram'. They took another length of metal and said 'that's a metre'. Instead of dividing the units up with random numbers, they decided to use powers of ten – so you can convert between (say) kilograms and grams and tonnes by simply moving the decimal point.

These scientists made your numeracy exam significantly easier, because the *metric system* they introduced is now the basis for almost all measurements around the world.

A few old-fashioned *imperial* units are still in use in the UK – most noticeably miles and pints, but also stones, pounds, feet and inches. These are becoming less common, though.

Weighing things up

Unless you're doing something incredibly scientific, you usually see weights in the metric system given in *kilograms* or *kg*. One kilogram weighs about the same as a one-litre bottle of water.

If you divided a kilogram into a thousand equal pieces, each of them would weigh a *gram* – that's about the same weight as one of those little sachets of sugar you get in a coffee shop.

Going the other way, a thousand kilograms weigh the same as a tonne – that's about the weight of a car.

You can do all the same sorts of questions with weight as you can with regular numbers, but the most common kind of question to come up in numeracy exams involves reading some kind of scale.

I'm willing to bet you've used a scale before – either to weigh yourself, or your vegetables in the supermarket, or your ingredients in the kitchen; you can see several of these in Figure 7-1.

Using a scale is easy: you just make sure it's set to zero, then put the thing you want to weigh on it. If it's a digital scale, you read off the weight from the display; if it's an analogue scale (one with a dial), you just find the number underneath the hairline.

Sometimes you're given a dial with two scales on it – perhaps kilograms and stones or grams and ounces. Make sure you're looking at the one the question asks for!

Figure 7-1: Several types of scale.

The long and short of it

Measuring length and distance is a very typical exam question, and something you have to deal with in real life too – if you're doing some home improvements, packing boxes or checking whether your fridge will fit through the door.

In the metric system, distances are usually measured in *metres* (m) – the top of a desk is a metre above the ground, give or take. A metre is divided up into 100 *centimetres* (or cm) – each of your fingers is probably about one centimetre wide. A thousand metres make a *kilometre* (km), which is two and a half laps of an athletics track.

In Britain, we still use a few old-fashioned imperial units of length, notably the *mile* (about 1.6 kilometres) and the *inch* (about 2.5 centimetres). You need to know that these things exist, but the conversion factors are given to you if you have to convert between them in the exam.

Converting between units

Converting is what you do any time a value is given in one unit and you need a different one – if you know a measurement in inches but you prefer centimetres, or you have a volume in pints that ought to be in litres, or a price in Chinese yuan that you need in Mexican pesos.

There's bad news, good news and better news in this topic. The bad news is, there are an almost infinite number of possible conversions you can do. The good news is that you only ever experience a handful of them in numeracy tests, and the better news is that you can use the Table of Joy (see Chapter 5 if you need help with that) on very nearly all of them.

The only kind of unit conversion where the Table of Joy doesn't work is temperature. If you have to do a temperature conversion, you're given the formula. In fact, you're given the conversion factor between units in most cases.

Converting units with the Table of Joy

A typical conversion question would ask you something like this:

> *An American drinks from a 16-ounce cup of coffee. An ounce of coffee is about the same as 30 millilitres. How much coffee is 16 ounces, in millilitres?*

Here are the steps you take to set up the Table of Joy:

1. **Draw out a noughts and crosses grid, giving yourself enough space for labels.** In this case, the column labels are 'ounces' and 'millilitres', and the row labels are 'conversion' and 'coffee'.

2. **Fill in the conversion rate.** You know that one ounce is 30 millilitres, so put '1' in the conversion/ounces square and '30' in the conversion/millilitres square.

3. **Fill in the other amount.** Here, you're interested in 16 ounces, so put '16' in the coffee/ounces square.

4. **Shade in the Table of Joy like a chessboard and write down the sum.** Have a look at Figure 7-2 to see what it looks like – the sum is $16 \times 30 \div 1$.

5. **Work out the sum.** The answer is 480 millilitres – I don't know about you, but I'd be bouncing off of the walls if I drank that much!

	ounces	millilitres
conversion	1	30
coffee	16	$\dfrac{30 \times 16}{1} = 480$

Figure 7-2: Coffee conversion with the Table of Joy.

Converting units the traditional way

The traditional way of converting units involves fewer steps but needs you to remember a bit more. It also only works when you have a conversion factor given as 'one thing equals some number of other things' – say, 'One mile is the same as 1.6 kilometres.' To make the recipe easier, it helps to think of the thing with a one by it as the *'one' side* of the conversion, and the thing on the other side as . . . well, the *other side*.

Here's how you'd do an example that wanted you to convert £75 into South African rand at the rate of one pound to 11 rand.

1. **Work out whether what you know is on the 'one' side of the conversion or the other side.** In this case, you know about pounds, which is on the 'one' side of the conversion – you're told that one pound equals some number of rand.

2. **If your number is on the 'one' side, multiply by the conversion factor, otherwise divide by it.** Here, you need to multiply 75 by 11 and get 825 rand.

Going the other way, if you had 583 rand that you wanted to convert back into pounds, you would divide by 11 – and get the answer of £53.

Converting temperature using algebra

The one unit conversion you can't do using the Table of Joy or even the traditional method is the conversion between Celsius and Fahrenheit and vice versa. (I tell the whole story about the different scales, involving Mrs Fahrenheit's armpit and a sneaky Mr Linnaeus turning everything around, in *Basic Maths For Dummies* (Wiley), but you'll need to buy the book to read it.)

If you need to convert between Fahrenheit and Celsius, you'll be given either a formula or a recipe – you don't need to remember them, just follow the instructions. The most common ways of writing the formulas are:

$$F = 1.8 \times C + 32$$

$$C = (F - 32) \times 5 \div 9$$

These follow the normal rules for formulas you may have seen in Chapter 5, but here are the recipes written out so you can see how they work. First up, suppose you want to convert 30°C to Fahrenheit:

1. **Multiply the Celsius number by 1.8.** In the example, $30 \times 1.8 = 54$.

2. **Add on 32.** $54 + 32 = 86$, so 30°C is 86°F.

Now, how about converting 50°F into Celsius?

1. **Take 32 away from the Fahrenheit number.** $50 - 32 = 18$.

2. **Multiply the result by 5.** $18 \times 5 = 90$.

3. **Divide your answer by 9.** $90 \div 9 = 10$, so 50°F is the same as 10°C.

Showing Shapes Who's Boss

Many numeracy tests ask you to describe shapes in some way. You may have to:

- ✔ Name the kind of shape in a picture.

- ✔ Say how many sides a named shape has.

- ✔ Work out the size of an angle in a shape.

- ✔ Figure out the area or perimeter of a shape, which could be a complicated one.

- ✔ Work out the volume or capacity of a simple 3-D shape.

- ✔ Determine how many boxes fit into a bigger box.

- ✔ Use a formula to work out any of these quantities.

Finding your angle

Angle is another word for corner.

Angles are measured in degrees. For example, if a car spins 360 degrees, it spins all the way round, while the latitude of London is 53 degrees north of the equator. Confusingly, angle degrees are completely different from temperature degrees – the context usually makes clear which type of degrees you need to work with (except possibly when talking about pointy icicles!).

The four key types of angle you need to know about, as shown in Figure 7-3, are:

✔ An *acute* angle is less than 90° – a small angle that looks quite pointy. Remember this by thinking that a 'cute' angle is little.

✔ A *right angle* is exactly 90°.

✔ An *obtuse* angle is more than 90° but less than 180°.

✔ A *reflex* angle is more than 180°. You can remember this by thinking of the doctor hitting the outside of your knee to test your reflexes – the angle on the outside of your knee is more than 180°!

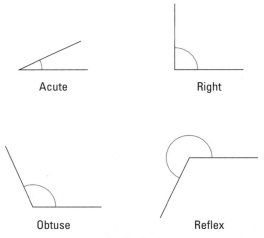

Acute   Right

Obtuse   Reflex

Figure 7-3: The four types of angle.

The shapes you need to know

The four basic *two-dimensional* (or flat) shapes you need to know and recognise are the square, rectangle, triangle and circle.

A few others you may need to know about are the pentagon (five sides), a hexagon (six sides) and an octagon (eight sides).

You may also need to know a few ways to describe triangles:

- An *equilateral* triangle has three sides of the same length ('equi-' means 'the same', and 'lateral' means 'side'). You may also need to know that each angle in an equilateral triangle is 60°.

- An *isosceles* triangle has two sides of the same length and one different (one of my students taught me to remember this as an i-sausages triangle, and to imagine two sausages leaning on each other). Two of the angles in an isosceles triangle are the same, and the other different – it's the one between the sausages that's different.

- A *scalene* triangle has sides of all different lengths.

- A *right-angled* triangle has one corner with an angle of 90° – a right-angled triangle can be either scalene or isosceles.

In three dimensions, the main shapes you need to know about are these:

- The cube: the shape of a die – a box where all six faces are equal-sized squares.

- The cuboid: the shape of a shoe box – all six faces are rectangles.

- The sphere: the shape of a ball.

- The cone: the shape of an ice cream cone (at least, the pointy bit!)

All about area

A very loose definition of area is 'how much stuff you could fit on the floor'. Depending on how big the shape you're looking at is, you measure area in square centimetres (cm^2), square metres (m^2) or (unusually) square kilometers (km^2).

Really easy rectangles and squares

Working out the area of rectangles is very straightforward: all you do is multiply together the height of the rectangle by its width.

If you're dealing with a square, you know the height and the width are the same, so you just multiply the length of the side by itself.

Trickier triangles

Triangles are a little more difficult to work out, but not all that difficult. Here are the steps you follow to find the area:

1. Find the length of the *base* of the triangle, the distance across the bottom.

2. Find the *height* of the triangle, the distance from the base to the top.

3. Multiply your answers from Step 1 and Step 2.

4. Halve your answer from Step 3. This is the area of the triangle.

If you tilt your head and narrow your eyes a bit, you may be able to see why this is the way to do it. A triangle is half as big as a rectangle with the same width and height, so its area is half of the rectangle's area. Also, if you're a remembering-formulas kind of person, you may like to remember 'half base times height' as the formula for the area of a triangle.

Combining rectangles

It's pretty unusual to get a question as simple as 'find the area of this rectangle' in a test. Most tests like to spice it up a bit and bundle two or more rectangles together and ask you to find the total area. You need to think a little harder for this kind of question, but the steps are pretty logical:

1. Split your complicated shape up into two rectangles (or more, if you need to).

2. Work out the height and width of each rectangle. You may need to add or take away some given lengths from each other to find all the information you need – look at Figure 7-4 to see how you do this.

3. Work out the area for each rectangle – multiply the width of each rectangle by its height.

4. Add up the areas you worked out in Step 3.

It doesn't matter how you split the rectangle up, you still end up with the right area! Figure 7-4 shows an example of finding the area of a compound rectangle.

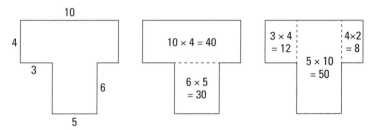

Figure 7-4: The area of a compound rectangle.

Surface areas

A variation on the compound rectangle is the *surface area* question. If the question asks you for the surface area of a three-dimensional shape (usually a box), it's really asking how much wrapping paper you would need to wrap it up – assuming you wrap things like I do, by cutting rectangles just big enough to cover each side and taping them together.

Oddly enough, that's exactly how you work out the surface area of any 3D shape:

1. Find the area of each face of the shape. All of the faces will be simple shapes, most likely rectangles but possibly triangles as well. Remember to include the faces hidden at the back of the drawing.

2. Add up all of the areas you worked out in Step 1. This is the total surface area.

Figure 7-5 shows an example surface area question.

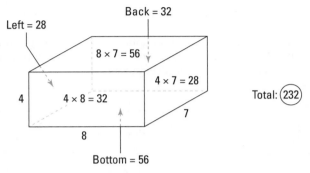

Figure 7-5: Surface areas.

Fiddling with formulas

The last kind of area question you're likely to see involves using a formula to find the area of a complicated shape. These look a bit intimidating, especially if you have bad memories of algebra from school, but if you take a deep breath and approach the problem systematically, you can pick up easy marks here.

So, taking it one step at a time:

1. Figure out which letter stands for which quantity – the question usually says what stands for what directly underneath the formula. I like to write each letter next to its value somewhere so I don't lose track.

2. Rewrite the formula, replacing each letter with the value it represents – so if you know h is 5, you replace all of the hs in the formula with 5. If there are two values next to each other without a +, −, × or ÷ in between them, there ought to be a ×, write it in!

3. Work out the sum you just figured out using the BIDMAS rules (check out Chapter 5 if you need to) – work out what's in the *brackets* first, then any *indexes* (powers), then any *multiplications or divisions*, then *additions or subtractions*.

An index is a little number above and to the right of another number, like this: 4^2. What this means is 'multiply a list of two 4s together', or $4^2 = 4 \times 4 = 16$. In the same way, $5^3 = 5 \times 5 \times 5 = 125$.

A walk around the perimeter

Once in a while you hear a news report from an airport or an army base that makes reference to the *perimeter fence*. This is a fence that goes all the way around the airport or base.

The *perimeter* of any shape is the distance all the way around it. You can work it out by just adding up the lengths of the sides.

For example, if you know a square has sides of length 10cm (just like the square in Figure 7-6), you can work out that the perimeter is 10cm + 10cm + 10cm + 10cm = 40cm.

The other shape in Figure 7-6 is a bit harder to figure out, but with a bit of thinking it all comes together. Here are the steps for working out the perimeter of a complicated shape:

1. **Find out which sides don't have a length marked.** In this case, the vertical side in the top-right and the horizontal side at the top have no length marked.

2. **Work out the length of those sides using other facts you know about the shape to help you.** The vertical side in the top-right has to be 5m because the two vertical sides on the right have to match up with the one vertical side on the left. The left side is 11m, and the lower-right side is 6m, so there's 11 – 6 = 5m left to fill. Using the same kind of thinking, the horizontal side at the top has to be 7m long.

3. **Write down all of the sides' lengths.** I like to circle them on the diagram as I go to make sure I don't miss any. Here, the sides are 10, 6, 3, 5, 7 and 11m long.

4. **Add the lengths up. The answer is the perimeter.** The sum is 10 + 6 + 3 + 5 + 7 + 11 = 42, which is the answer.

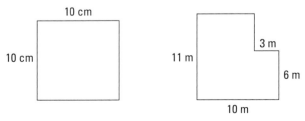

Figure 7-6: A square and a more complicated shape.

How much things hold

You'd be forgiven for thinking that examiners had an obses-
sion with putting things in boxes. The two things numeracy
tests often ask about the *capacity* of boxes (in other words,
how much they hold) are:

- ✔ The *volume* of the box (roughly, how much liquid you
could fit in it).

- ✔ How many objects of a given size fit in it.

In numeracy tests, you usually measure volume and capacity
in either millilitres (ml) or centimetres cubed (cm^3) – they're
actually two different ways of saying the same size.

You may also see litres (1000ml) or metres cubed (m^3), which
work out to be the same as 1000 litres or $1,000,000cm^3$.

Working out the volume of a box is very straightforward:

1. Work out the three *dimensions* – the *height*, *width* and
   depth of the box – make sure they're all in the same
   units (usually centimetres). Look at Figure 7-7 to see
   which is which.

2. Multiply the height by the width, and the result by the
   depth. That's your answer – if you measured everything in centimetres, your answer is in cm^3; if everything was in metres, your answer would be in m^3.

It doesn't matter which order you multiply the three dimensions in (because the volume doesn't change if you rotate the
box), so feel free to change the order if you can come up with
an easy sum first!

Working out how many boxes fit into a bigger box is a slightly
trickier problem. You'll normally be given something like
Figure 7-7, showing the dimensions of a big box and a smaller
box – luckily, the smaller box will be facing in the direction
you'll be packing it (so you don't need to worry about twisting it
around).

If you've ever moved house, you'll know that you can fit more
cuboids – boxes or books – into a big box if you twist some
of them around. As far as numeracy tests go, you can safely
ignore this strategy – the question just asks about packing
boxes in a boring fixed orientation.

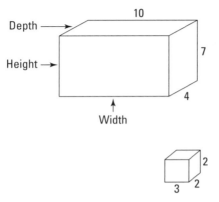

Figure 7-7: Boxes in boxes.

Here are the steps:

1. Work out how many small boxes fit along the front of the bigger box. Divide the width of the big box by the width of the smaller box. If the number doesn't go exactly, you round *down*, no matter how close you are to the higher number. Write this number down. In the example in Figure 7-7, three small boxes fit across the front of the big box.

2. Work out how many boxes fit along the side. Divide the depth of the big box by the depth of the smaller box. Again, round down if it doesn't go exactly. Write this number down as well. In Figure 7-7, two boxes fit along the side.

3. Work out how many boxes fit the height. Divide the height of the bigger box by the height of the smaller box. Once more, round down if you need to, and write the number down. In Figure 7-7, three boxes fit.

4. Multiply your answers from Steps 1, 2 and 3. This is the number of boxes that will fit in the big box. For Figure 7-7, this is $3 \times 2 \times 3 = 18$ boxes.

I like to think about this recipe as stacking layers. The first step tells you how many boxes fit along the front, and multiplying that by the number of boxes along the side tells you how many boxes all together fit on the floor – the number of boxes in a layer. The number of boxes up the height tells you how many layers there are, so if you multiply that by the number of boxes in a layer, you get the number of boxes all together.

Working with speed, distance and time

You can see that speed is related to distance and time if you just think about the units you use for it: you typically give a speed in miles per hour (or in kilometres per hour).

In fact, the units give you a clue as to the formula: if you translate 'per' as 'divide by', it tells you that the speed (in miles per hour) is the distance (in miles) divided by the time taken (in hours). Put another way, speed = distance ÷ time.

I find it a bit easier to remember the equation with a formula triangle like the one in Figure 7-8 – I use the mnemonic **S**kinny **D**enim **T**rousers to remember which letter goes where, but feel free to come up with your own. Rude ones tend to be more memorable!

$$D = S \times T$$
$$S = D \div T$$
$$T = D \div S$$

Figure 7-8: A formula triangle for speed, distance and time.

Typical speed-distance-time questions ask you to work out one of the three quantities, given the other two. The three types of question are:

- ✔ **Find the speed, given the distance and time.** Looking at the formula triangle, you can work out that the speed is the distance divided by the time.

- ✔ **Find the distance, given the speed and the time.** Again, if you look at the formula triangle, you can see that you get distance by multiplying speed by time.

- ✔ **Find the time, given the speed and the distance.** The formula triangle in Figure 7-8 says that you get the time by dividing distance by speed.

Sometimes, an exam tries to trip you up by giving a time in minutes rather than hours. Always make sure you convert times into hours before you try to do any sums in miles per hour or kilometres per hour. And remember an hour has 60 minutes, not 100!

Finding the speed

Here are the steps for finding the speed if you know the distance and time:

1. Draw the SDT triangle as in Figure 7-8.

2. Cover up the thing you're trying to find (the S for Speed).

3. Read off the sum you need to do: D ÷ T, or distance divided by time. (The D is above the T, so you divide.)

4. Write down the sum with the numbers you're given for distance and time, and work out the answer!

Finding the distance

Here are the steps for finding the distance if you know the speed and time:

1. Draw the SDT triangle as in Figure 7-8.

2. Cover up the thing you're trying to find (the D for Distance).

3. Read off the sum you need to do: S × T, or speed times time. (The S and T are on the same level, so it's a multiplication.)

4. Write down the sum with the numbers you're given for speed and time, and work out the answer!

Finding the time

Getting familiar? Here are the steps for finding the time if you know the distance and speed:

1. Draw the SDT triangle as in Figure 7-8.

2. Cover up the thing you're trying to find (the T for Time).

3. Read off the sum you need to do: D ÷ S, or distance divided by speed.

4. Write down the sum with the numbers you're given for distance and speed, and work out the answer!

Chapter 8

Interpreting Data

. . . .

In This Chapter

▶ Grasping graphs

▶ Tackling tables

▶ Dealing with distance, speed and time

. . . .

*A*ll the numeracy tests you're likely to come across ask you to deal with information in graphs and tables and to be able to work out basic statistics such as averages and the range.

Graphs and tables are useful topics in everyday life – if you pick up a newspaper or watch the news, you're almost certain to see a graph somewhere; you might also read price information from a table and have to figure out when to catch your bus or train.

In this chapter, I take you through the different types of graph you may need to know about and show you a few kinds of table that may crop up in your test.

Getting on Top of Graphs

A *graph* is just a picture that describes a set of data. Graphs come in all manner of different types, from fairly simple bar charts and pictograms to more complicated scatter graphs and line graphs.

The one thing nearly all the graphs you need to care about have in common is that the *size* or the *position* of some element of the picture describes one of the values in the data. In a bar chart, the height of each bar tells you how much or how many things that bar represents; in a pie chart, it's the angle of each slice.

The exceptions to this rule are the box plot and the cumulative frequency graph, which work differently and I explain them later in this chapter. Fortunately, you only care about those if you're doing the QTS numeracy test – otherwise, you can skip those sections completely.

In this section, I run through the various types of graphs and how to read them. You may be relieved to learn that you don't have to draw graphs in a numeracy exam, just read them.

Which graph to use

One of the most fear-inspiring questions I've seen in a numeracy test is 'Which type of graph would you use to display this data?' It gives me the chills each time, partly because two or more answers are often perfectly acceptable.

To answer the question, you need to know the difference between categorical and numerical data: *categorical data* is data that's in groups (such as eye colour, or regions of a country), while *numerical data* is data that's counted or measured (like money or weight).

Figure 8-1 gives a table of which kind of graph I'd use in which situation – I wish I could give you more interesting advice than 'learn this table', but sadly, I can't. Learn the table.

In the table, I talk about the number of *data sets* involved in a graph. A data set is simply a collection of data with something in common such as the number people living in each house in a particular town or the test scores of all the students in a class. Some graphs tell you about a single data set, while others let you compare several different data sets (for example, you might want to see if your class has better test scores than your friend's!).

Data type	Data sets	What you're interested in	Example	Graph
Categorical	One	How many things per group	People with different eye colours	Bar chart, pictogram or tally chart
Categorical	Several	How many things per group	People with different eye colours in different towns	Multiple bar chart
Categorical	One	Proportions	Votes in a general election	Pie chart
Categorical	Several	Proportions	Votes in several different towns	Stacked bar chart
Numerical	One	Values	Temperature over a day	Line graph
Numerical	Several	Values	Temperature over a day in several cities	Multiple line graph
Numerical	-	Details of observations	Heights and ages of students	Scatter graph

Figure 8-1: Which graph to use when.

Battling with bar charts

A bar chart looks a bit like the skyline of a city with lots of skyscrapers. (They can also be sideways-on, so they look like a picture of a skyline with skyscrapers going sideways. I suppose that would make them horizon-scrapers.) Each of the skyscrapers (bars) represents a group or a category – say, the number of people with green eyes, or the maximum speed of a particular car, or the percentage of late trains in a particular month. The bar charts in Figure 8-2 show the profit made by some fictional companies, in both horizontal and vertical style.

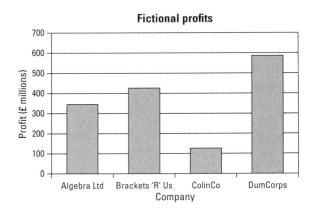

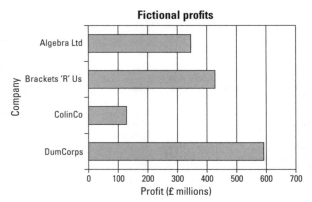

Figure 8-2: Bar charts with vertical bars (left) and horizontal bars (right).

How to read a bar chart

Reading a bar chart is pretty straightforward. Here's what you do:

1. **Find the bar you're interested in.** The bars are usually either labelled on the graph or on the x-axis at the bottom of the graph (or, if it's a horizontal bar chart, on the y-axis on the left). There may be a key that tells you which colour or shading belongs to which group.

2. **Place a ruler horizontally at the top of the bar (or vertically at the end if you're looking at a horizontal bar chart).**

3. **Read the relevant number off the scale.** If you're lucky, the ruler will lie on a marked number on the axis – if not, you need to estimate as best you can.

For example, in Figure 8-2, the value of DumCorps's sales is a little short of £600 million.

Multiple bar charts

A variation on the simple bar chart is the *multiple bar chart*, one of the ugliest graphs known to science. The difference between the multiple bar chart and the regular bar chart is (unsurprisingly) the number of bars. You can see this in Figure 8-3.

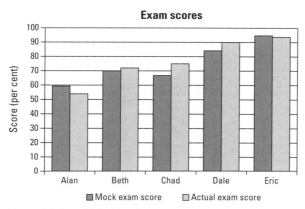

Figure 8-3: A multiple bar chart.

The idea of a multiple bar chart is to compare similar information in two different scenarios – a school's inspection rankings in two different years, the distribution of ages of the populations of two different cities or (as in Figure 8-3) the difference between students' mock and actual exam scores.

Multiple bar charts work just like regular bar graphs – the only extra step you need to take is to make sure you're using the correct bar before you read off the value. For example, in Figure 8-3, you can see that Beth scored 70% in her mock exam and a little higher (in fact, 72%) in her actual exam.

Making pie charts a piece of cake

A *pie chart* gets its name because (surprise, surprise) it looks like a pie – a circle divided into slices of various sizes. It shows you at a glance which groups among the data are the biggest and smallest, and the size of the angle at the point of each slice tells you how big the group it represents is. Figure 8-4 shows you a typical pie chart.

Favourite types of pies
(Survey of 35 people)

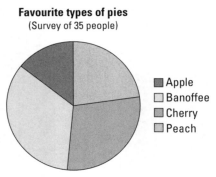

Apple
Banoffee
Cherry
Peach

Figure 8-4: A pie chart.

The three things you may have to do with a pie chart in a numeracy test are to convert between:

✔ The angle and the size of each group.

✔ Percentages and the size of each group.

✔ The angles and percentages.

Luckily, the Table of Joy (which I explain in Chapter 5) works brilliantly for all three types of question, whichever way you have to work them out.

The three key numbers you need to know are: the number of people or things the chart represents (this may be given to you in the question or marked somewhere on the graph); the number of degrees in a circle (360); and the number of per cent in a whole thing (100).

In all three cases, you follow the same recipe:

1. Draw out your Table of Joy noughts and crosses grid.

2. Label the left side with 'slice' and 'whole thing', and the top with the things you're measuring – for example, 'angle' and 'size'.

3. Fill in the information you know in the appropriate squares – see Figure 8-5 for an example.

4. Shade the grid like a chess-board and write out the Table of Joy sum: multiply the two numbers on the same colour squares and divide by the other number.

5. Work out the sum to get your answer!

Figure 8-5 shows how to work out the size of the angle representing 7 out of 35 people.

	Angle	People
Whole thing	360	35
Slice		7

$$\frac{360 \times 7}{35} = 72°$$

Figure 8-5: A pie chart worked example.

Living with line graphs

A *line graph* shows how one quantity responds to changes in another – often, but not always, time. A line graph might show how prices change over time, the expected weight of a cow given its size or how fast a chemical reaction takes place as you change the concentration of one of the ingredients.

Reading a line graph is simple and (hopefully) fairly obvious. You're normally given one value (say, the time) and have to find the other (say, the temperature).

You may be given a graph with several different lines on it, such as Figure 8-6. Multiple line graphs can be confusing, even for the pros, but they're not too bad if you can keep your head. All you have to do is make sure you're looking at the correct line – the graph will have a key beside it telling you which graph is which; in this example the different colours show London and Edinburgh.

This recipe assumes you're working on paper. If you're working on a computer, you can follow a ruler instead of drawing an actual line. I don't want you kicked out of the exam hall for graffiti-ing the computers!

Here's the recipe, which shows you how to use Figure 8-6 to find the temperature in Edinburgh at 1600:

1. Check which axis the value you're given is on. Look at the labels to help you decide. In this example, you're given a time, so you need to look along the bottom axis, marked 'Time'.

2. Find the value on that axis. It's near the middle.

3. If the graph has more than one line on it, pick which line you're interested in. Here, you care about Edinburgh, so you have to pay attention to the darker line.

4. If your value is on the horizontal axis, draw a line (or follow a ruler) directly up until it meets the graph; if your value is on the vertical axis, draw a line (or follow a ruler) directly to the right until it meets the line. Here, you draw a line upwards from 16 until it hits the darker line.

5. If you just drew upwards, draw a line to the left until you reach the vertical axis; if you just drew to the right, draw a line downwards to the horizontal axis. In this example, you draw a line to the right until it hits the vertical axis.

6. Read the value off of the axis. This is your answer. For this example, you'd get 17°C.

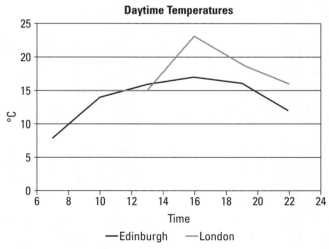

Figure 8-6: A multiple line graph.

Scatter graphs

A *scatter graph* is quite similar to a line graph except that it doesn't usually have a line on it! Instead, it has many dots or crosses. Each mark on the graph represents one thing – for example, a person or an experiment; its position on the graph shows you two values associated with it.

If a scatter graph compared people's heights and weights, the mark representing me would be around 1.7 metres (on the height axis) and around 80 kilograms (on the weight axis).

You read scatter graphs exactly the same way as line graphs, so you can follow the recipe from the previous section.

Beating box plots

Box plots are part of the teacher training numeracy tests, but not any of the others that I'm aware of. Unless you're doing the QTS test, you can safely skip this topic.

Quick quartiles

Quartiles are values that divide a data set up into *four equal parts* – so if you have 100 people arranged by height, 25 of them will be shorter than the lower quartile, and 25 will be taller than the upper quartile.

The easy way to find quartiles is to start by finding the median (especially if you're doing a box plot, you're going to need that anyway – refer to Chapter 5 for more on the median). This divides your data into two equal halves. If you then find the median of the top half, that gives you the upper quartile; the median of the bottom half is the lower quartile. Easy.

The usual reason for finding the quartiles is to work out the *interquartile range*, which is a measure of how spread out, or varied, your data set is.

For example, if your data set was the number of wheels on cars in a city, you'd expect a very small interquartile range because nearly all cars have four wheels – there's not much variation. On the other hand, if you were to look at the number of miles cars in a city had travelled, you'd have a large interquartile range because of the difference between well-travelled vehicles and city runarounds.

A *box plot*, also known as a *box and whiskers* plot, looks a little bit like a syringe. It gives you information about the *distribution* of a data set. In particular, it tells you about the highest and lowest values, as well as the median and the *quartiles* – see the 'Quick quartiles' sidebar to learn more about these.

You may see box plots going from left to right or from bottom to top (see Figure 8-7 for an example of each); in either case, they work the same way: you have a *box* in the middle of the graph with a line in the middle, and two *whiskers* at the ends of the box, each with a line at the end. Here's what they mean:

- ✔ The leftmost or lowest line on the graph is the smallest value in the data set. In Figure 8-7, the lowest value is 33.

- ✔ The rightmost or highest line on the graph is the largest value in the data set. In Figure 8-7, the highest value is 80.

- ✔ The line in the middle of the box represents the median of the data set. In Figure 8-7, the median value is 47.

- ✔ The left or lower end of the box is the lower quartile. In Figure 8-7, the lower quartile is 42.5

- ✔ The right or higher end of the box is the upper quartile. In Figure 8-7, the upper quartile is 60.

You may be asked to work out the *range* from a box plot; this is the largest value take away the smallest value, and you can simply read both values off of the graph (they're the ends of the whiskers). In Figure 8-7, the range is 47.

You may also be asked to find the *interquartile range*, which is very similar to the range, except that you find the difference between the upper and lower quartile – again, you can just read these off of the graph, as these values are at the ends of the box. In Figure 8-7, the interquartile range is 17.5.

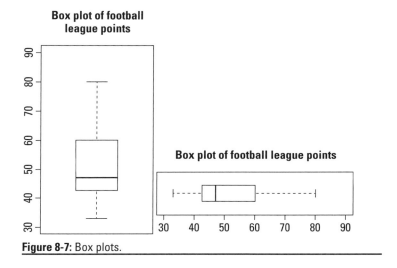

Figure 8-7: Box plots.

Conquering cumulative frequency

Cumulative frequency graphs are part of the teacher training numeracy tests, but not any of the others that I'm aware of. Unless you're doing the QTS test, you can safely skip this topic.

The word *cumulative* comes from the same root as *accumulate*, which means 'to build up'. A cumulative frequency graph, like the one in Figure 8-8, shows how many people or objects have a smaller value than the number on the horizontal axis.

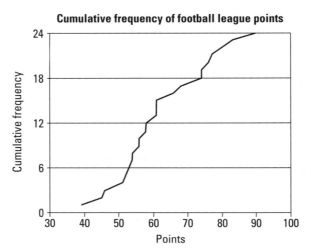

Figure 8-8: A cumulative frequency graph.

Reading a cumulative frequency graph is much like reading a line graph (see the section on 'Living With Line Graphs'). The only tricky thing about cumulative frequency graphs is figuring out which way you need to read the graph!

The two main kinds of question to do with cumulative frequency are ones that ask you to find *how many* things are below or above a particular value, and ones that want to know the *value* that corresponds to a certain cumulative frequency (or, as the pros call it, 'numbered thing').

Finding the cumulative frequency

You find the cumulative frequency when a question asks 'how many things have a value below (or above) a given value?' Looking at Figure 8-8, the exam may ask 'How many teams scored 60 points or more?' Here's a recipe to work it out:

1. Find the value (here, 60 points) on the horizontal axis.

2. Draw a straight line up from that value to the curve, and then a straight line left to the vertical axis.

3. Read off the value from the axis (for this question, you get 13). If your question asks 'or fewer', this is your answer.

4. If your question asks 'or more', take your answer from Step 3 away from the total number of teams. There are 24 teams, so the answer is 11.

Instead of 'how many', the question may sometimes ask 'what percentage' or 'what fraction'. In this case, you find out what percentage or fraction your answer is of the total – check out Chapter 5 for a refresher on how to do that.

Finding a value (or, medians, quartiles and the interquartile range)

If a question asks you to find the median, or quartiles from a cumulative frequency graph, you need to read the graph the other way around. Here's how you do it:

1. If you want the median, find the number that's half of the total number of things (in Figure 8-8, half of 24 is 12). If you want the lower quartile, find a quarter of the total (which would be 6), and if you want the upper quartile, you find three quarters of the total (18).

2. Find the number you worked out in Step 1 on the vertical axis.

3. Draw a line straight to the right until it reaches the curve, then a vertical line down to the horizontal axis.

4. Read the value off of the horizontal axis – this is your answer! (The median in the figure is about 58 points, the lower quartile 53 and the upper quartile about 75).

If you have to find the interquartile range, that's not much more difficult: you simply find the difference between the upper and lower quartiles – the sum for Figure 8-8 would be 75 – 53 = 22 points.

Whenever the question wants a value (something you'd expect to find on the horizontal axis), you need to start from the vertical axis.

Drilling into Data Tables

Tables are one of the most obvious ways of representing complicated data in a simple and easy-to-read format. You see them all over the place, from food packaging to price charts to league tables.

In this section, I run through the ins and outs of data tables (which are usually easy if you take care) and the kinds of sums you have to do with them (which may be a little trickier).

Tackling two-way tables

Two-way tables are a particular kind of table that I've only ever seen in maths exams and statistics textbooks. The idea of a two-way table is to show the numbers of observations split across two separate categories and (importantly) the totals of each.

A good example a two-way table is in Figure 8-9, comparing the numbers of people in a survey who exercise regularly and who normally eat a healthy breakfast. You can see that the bottom number in each column (in the row marked 'total') is the sum of the numbers above it, and the last number in each row (in the column marked 'total') is the sum of the numbers to its left.

You may need to find the missing numbers in a two-way table such as Figure 8-9, in which case you should do this:

1. Find a row or column which only has one number missing.

2. If the missing number is the last number in the row or column, simply add up the other numbers in your row or column – this is the answer.

3. Otherwise, add up all of the numbers in the row or column apart from the last one, then take your answer away from the last one. This is the answer.

		Regular exercise		
		Yes	No	Total
Healthy breakfast	Yes	8	9	17
	No	8	5	13
	Total	16	14	30

Figure 8-9: A two-way table.

Tallying up

A *tally chart*, like the one in Figure 8-10, is something you might use to record data – for example, if you were doing a survey on Internet browsers or recording different types of plant life in a forest.

Chrome	ЖНТ IIII
Firefox	ЖНТ ЖНТ ЖНТ ЖНТ III
Internet Explorer	III
Safari	IIII
Other	ЖНТ IIII

Figure 8-10: A tally chart.

You don't need to know how to make a tally chart for a numeracy test, but you do need to be able to read it. Here's how you figure out how many things were counted in each category:

1. Find the category labelled on the left.

2. Count the number of crossed-off fences (usually they look like four vertical lines crossed by one horizontal one (each crossed-off fence represents 5 observations). Multiply the number by five.

3. Count the number of left-over marks after the fences. Add this number on to your answer from Step 2. This is your answer!

Dealing with data tables

A loose, but workable, definition of a data table is any kind of information that's presented in a grid. If you look at any food packaging, you'll probably see a table listing the nutritional values of a serving of the food. If you watch a presentation, the chances are the presenter will include a table full of data somewhere in it. If you research information on a town, you may see tables showing its ethnic, religious and economic make-up.

All you need to do to find a value in a table – for example, finding the amount of protein in 100 grams of tomatoes – is this:

1. Find the labels you're looking for on the left and at the top of the table. In this case, I'd look for 'per 100g' at the top and 'protein' on the left.

2. Find the value that's in the same row and column as your labels. That's your answer!

You may have to find several values and do further sums with them. In which case, read on!

Taming table sums

It's quite common for a numeracy exam to ask you to do a little more work once you've read a value (or several values) from a table or graph. This can range from the quite simple, 'Which of these values is the smallest?' to the quite involved, 'What is the range of the values in the table?'.

Here are some general principles you can follow for doing sums with data in tables or graphs:

✔ Find all the data you need and write it out clearly.

✔ Check that the data you've written down makes sense.

✔ Keep your working as neat as possible so you don't get confused.

✔ Work through the sum as normal – the rules of maths don't change just because the data comes from a table or graph!

Moving Swiftly Along: Working with Time-Based Questions

You need to be a little more careful than usual when a question asks you to work with a table or graph that's time-related and may involve:

- ✔ Transport timetables.
- ✔ Table of expected times to complete a task.
- ✔ A distance-time graph.

As with most numeracy sums, if you stay calm and think the problem through, there's nothing too complicated here.

Reading timetables

Common timetable questions are:

- ✔ If you leave somewhere at a given time, when will you arrive at your destination?
- ✔ What's the last bus you can catch from one place to arrive somewhere else by a certain time?
- ✔ How long does it take to get from Point A to Point B?

Timetables are usually given using the 24-hour clock – be careful not to mix up morning and afternoon times!

When will you get there?

This is an easy, three-step process:

1. Find the place you're leaving from on the timetable.

2. Read across until you find a time as soon as possible after when you want to leave.

3. Read down the column until you reach the time corresponding to where you're going. That's your arrival time.

Arriving on time

Finding the last journey that arrives before a given time is a very similar recipe to the previous one, just a little backwards:

1. Find your destination on the timetable.

2. Read across until you find the last time that's before you want to arrive.

3. Read *up* the column until you find the time corresponding to where you're starting. That's your departure time.

How long does it take?

Finally, finding how long it takes to travel between two places is just another variation on the theme:

1. Find a time corresponding to your starting place in the timetable.

2. Find the time in the same column corresponding to your destination.

3. Work out the time difference between them.

Be careful when you're working out a time difference – remember there are 60 minutes in an hour, not 100!

Part III
Practice Tests

'Right — you were pretty good on the speed tests — now we come to the intelligence test ....'

In this part . . .

The best way to get good at numeracy tests is to do lots of them. To help you with that, I include lots of them here. Each exam has a target time and a suggestion about whether to use a calculator or not – but feel free to study in whatever way suits you best.

Chapter 9

Mental Arithmetic Tests

● ●

In This Chapter

▶ Working with shapes, charts and measurements

▶ Honing your mental arithmetic

● ●

*T*his chapter contains four mental arithmetic tests for
you to practise, followed by worked answers. They're
designed to mirror a typical mental arithmetic numeracy test.

In the real tests, you're typically allowed to write down your
working out, but you're not permitted to use a calculator.

Test A: Armed Forces and Emergency Services

This test is around the same level as the entrance exams for
the armed forces and emergency services. These tests vary in
length, but in this sample test you have 25 minutes to answer
25 questions.

In the test, some of the questions are multiple choice, while
others ask you to type or write in your answer.

Test A Questions

Figure 9-1: Quinn's pizza.

1. Quinn cuts a delicious grey pizza into six slices and eats four of them. Which of the pizzas in Figure 9-1 is his?

2. Trainees are grouped by age and sex for a team-building exercise. Group A consists of men under 21; Group B consists of men 21 and over. Group C consists of women under 21, and Group D consists of women over 21. Karen is 19 – which group is she placed in?

3. Which of these numbers is seventy-four?

A: 704   B: 74   C: 47   D: 774   E: 740

4. Paul is buying cans of lemonade for his son's football team. Cans are sold in packs of six. He buys four packs. How many cans does he buy in total?

A: 16   B: 24   C: 10   D: 20   E: 30

A   B   C   D   E

Figure 9-2: Shapes for Question 5.

5. Which of the shapes in Figure 9-2 is a hexagon?

6. How many sides does a rectangle have?

7. A sum is written in words as 'start with nine, divide it by three, then add seven'. Which of the following matches it?

A: $9 \times 3 + 7$ B: $9 \div 3 + 7$ C: $9 \div 3 \times 7$ D: $9 - 3 + 7$

Oxford	09:00	09:30	10:00	10:30	11:00	11:30	12:00
Reading	09:30	10:00	10:30	11:00	11:30	12:00	12:30
London	10:10	10:40	11:10	11:40	12:10	12:40	13:10

Figure 9-3: Keith's timetable.

8. Keith is taking a train from Oxford and needs to be in London before noon. He looks at the timetable in Figure 9-3. Which is the latest train he can catch?

9. A car is travelling at 76 km/h. What is this to the nearest ten kilometres per hour?

10. Alex buys a burger for £2.70 and a portion of chips for £1.20. How much change does he get from £10?

A: 10p   B: £5.10   C: £6.10   D: £3.90

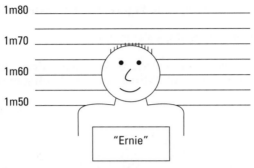

Figure 9-4: A mugshot of Ernie.

11. Figure 9-4 shows a picture of Ernie. How tall is he, to the nearest 10cm?

12. What is the next number in this sequence: 570, 470, 370, 270, . . . ?

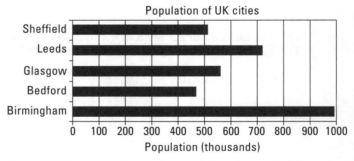

Figure 9-5: A bar chart showing the population of several cities.

13. Look at the chart in Figure 9-5. Which city is bigger than Glasgow but smaller than Birmingham?

14. Which of the following fractions has the same value as ⅓?

A: ⅖   B: ½   C: ⅚   D: ⅔   E: ³⁄₁₀

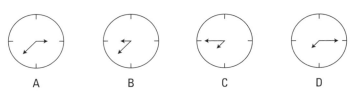

Figure 9-6: Several clocks.

15. Which of the clocks in Figure 9-6 shows the time 19:45?

16. Stu's restaurant bill came to £19.30. He wants to leave a 10% tip – how much should he add on?

A: £2.00   B: 19p   C: 20p   D: £19   E: £1.93

17. Beth is trying to raise £1,500 to take part in a charity walk. So far, she has raised £200 from a car boot sale, £700 from sponsorship and £45 from a raffle. How much more does she need to raise?

18. Four-fifths is the same as:

A: 0.45   B: 40%   C: ¾   D: 80%   E: 0.9

Monday	Tuesday	Wednesday	Thursday	Friday
8	8.5	8	8	5

Figure 9-7: Will's timesheet.

19. Figure 9-7 shows Will's timesheet. How many hours did he work in total?

20. Victoria is allowed 30 days of leave a year. So far, she has taken 12 full days and three half-days. How many days of leave does she have left?

21. A day trip costs a total of £360 for twelve people. How much does it cost per person?

22. The cost of a train ticket is £20. If it goes up by 15%, what is the new price?

23. Yvonne leaves home at 07:45 and arrives at her destination at 10:05. How long did her journey take?

24. Simon notices that about one email in every seven he receives is spam. If he receives 42 emails in a day, how many would you expect to be spam?

25. Christine travels 180 miles in three hours. What is her average speed for the journey?

Worked Answers for Test A

1. **A.** If Quinn eats four of the six slices, he has two left.

2. **Group C.** Karen is a woman under 21.

3. **B: 74.**

4. **B: 24.** $6 \times 4 = 24$.

5. **D.** A hexagon has six sides.

6. **4.**

7. **B: 9 ÷ 3 + 7.** This is just replacing words with the right symbols, no funny business!

8. **10.30.** The 11:00 train doesn't arrive until after 12:00.

9. **80 km/h.** 76km/h is closer to 80km/h than to 70km/h so you round up.

If the speed was 75km/h, exactly halfway between – you round up.

10. **C: £6.10.** The meal costs £3.90, and £10.00 – £3.90 = £6.10.

11. **1 metre 70.** Ernie is closer to 1 metre 70 than 1 metre 60.

12. **170.** The numbers go down by 100 each time.

13. **Leeds.**

14. **D: ⅖.** You can divide the top and bottom by two to get ⅓.

15. **C.** The minute (big) hand is pointing at 9 and the little hand between 7 and 8.

16. **E: ₤1.93.** To find 10%, you divide ₤19.30 by 10.

17. **₤555.** So far, Beth has raised ₤945. She is ₤1500 − ₤945 = ₤555 short of her goal.

18. **D: 80%.** To get from fifths to percentages (hundredths) in this question, you multiply the top and bottom of the fraction by 20, because 5 x 20 = 100. See Chapter 4 for more on converting fractions to percentages.

19. **37.5.** 8 + 8.5 + 8 + 8 + 5 = 37.5.

20. **16.5.** She's used 13.5 days of leave so far, and 30 − 13.5 = 16.5.

21. **₤30.** The sum is ₤360 ÷ 12. The easiest way to do this is by cancelling, and saying 360 ÷ 12 = 180 ÷ 6 = 90 ÷ 3 = 30. Chapter 4 explains cancelling down in more detail.

22. **₤23.** The Table of Joy sum to find the increase is 15 × 20 ÷ 100. Fifteen times 20 is 300, and 300 ÷ 100 = 3. You add this on to the 20 to get ₤23. (Chapter 5 explains the fantabulous Table of Joy.)

23. **2 hours 20 minutes.** Two hours after she sets off, it's 09:45; 15 minutes after that it's 10:00; and five minutes after that is 10:05. That's a total of 2 hours and 20 minutes.

24. **About 6.** The sum to do is 42 ÷ 7.

25. **60 miles per hour.** The sum is 180 ÷ 3.

Test B: ALAN

The questions in Test B are the same level as the ones in the ALAN exams that don't involve graphs and tables or large numbers of steps. (For more involved questions, see Chapter 10; for questions with graphs and tables in, see Chapter 11; and for a full range of ALAN-style questions, see Chapter 12. Don't say I'm not good to you!) This test contains 25 questions and you have 25 minutes for it. Remember, you can't use a calculator in ALAN tests.

Test B Questions

1. A sign says the road ahead narrows to 9 feet. One foot is about 30 cm. What is 9 feet in metres?

A: 27m   B: 2.7m   C: 3m   D: 0.3m   E: 2.5m

2. A 750ml bottle of water fills three glasses. How many glasses would a three-litre bottle fill?

A: 12   B: 10   C: 15   D: 20   E: 25

3. The temperature in Reykjavik is −7°C. The temperature in Moscow is −2°C. How much warmer is Moscow than Reykjavik?

A: 9°C   B: −9°C   C: 3°C   D: 5°C   E: −5°C

4. A recipe for a smoothie that serves ten people calls for 300ml of pineapple juice. If Nicky wants to make the smoothie for four people, how much pineapple juice should he use?

A: 30ml   B: 1200ml   C: 150ml   D: 100ml   E: 120ml

5. Stefan needs to catch a plane which leaves at 12.15 p.m. He wants to allow 20 minutes to drive to the airport and 90 minutes to clear security. What is the latest he should set off?

A: 11.05 a.m.   B: 10.05 a.m.   C: 10.25 a.m.   D: 11.25 a.m.
E: 10.45 a.m.

6. Jo lives three quarters of a mile from the nearest station. One mile is about 1,600 metres. Roughly how many metres does she live from the station?

A: 400m B: 800m C: 1,000m D: 1,200m E: 1,500m

7. Christina's journey to work takes 50 minutes. She notices that she spends ten minutes of the journey stopped at traffic lights. What percentage of her journey did she spend stopped at the lights?

A: 10% B: 15% C: 20% D: 50% E: 80%

8. Barry is buying a suit. The suit normally costs £600, but is on sale for £500. The price is reduced by what fraction?

A: $\frac{1}{10}$ B: $\frac{1}{6}$ C: $\frac{1}{5}$ D: $\frac{4}{5}$ E: $\frac{5}{6}$

9. Will earns £25 for each computer he repairs. One day, he repairs seven computers. How much does he earn?

A: £140 B: £150 C: £165 D: £175 E: £200

10. A train ticket normally costs £45. Patrick's railcard gives him $\frac{1}{3}$ off the fare. How much does he save if he uses the railcard?

A: £12.50 B: £15 C: £22.50 D: £30 E: £32.50

11. Ramit and Scott decide to split their company's profits in the ratio 5:2. If the company's profit was £35,000, how much would Scott receive?

A: £10,000 B: £14,000 C: £17,500 D: £25,000
E: £28,000

12. A state in the USA has a sales tax of 15%. What is 15% as a fraction?

A: $\frac{1}{15}$ B: $\frac{1}{10}$ C: $\frac{3}{20}$ D: $\frac{1}{6}$ E: $\frac{1}{5}$

13. A student notices his bank balance is –£15. He pays in £100. What is his new balance?

A: –£115 B: –£85 C: £85 D: £100 E: £115

14. Gareth is on holiday in Spain and pays for a meal that costs €35. If one euro is the same as 80p, how much does his meal cost in pounds?

A: £2.80   B: £3   C: £24   D: £28   E: £30

15. A bus journey costs £1.80 for an adult ticket and £1 for a child ticket. How much does the journey cost for a family of two adults and three children?

A: £2.80   B: £3.60   C: £4.60   D: £6.60   E: £7.40

16. An American recipe asks for two and a half cups of water. A cup is about the same as 220 millilitres. How many millilitres is 2.5 cups?

A: 55   B: 88   C: 500   D: 550   E: 880

17. A recreational football league has 400 registered players, of whom 20 are qualified referees. What proportion of the players are also referees?

A: 0.05   B: 0.2   C: 0.5   D: 0.8   E: 0.95

18. Lisa goes out for a walk at 6.45 p.m. She knows that sunset is at 8.25 p.m. How long does she have before the sun goes down?

A: 2 hours 20 minutes   B: 1 hour 40 minutes
C: 2 hours 40 minutes   D: 1 hour 20 minutes   E: 2 hours

19. Kerry works a 40-hour week. She spends five-eighths of her time working on a project. How many hours does she spend *not* working on the project?

A: 5   B: 15   C: 20   D: 25   E: 35

20. Rob has five litres of coffee to serve twenty people. If he gives everyone an equal amount of coffee, how much do they each get?

A: 20ml   B: 25ml   C: 200ml   D: 250ml   E: 400ml

21. Anja pays 1.4p per minute for phone calls. How much would a one-hour call cost her?

A: 1.4p   B: 8.4p   C: 14p   D: 84p   E: £1.40

22. A cinema ticket costs £5.50 for a matinee performance, and £2.20 extra for an evening show. What fraction of the evening cost is the matinee cost?

A: ⅕   B: ⅔   C: ⅖   D: ½   E: ¾

23. A plane travels 5,000 miles from London to Seattle in 8 hours. What is its average speed?

A: 60mph   B: 62.5mph   C: 500mph   D: 600mph
E: 625mph

24. A computer costs £400 plus 20% VAT. What is the total cost of the computer, including VAT?

A: £404   B: £408   C: £420   D: £440   E: £480

25. Denver airport is about 5,000 feet above sea level. One foot is about 30 centimetres. Approximately how many metres above sea level is Denver airport?

A: 15m   B: 150m   C: 1,500m   D: 15,000m
E: 150,000m

Worked Answers for Test B

1. **B: 2.7m.** The sum is $9 \times 30cm = 270cm = 2.7m$.

2. **A: 12.** One glass is 250ml ($750 \div 3$), so four glasses are the same as one litre. Three litres would be $3 \times 4 = 12$ glasses.

3. **D: 5°C.** See the number line in Figure 9-8. The gap between –7 and –2 is five spaces.

Figure 9-8: Number line to answer Question 3.

4. **E: 120ml.** One serving of the smoothie needs 30ml ($300 \div 10$), so four servings would be $4 \times 30 = 120ml$.

5. **C: 10.25.** He needs to allow one hour and 50 minutes for the journey. Fifty minutes before 12.15 is 11.25, and an hour before that is 10.25.

6. **D: 1,200m.** A quarter of a mile is 400m, so three-quarters of a mile is $3 \times 400 = 1,200m$.

7. **C: 20%.** Ten per cent of 50 minutes is 5 minutes, so 20% of 50 minutes is 10 minutes.

8. **B: ⅙.** The price is reduced by £100 out of the original price of £600. $100 \div 600 = ⅙$.

9. **D: £175.** The sum is $£25 \times 7$. Twenty times seven is 140; five times seven is 35; added together, that's 175.

If you want to get really good at your 25, 50 and 75 times tables, play the numbers game on television show *Countdown*. In fact, it's really good practice for all of your arithmetic skills – and a little bit more exciting than regular sums.

10. **B: £15.** $£45 \div 3 = £15$.

11. **A: £10,000.** They divide the profit into seven shares, so each share is $£35,000 \div 7 = £5,000$. Scott receives two of them, making £10,000. You can also do this with the Table of Joy; the sum is $35,000 \times 2 \div 7 = 70,000 \div 7 = 10,000$.

12. **C: ³⁄₂₀.** Ten per cent is ¹⁄₁₀, so 5% is ¹⁄₂₀. 15% is three times as big, making ³⁄₂₀.

13. **C: £85.** The first £15 takes his balance to zero, and then you add the remaining £85.

You can't rely on the exchange rate being the same every time! It might be that in another question, the exchange rate is 90p to the euro, or €1.10 to the pound, or something else entirely – make sure you work it out fresh each time!

14. **D: £28.** Ten euros is the same as £8, so €30 is £24. Five euros is the same as £4, which you add on.

15. **D: £6.60.** The adults cost 2 × £1.80 = £3.60 and the children cost 3 × £1 = £3. The total is £6.60.

16. **D: 550ml.** Two cups is 440ml, and half a cup would be 110ml. That makes 550ml all together.

17. **A: 0.05.** 20 ÷ 400 is the same as 1 ÷ 20 = 0.05. You can work that out by saying 1 ÷ 10 is the same as 0.1, and 1 ÷ 20 is half of that.

18. **B: 1 hour and 40 minutes.** After one hour, it'll be 7.45. After another 15 minutes, it's 8 o'clock, and after another 25 minutes, it'll be 8.25. That's a total of one hour and 40 minutes.

19. **B: 15 hours.** One-eighth of 40 is 40 ÷ 8 = 5, so five-eighths is 25 hours. You want the time left over after she works 25 of the 40 hours, so you work out 40 − 25 = 15.

20. **D: 250ml.** Five litres is the same as 5,000ml, which Rob needs to divide by 20. 5,000 ÷ 20 = 500 ÷ 2 = 250.

21. **D: 84p.** The sum to do is 60 × 1.4 = 6 × 14. Six times ten is 60 and six times four is 24, making 84p altogether.

22. **E: ⁵⁄₇.** The matinee price is £5.50 and the evening price is £7.70. The fraction is 5.5/7.7 = ⁵⁵⁄₇₇ = ⁵⁄₇.

23. **E: 625mph.** The sum is 5,000 ÷ 8 = 2,500 ÷ 4 = 1,250 ÷ 2 = 625.

24. **E: £480.** Ten per cent of £400 is £40, so 20% is £80. Add this on to £400 to get £480.

25. **C: 1,500.** If one foot is 30cm, ten feet make three metres, and 1,000 feet make 300 metres. Five thousand feet is about the same as 1,500m.

Test C: Qualified Teacher Status

This test is roughly the same level as the mental arithmetic section of a Qualified Teacher Status exam, in which you have 12 minutes to answer 12 questions. Remember to stay calm and work through the questions methodically. QTS questions are not normally multiple choice.

Test C Questions

1. In a year group of 120 students, 48 study French. What proportion of the students do not study French? Give your answer as a decimal.

2. In a group of 150 students, 90% travel to school on foot or by bike. If 70 students travel by bike, how many walk?

3. Eighty students took their maths GCSE and 28 of them achieved A* grades. What percentage of the students achieved an A*?

4. A school talent show consists of eight ten-minute acts and six five-minute acts, plus a twenty-minute interval. If the show begins at 6.45 p.m., when should it finish?

5. At a rugby tournament, six teams arrive with squads of 20 players, and two teams arrive with squads of 22. How many players are at the tournament?

6. A class takes part in a sponsored walk and raises £1.20 for every mile walked. The class contains 25 students, and each student walks an average of three miles. How much does the class raise altogether?

7. For a cookery lesson, each student needs 300 grams of rice. There are thirty students in the class. Rice is sold in bags of 1.5kg. How many bags of rice does the class need?

8. Of the forty teachers in a school, six are left-handed. What percentage of the teachers are left-handed?

9. What is 425 ÷ 0.1?

10. Javier pays an excess baggage fee of €40. If one euro is approximately the same as 90p, how much was the fee in pounds?

11. A student achieves 60 marks out of 75 in an exam. What is this as a percentage?

12. Forty sixth-form students take part in a university open day. There are 120 students in the sixth form altogether. What fraction of the sixth form takes part?

Worked Answers for Test C

1. **0.6.** You have (at least) two ways of doing this sum. You can work out how many students don't study French (72) and divide that by the total (120) – the sum is $72 \div 120 = 36 \div 60 = 6 \div 10 = 0.6$. Alternatively, you can work out the proportion that do study French ($48 \div 120 = 0.4$) and take the answer away from 1 ($1 - 0.4 = 0.6$).

2. **65.** 90% of 150 is $15 \times 9 = 135$ students who walk or cycle. If 70 cycle, then there $135 - 70 = 65$ who walk.

3. **35%.** The Table of Joy sum is $28 \times 100 \div 80 = 2800 \div 80 = 280 \div 8 = 140 \div 4 = 70 \div 2 = 35$. (Chapter 5 explains the Table of Joy.)

4. **8.55 p.m.** The ten-minute acts take up 80 minutes. The five-minute acts take up 30 minutes. Altogether, the acts take up 110 minutes; adding the interval makes 130 minutes, or 2 hours and 10 minutes. Two hours and ten minutes after 6.45 is 8.55 p.m.

5. **164.** The six squads of 20 make up 120 players. The two squads of 22 make up 44 players. Adding those together makes 164.

6. **£90.** The sum is $25 \times 1.2 \times 3$. To work out 25×1.2, you ignore the decimal point and do $25 \times 12 = 300$, then put the point back in one place from the end to get 30 (see Chapter 4 if you need a refresher on decimal multiplying!). Then you multiply the answer by 3 to get 90.

7. **6.** They need a total of $300 \times 30 = 9{,}000$g, or 9kg. The sum is $9 \div 1.5 = 18 \div 3 = 6$.

8. **15%.** The Table of Joy sum is $6 \times 100 \div 40 = 600 \div 40 = 60 \div 4 = 15$.

9. **4250.** To work out $425 \div 0.1$, multiply top and bottom by 10 to get $4250 \div 1 = 4250$. Another way to think of it: the question is asking 'how many 10ps make up £425?'. You know that ten 10ps make one pound, so £425 would be 425 batches of 10, and $425 \times 10 = 4250$.

Whenever you want to divide by a decimal, it's almost always a good idea to multiply top and bottom by the same number – usually ten or two. This makes a horrible decimal division into a nice whole number division.

10. **£36.** Ten euros is the same as £9, so €40 is $4 \times 9 = $ £36.

11. **80%.** The sum is $60 \times 100 \div 75 = 6,000 \div 75 = 2,000 \div 25 = 400 \div 5 = 80$. See Chapter 5 for more about working out percentages.

12. **⅓.** The sum is $40 \div 120 = 4 \div 12 = 1 \div 3$.

Test D: General Mental Arithmetic

Test D is designed to be at a level useful to all numeracy students. It contains 25 questions and your target time is 25 minutes.

Don't worry if it takes longer than that – work on getting questions right and then on improving your speed.

Test D Questions

1. Evelyn books accommodation for a holiday. She spends three nights at a hotel in Edinburgh that charges £95 per night, and four nights at a hotel in St Andrews that charges £105 per night. How much does she pay for accommodation?

2. Karim buys 6.5 kilograms of potatoes, 250 grams of cheese and one kilogram of mushrooms. How much does his shopping weigh altogether, in kilograms?

3. Henry planned to arrive at the picnic at 2.45 p.m., but is held up by a traffic jam which adds 45 minutes to his journey and a diversion that adds half an hour. What time does he arrive?

Sheffield	07:10	07:40	08:10	08:40	09:10	09:40
Stockport	08:10	08:40	09:10	09:40	10:10	10:40
Manchester	08:22	08:52	09:22	09:52	10:22	10:52

Figure 9-9: A train timetable.

4. Figure 9-9 shows a train timetable. Frank needs to be in Manchester before 10 a.m. for a meeting. What is the latest train he can catch from Stockport?

5. Stephanie buys cards to send to her clients. Each card costs 39p, and she wants to buy 82. She rounds the price per postcard to the nearest 10p and the number of clients to the nearest ten to work out roughly how much she'll need to spend. Roughly, how much does she expect to spend?

6. Justin buys four large envelopes for 75p each, four air-mail stamps for £2.30 each and a bar of chocolate for 50p. He pays with a £20 note; how much change does he get?

7. In his last four cricket matches, Ian has made scores of 38, 44, 50 and 56. He notices that his scores follow a pattern – what would he expect to score in his next match, if the pattern continues?

8. A computer is advertised for sale at £320 plus VAT at 20%. What is the total price of the computer, including VAT?

9. Susie organises a trip to a concert for a group of 16 people. The total cost is £336. How much is that per person?

10. Paolo sits an exam and scores 64 out of 72. What fraction of the total marks did he get, in its simplest form?

11. Kim drives 30 miles in 40 minutes. What was her average speed in miles per hour?

12. A fitness enthusiast buys a five-pound weight from an exercise equipment shop. She knows one pound is roughly 450 grams. How heavy is the five-pound weight in kilograms and grams?

13. One serving of cereal is 40 grams. How many servings are there in a one kilogram bag of cereal?

14. In a card game, Louise starts with –25 points. In the first round, she scores 45 points. What is her score after the first round?

15. Pepe knows that four big pizzas are usually enough to serve ten people. He has to organise pizza supplies for a party of 75 people. How many pizzas does he need to order?

16. A football match consists of two 45-minute halves and a 15-minute half-time break. It takes Roger 25 minutes to walk home from the stadium. If a game starts at 5.30 p.m. and Roger walks home immediately after the final whistle, what time does he get home?

17. Barney decides to take a train to Scotland. The full-price ticket costs £150, but if he buys a railcard for £28, he can save ⅓ of the price. How much would he save overall by buying the railcard?

18. An athlete divides his training time between jogging, walking and speed work in the ratio 5:1:2. One week, he spends 30 minutes on speed work; how long did he spend jogging?

19. Kirsten is planning a holiday to Japan. The exchange rate is 125 yen to one pound. If she wants to take £400 in spending money, how many yen does she require?

20. A driving test centre processes 800 driving tests in a given week. 560 of the tests are successful. What proportion of the tests are unsuccessful? Give your answer as a decimal.

21. What is 0.7×500?

22. Jeff buys three train tickets at a total cost of £9.60. How much was each ticket?

23. A carton of juice normally contains 500 millilitres, but the juice company runs a promotion using cartons that contain 20% more juice than usual. How much does each promotional carton contain?

24. Three princesses share an inheritance in the ratio of 4:2:1. If the inheritance was £21 million, how much does the first princess receive?

25. A truck driver travels for eight hours at an average speed of 55 miles per hour. How many miles does she travel?

Worked Answers for Test D

1. **£705.** The sums are $3 \times 95 + 4 \times 105 = 285 + 420 = 705$.

2. **7.75kg.** You can do the sum either in kilograms (6.5 + 0.25 + 1 = 7.75) or in grams (6500 + 250 + 1000 = 7750) – if you do it in grams, remember to convert back to kilograms at the end.

3. **4.00 p.m.** He's delayed by a total of 1 hour and 15 minutes. One hour after 2.45 is 3.45, and fifteen minutes after that is 4.00.

4. **9:40.** This is the last train from Stockport that gets in before 10 a.m. Make sure you look at the Stockport times and not the Sheffield times!

5. **£32.** The sum is 40p $\times$ 80 = 3200p = £32. (The exact answer is £31.98).

6. **£7.30.** $4 \times 75p = £3$; $4 \times £2.30 = £9.20$, and £3 + £9.20 + 50p = £12.70. Lastly, £20 – £12.70 = £7.30.

7. **62.** His scores are going up by six each time. Of course, there's no guarantee the pattern will continue!

8. **£384.** Ten per cent of £320 is £32, so 20% is £64. Adding the VAT onto the price gives £320 + £64 = £384.

9. **£21.** The sum is £336 ÷ 16. You can cancel that down to 168 ÷ 8 = 84 ÷ 4 = 42 ÷ 2 = 21.

10. **⁸⁄₉.** You can divide both 64 and 72 by 8 to get 8 and 9. Alternatively, you can repeatedly halve both numbers to get $^{32}\!/_{36} = {}^{16}\!/_{18} = {}^8\!/_9$.

11. **45mph.** You have several ways to do this, including the Table of Joy, for which the sum would be 30×60 (minutes) ÷ 40 = 1800 ÷ 40 = 180 ÷ 4 = 90 ÷ 2 = 45.

12. **2 kilograms and 250 grams.** The sum is $5 \times 450g = 2250g = 2$ kilograms and 250 grams.

13. **25.** One kilogram is 1000 grams, and 1000 ÷ 40 = 100 ÷ 4 = 25.

14. **20.** –25 + 45 is the same as 45 – 25 = 20. Alternatively, you can look at the number line in Figure 9-10.

◄- - - - -25 points until 0 - - - - -► ◄- - - - -20 points until 45- - - - -►

| -25 | -20 | -15 | -10 | -5 | 0 | 5 | 10 | 15 | 20 | 25 |

Figure 9-10: Number line for Question 14.

15. **30.** There are many ways to do this. The easiest is to say that if 10 people need 4 pizzas, then 70 people would need $7 \times 4 = 28$ pizzas. The five people left over would need only two pizzas.

16. **7.40 p.m.** The first half finishes at 6.15, the second half starts at 6.30 and the final whistle goes at 7.15 p.m. 25 minutes after that is 7.40 p.m. Alternatively, you may spot that the game takes 90 minutes, the break and the walk together take 40 minutes, making a total of 130 minutes (which is 2 hours and 10 minutes). Adding 2 hours and 10 minutes to 5.30 p.m. takes you to 7.40 p.m.

17. **£22.** The price of the ticket after the reduction is £100 (the discount is £150 ÷ 3 = £50, so the ticked costs £150 – £50 = £100), so he'd spend £128 instead of £150. The difference is £22.

18. **1 hour 15 minutes.** One 'share' is 30 ÷ 2 = 15 minutes, so five shares is $5 \times 15 = 75$ minutes. That's an hour and a quarter.

19. **50,000 yen.** The sum is $400 \times 125 = 50,000$ yen. The easiest way to do this is to say that £4 is 500 yen, so £400 is a hundred times larger.

20. **0.3.** If 560 tests out of 800 are successful, 240 are unsuccessful. 240 ÷ 800 = 0.3. (Alternatively, you can say 240 is 30% of 800, which is the same as 0.3.)

21. **350.** You have several ways to do this. For example, 0.7 × 100 = 70, so 0.7 × 500 is five times as large, giving $70 \times 5 = 350$.

22. **£3.20.** £9 ÷ 3 = £3 and 60p ÷ 3 = 20p.

23. **600ml.** Ten per cent of 500ml is 50ml, so 20% is 100ml. Adding this on to the original 500ml gives 600ml.

24. **£12 million.** One share is £21 million ÷ 7 = £3 million, so four shares would be £12 million.

25. **440 miles.** The sum is simply $55 \times 8 = 440$. You can split this up as $8 \times 50 = 400$ and $8 \times 5 = 40$.

Answers at a Glance

Test A

1. **A.**

2. **Group C.**

3. **B. 74.**

4. **B: 24.**

5. **D.**

6. **4.**

7. **B: 9 ÷ 3 + 7.**

8. **10.30.**

9. **80 km/h.**

10. **C: £6.10.**

11. **1 metre 70.**

12. **170.**

13. **Leeds.**

14. **D: ⅖.**

15. **C.**

16. **E: £1.93.**

17. **£555.**

18. **D: 80%.**

19. **37.5.**

20. **16.5.**

21. **£30.**

22. **£23.**

23. **2 hours 20 minutes.**

24. **6.**

25. **60 miles per hour.**

Test B

1. **B: 2.7m.**

2. **A: 12.**

3. **D: 5°C.**

4. **E: 120ml.**

5. **C: 10.25.**

6. **D: 1,200m.**

7. **C: 20%.**

8. **B: ⅙.**

9. **D: £175.**

10. **B: £15.**

11. **A: £10,000.**

12. **C: ³⁄₂₀.**

13. **C: £85.**

14. **D: £28.**

15. **D: £6.60.**

16. **D: 550ml.**

17. **A: 0.05.**

18. **B: 1 hour and 40 minutes.**

19. **B: 15.**

20. **D: 250ml.**

21. **D: 84p.**

22. E: ⁵/₇.

23. E: 625mph.

24. E: £480.

25. C: 1,500.

Test C

1. **0.6.**

2. **65.**

3. **35%.**

4. **8.55 p.m.**

5. **164.**

6. **£90.**

7. **6.**

8. **15%.**

9. **4250.**

10. **£36.**

11. **80%.**

12. ⅓.

Test D

1. **£705.**

2. **7.75kg.**

3. **4.00 p.m.**

4. **9:40.**

5. **£32.**

6. **£7.30.**

7. **62.**

8. **£384.**

9. **£21.**

10. ⁸/₉.

11. **45mph.**

12. **2 kilograms and 250 grams.**

13. **25.**

14. **20.**

15. **30.**

16. **7.40 p.m.**

17. **£22.**

18. **1 hour 15 minutes.**

19. **50,000 yen.**

20. **0.3.**

21. **350.**

22. **£3.20.**

23. **600ml.**

24. **£12 million.**

25. **440 miles.**

Chapter 10

Testing Real-World Maths

· ·

In This Chapter

▶ Distances, volume and schedules

▶ Fractions and percentages

· ·

*T*his chapter gives you the chance to test your real-world maths knowledge such as calculating distances, reading timetables and figuring out change, based mainly on the material in Chapter 7. Each practice test is designed to be about the same level as the 'real' numeracy tests, and I give a target time for each of them – although you're free to work without a time limit if you prefer while you practise.

In this kind of test, you're usually allowed to use a calculator (more often than not one that's on the computer you're using).

A few of the questions are marked with an asterisk (*) – these are questions where I've given more detailed worked answers because I don't cover them elsewhere in the book.

Test A: British Army Technical Skills Test

This test is designed to be around the same level as the Technical Skills Test for the British Army. It contains 25 questions and the target time for it is 25 minutes.

Test A Questions

1. Rob is planning a sponsored cycle from Land's End to John o'Groats. His planned route covers 924 miles, which he wants to cover in 14 days. How far does he need to cycle each day?

2. Kevin starts with one litre of water. He drinks 0.3 litres and uses 25 millilitres to wash his cup. How many millilitres of water does he have left?

3. Vanessa earns £8.97 per hour and works for 21 hours one week. She rounds each value to one significant figure to find an estimate of how much she made that week. What is her estimate?

4. Estimate the value of $20.2 \times 4.8 \div 50.5$. Give your answer to one significant figure.

5. Project A is expected to take $3\frac{1}{3}$ days. Project B should take $2\frac{3}{4}$ days. How long should the two projects take altogether?

6. You have $2\frac{1}{4}$ hours before you have to catch a train. You talk on the phone for 35 minutes. How long do you still have to wait? Give your answer in hours and minutes.

7. What is $\frac{9}{10} - \frac{1}{3}$?

8. An author has $3\frac{1}{2}$ pages to write to meet her deadline. She wants to have half of the pages written by lunchtime. How many pages must she write before lunch?

9. Tammy has bought six pizzas for a party. She knows that each party guest will eat $\frac{2}{3}$ of a pizza. How many people will the pizzas feed?

10. Express $\frac{3}{4}$ as a decimal.

11. Phil needs 50ml of mouthwash. What is 50ml in litres?

12. Four people have a mean age of 27. The mean age of three of them is 28. What is the age of the other person?

13. An army training organisation keeps its ratio of experts to trainees at 2:5. If it has 700 members in the organisation, how many of them are experts?

14. A physics class builds a model of a Roman catapult on a scale of 1:24. The model catapult is 50cm long. How big would the original catapult have been in real life?

15. In a competition, 20% of the competitors are eliminated after the first round. If there were 350 competitors to begin with, how many are left after the first round?

16. Andrew is supposed to read a meter every hour and records the readings. Unfortunately he falls asleep and misses two readings. Oops. The readings he made were: 438, 431, 424, . . . , . . . , 403. What were the missing readings?

17*. What is 86,400 in standard form?

18. A *knot* is defined as 1.852 kilometres per hour. What is this to two significant figures?

19. Peter is packing his Rubik's Cube collection into a box. Each cube has a side of 5.5 centimetres. The box he wants to pack them into is 11cm high, 33cm wide and 38.5cm long. How many cubes can he fit into the box?

20*. Solve the following simultaneous equations:
$$5x - 3y = 9$$
$$3x - y = 7.$$

21*. Factorise $x^2 - 2x - 8$.

22. A room has two walls which are each three metres long and two walls which are 8 metres long. The ceiling is 2.5m above the floor. How much paint would you need to paint the walls, ignoring doors and windows? Give your answer as an area in m^2.

23. A four-sided shape has two right angles and a 60° angle. What is the size of the fourth angle?

24*. If $z = (x - m) / s$, what does s equal?

25. Work out $-7(3+9) \div (1 + 5) - 1$.

Solving simultaneous equations

The only numeracy test I know of where simultaneous equations come up is the Army Technical Test. If you're not doing that, you can probably skip this sidebar.

Simultaneous equations are two equations written together, something like:

$2x + 3y = 11$

$5x + 5y = 20$

Unlike normal equations, simultaneous equations need you to give two answers, one for x and one for y. They're a bit fiddly, but here's how you do them – follow these steps and you'll be fine.

1. Multiply everything in the first equation by the number in front of the x in the second equation. Here, you multiply the first equation by 5 to get $10x + 15y = 55$.

2. Multiply everything in the second equation by the number in front of the x in the first equation. Here, you multiply the second equation by 2 to get $10x + 10y = 40$.

3. Find the number of ys in your answer to Step 1 (here, 15) and the number of ys in your answer to Step 2 (here, 10), and take them away – for this example, you get 5.

4. Find the number without any letters in Step 1 (here, 55) and the number without any letters in your answer to Step 2 (40) and take them away. You get 15.

5. Divide your answer from Step 4 by your answer from Step 3 – this is your answer for y. In this example, you get $y = 3$.

6. Replace the y in the very first equation with the value you worked out in Step 5 – in this example, you get $2x + 9 = 11$ (because $3 \times 3 = 9$). If the second equation looks easier, you can use that instead.

7. Find the number without any letters beside it on the left hand side of the equation (here, it's 9). If it has a plus before it, take it away from both sides (in this case, you get $2x = 2$); if it has a minus before it, add it to both sides.

8. Divide the right hand side by the number before the x. This is your answer for x. In this case, you do $x = 2 \div 2 = 1$. Your final answer is $x = 1$, $y = 3$.

Phew! That may seem like a lot of work, but once you've done a few of them, you'll start to find them easy.

Worked Answers for Test A

1. **66 miles.** You can do this as $924 \div 14 = 462 \div 7 = 66$. Alternatively, you can do it using the chunking method from Chapter 4 like this:

$$14 \times 2 = 28 \qquad 14 \times 20 = 280$$
$$14 \times 5 = 70 \qquad 14 \times 50 = 700$$
$$14 \times 10 = 140 \qquad 14 \times 100 = 1400$$

$$
\begin{array}{rl}
924 & \\
-\,700 & = 14 \times 50 \\
\hline
224 & \\
-\,140 & = 14 \times 10 \\
\hline
84 & \\
-\,70 & = 14 \times 5 \\
\hline
14 & \\
-\,14 & = 14 \times 1 \\
\hline
0 & \\
& 50 + 10 + 5 + 1 = 66
\end{array}
$$

2. **675ml.** The easiest way to do this is to convert everything into millilitres. Kevin starts with 1,000ml then uses a total of 325 (0.3 litres = 300ml). $1,000 - 325 = 675$.

3. **£180.** She rounds this off to $9 \times 20 = 180$.

4. **2.** Rounding the numbers to one significant figure gives an estimate of $20 \times 5 \div 50 = 2$. (The exact answer is 1.92). Note that 50.5 to one significant figure is 50: it's nearer to 50 than it is to 60.

5. **6$\frac{1}{12}$ days.** The whole days add up to 5. Three quarters is the same as nine twelfths; a third is the same as four twelfths. All together, that's $5\frac{13}{12}$, which is the same as $6\frac{1}{12}$.

6. **1 hour and 40 minutes.** You had 2 hours and 15 minutes, and used up 35, leaving one hour and 40 minutes.

7. **$\frac{17}{30}$.** You need to make the bottoms of the fractions the same. $\frac{9}{10}$ is the same as $\frac{27}{30}$, and a third is the same as $\frac{10}{30}$. Taking away, you're left with $\frac{17}{30}$.

8. **1$\frac{3}{4}$.** Half of 3 is $1\frac{1}{2}$, and half of $\frac{1}{2}$ is $\frac{1}{4}$. $1\frac{1}{2} + \frac{1}{4} = 1\frac{3}{4}$.

9. **9.** Six divided by $\frac{2}{3}$ is the same as $6 \times \frac{3}{2} = \frac{18}{2} = 9$. Alternatively, you can work out that two pizzas would feed three guests, so six pizzas would feed $3 \times 3 = 9$.

Factorising quadratic expressions

The only numeracy test I know of where factorising quadratics comes up is the Army Technical Test. If you're not doing that, you can probably skip this sidebar.

A *quadratic expression* is (as far as you're concerned) something with an x^2 in it. (Don't worry about a more precise technical definition – you're not going to see anything more complicated than this. A typical question will ask you to *factorise* it – which just means 'put it into brackets'.

You need to know about two types of expression: ones that have a plus sign before the last number (such as $x^2 - 8x + 15$) and ones that have a minus sign before the last number (for example, $x^2 + 3x - 18$).

Here are the steps if you have a plus sign (like with $x^2 - 8x + 15$):

1. Write down two brackets with plenty of space between them like this: $(x \quad)(x \quad)$.

2. Find which sign is before the middle number and write this after both of the xs. Here, you'd have $(x -)(x -)$.

3. Look for pairs of numbers that multiply together to make the number at the end. Here, you could have 1 and 15 or 3 and 5. (There aren't usually all that many options).

4. Add up each pair of numbers. Here, you'd have 16 and 8.

5. Pick the pair that adds up to the number in the middle and put them after the signs in the brackets. Your answer to this example would be $(x - 3)(x - 5)$.

If you have a minus sign at the end (such as with $x^2 + 3x - 18$), it's slightly different:

1. Write down two brackets with plenty of space between them like this: $(x \quad)(x \quad)$.

2. Put a plus after one x and a minus after the other, like this: $(x +)(x -)$.

3. Look for pairs of numbers that multiply together to make the number at the end. Here, you could have 1 and 18, 2 and 9, or 3 and 6. (There aren't usually all that many options).

4. Find the difference between each pair of options. Here, you have 17, 7 and 3.

5. Pick the pair whose difference is the number in the middle. Here, you want 3 and 6.

6. If the sign before the middle number is a plus, put the bigger number next to the plus in the brackets and the smaller number next to the minus. That's your answer. In this case, it's $(x + 6)(x - 3)$.

7. If the sign before the middle number is a minus, put the bigger number next to the minus in the brackets and the smaller number next to the plus. That's your answer.

10. **0.75.** One quarter is 0.25, so three-quarters is 0.75.

11. **0.05 litres.** Half a litre (0.5 litres) is 500ml, so 50ml is 0.5 ÷ 10 = 0.05 litres.

12. **24.** The four people have a total age of 27 × 4 = 108. The three people have a total age of 28 × 3 = 84. The last person's age must be 108 − 84 = 24. Chapter 5 explains the mean, mode and median.

13. **200.** For every seven members, two are experts; out of every seven hundred members, two hundred are experts. Another way to do this is to say that the ratio adds up to seven, so the total is made up of seven 'shares'. Each share is 700 ÷ 7 = 100, and the experts make up two shares: 200 people altogether.

14. **12 metres.** If you're happy with decimals, you can do 0.5m × 24 = 12. If not, you can say that one centimetre on the model is 24 in real life, so 50cm corresponds to 50 × 24 = 1200cm in real life, which is 12 metres.

Beware of trick answers in a multiple-choice exam – in this example you might well be given 1200m as an option. Make sure you pay attention to the units, and check that the answer is sensible. A 1200 metre catapult would do some serious damage, but probably only to itself!

15. **280.** Ten per cent of 350 is 35, so 20% is 70. If you eliminate 70 competitors, you end up with 350 − 70 = 280 still in the competition. You could also work out 80% of 350, which (using the Table of Joy, explained in Chapter 5) is 80 × 350 ÷ 100 = 28,000 ÷ 100 = 280.

16. **417, 410.** The readings are dropping by seven each time.

17. **8.64×10^4.** A *standard form* number comprises two parts – a number between 1 and 10, and 10 to the power of something. To make 86,400 into a number between 1 and 10, you have to move the decimal point 4 places to the left (so it's just after the 8). That means the number part is 8.64, and the four – the number of spaces you moved – is above the ten to give you 8.64×10^4.

18. **1.9 kilometres per hour.** With significant figures, you start counting at the first digit that isn't zero, so you round off after the 8. The next digit is 5, which is a high number, so you round the 8 up to 9.

19. **84.** He can fit two cubes up the way, six across the way and seven back, so the sum is $2 \times 6 \times 7 = 12 \times 7 = 84$.

20. $x = 3$, $y = 2$. Rearranging the second equation gives $y = 3x - 7$, or $3y = 9x - 21$. Rearranging the first equation gives $3y = 5x - 9$. That means $9x - 21 = 5x - 9$ or $4x = 12$, so $x = 3$. Since $y = 3x - 7$, $y = 2$.

21. $(x - 4)(x + 2)$. You need to find two numbers that multiply to make -8 but add to make -2. The only pair that works is -4 and 2, so these go with the xs in the brackets.

In a multiple-choice test, it may be easier just to multiply out each of the possible answers and see which one gives you the same expression as in the question.

22. **55m².** Two of the walls have an area of $3m \times 2.5m = 7.5m^2$, making $15m^2$; the other two walls have an area of $8m \times 2.5m = 20m^2$, making $40m^2$. Altogether, that's $55m^2$ of wall to paint. Another way to do this is to multiply the perimeter by the height. The perimeter is $3 + 3 + 8 + 8 = 22m$; $22m \times 2.5m = 55m^2$.

23. **120°.** The angles in a four-sided shape add up to $360°$, and the three angles you know about add up to $90 + 90 + 60 = 240°$. The remaining angle is $360 - 240 = 120°$.

24. $s = (x - m) / z$. Whenever you have a simple divide sum in algebra, you can turn it into a formula triangle like the one in Figure 10-1. The thing on top (here, $(x - m)$) goes on the top of the triangle. You cover up the thing you want to find and bingo! The rearrangement almost jumps out at you.

25. **–15.** Start with the brackets to get: $-7 \times 12 \div 6 - 1$. Now do the multiplications and divisions from left to right: $-84 \div 6 - 1 = -14 - 1$, which is -15. I explain BIDMAS in Chapter 5.

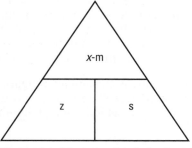

Figure 10-1: A formula triangle for Question 24.

Test B: Qualified Teacher Status Numeracy Test

Test B is around the same level as the on-screen questions in the Qualified Teacher Status numeracy test, avoiding questions with graphs and tables (you can practise these in Chapters 12 and 13). This test consists of 12 questions and your target time is 18 minutes. You may use a calculator.

In the QTS test, some questions are multiple choice and others ask that you type in your answer.

Test B Questions

1. A teacher plans a trip to a local historic site. A total of 30 people go on the trip. Group entrance for 30 people costs £183, and travelling by bus to the site costs £2.40 per person. How much does the trip cost per person?

2. A French high speed train travels at an average of 180 miles per hour. Paris and Avignon are 600km apart, and eight kilometres are roughly the same as five miles. How long would it normally take the train to get from Paris to Avignon?

3. A set of textbooks cost £3.75 each, with a 15% discount if you buy ten or more. Postage is £1.40 per pack of five books. How much do 20 books cost, including the discount and postage?

4. A teacher plans a minibus trip to a university open day. The university is 107 miles away. The minibus's fuel consumption is listed as 33 miles per gallon. At the time, petrol costs £1.35 per litre. One gallon is 4.546 litres. How much money should she budget for the trip there and back, to the nearest pound?

5. A drama teacher is looking into the cost of producing 250 programmes for a school play. Each programme consists of two black-and-white pages and one colour page. AutoPrint charges 2p per black-and-white page and 5p per colour page, plus a £10 set-up fee. PrestoPress quotes £30 for the whole order. What is the difference in price?

A: Autoprint is £7.50 cheaper   B: Autoprint is £2.50 cheaper
C: There's no difference   D: PrestoPress is £2.50 cheaper

6. A PE teacher has been asked to look after the school swimming pool. He knows the pool is 25 metres long, 10 metres wide and 1.8 metres deep. He needs to add at least one purification tablet for every hundred cubic metres of water in the pool. What is the least number of tablets he needs to use?

A: 4   B: 5   C: 45   D: 450

7. A school day consists of five hour-long classes, a 20-minute break in the morning, a 50-minute lunch break, and a 15-minute registration period. If the school day starts at 8.45 a.m., when does it finish?

A: 3.10 p.m.   B: 2.50 p.m.   C: 4.10 p.m.   D: 2.30 p.m.

8. A teacher decides to redecorate her classroom. The room is 2.2 metres high, 4.6 metres wide and 6.8 metres long. One can of paint is enough to cover 11m² of wall. How many cans of paint does she need to buy, ignoring doors and windows?

A: 3   B: 5   C: 6   D: 7

	Company A	Company B	Company C
Bumper packs (each)	£2.50	£2.20	£2.80
Individual worksheets (each)	£0.20	£0.25	£0.10

Figure 10-2: Price of teaching supplies.

9. The table in Figure 10-2 shows the prices of teaching supplies from three different companies. A teacher needs 5 bumper packs and 25 individual worksheets. Which company gives the best deal?

A: Company A   B: Company B   C: Company C
D: It's a tie

10. A student brings in a €20 note for show and tell. One euro is worth 87p. How much is the €20 note worth?

A: £1740   B: £0.23   C: £17.40   D: £22.99

11. A teacher takes, on average, 8 minutes to mark a student's homework. He has a class of 28 students. He sits down to start marking at 4 p.m. on Sunday, and plans to take a break of an hour to watch *Doctor Who* before finishing marking. When should he finish his marking?

A: 8.44 p.m.   B: 7.44 p.m.   C: 6.44 p.m.   D: 5.44 p.m.

12. A sixth-former says that her car's fuel tank holds nine gallons of petrol, and she knows that one litre is 0.22 gallons. How many litres of petrol does her fuel tank hold?

A: 1.98 litres   B: 40.9 litres   C: 19.8 litres   D: 4.09 litres

Worked Answers for Test B

1. **£8.50.** The booking costs £183, and the travel costs a total of £2.40 × 30 = £72. All together, that's £255. Split between 30 people, the cost is £255 ÷ 30 = £8.50 each.

2. **2 hours and 5 minutes.** Using the Table of Joy (explained in Chapter 5), 600km is the same as 600 × 5 ÷ 8 = 3,000 ÷ 8 = 375 miles. To get the time, you divide 375 by 180 to get 2.083 hours. That's a horrible number, so multiply by 60 to get 125 minutes, which is 2 hours 5 minutes.

3. **£69.35.** The base price is £3.75 × 20 = £75. 15% of £75 is £75 × 15 ÷ 100 = £11.25, which you take off to get £63.75. You're ordering four packs of books, making the postage 4 × £1.40 = £5.60. Lastly, do £63.75 + £5.60 = £69.35.

4. **£40.** The trip should use up 107 ÷ 33 = 3.24 gallons of fuel. In litres, that's 3.24 × 4.546 = 14.74 litres. Each litre costs £1.35, so the total fuel cost (one way) is 14.74 × 1.35 = £19.90. The return trip would cost £39.80, which is £40 to the nearest pound.

I've worked out the exact values in Question 4 using a calculator but only written down a couple of decimal places in my answer – if you have decided to practise these questions without a calculator, your answers may be slightly different, but you should still end up with £40.

5. **D: PrestoPress is £2.50 cheaper.** AutoPrint charges 9p per programme, and 9p × 250 = 2250p = £22.50. Adding the setup charge of £10, that's £32.50, so PrestoPrint's £30 quote is £2.50 cheaper.

6. **B: 5.** The volume of the pool is 25 × 10 × 1.8 = 450m³. He needs more than 450 ÷ 100 = 4.5 tablets for the pool, so he should use 5.

7. **A: 3.10 p.m.** It doesn't matter what order you add the times in, as long as you get them all. The easiest way (I think) is to add on the 15 minutes first (taking you to 9 a.m.), then the five hours of classes (2 p.m.), then one hour and ten minutes of breaks, getting you to 3.10 p.m.

8. **B: 5.** The perimeter of the classroom is 4.6 + 6.8 + 4.6 + 6.8 = 22.8 metres, so the area of the walls is 22.8 × 2.2 = 50.16m². If

each paint can covers 11m², the teacher needs 50.16 ÷ 11 = 4.56 cans, so she needs to buy five.

9. **C: Company C.** Five bumper packs from Company A cost £12.50; 25 worksheets cost £5, making £17.50. Five bumper packs from Company B cost £11, and 25 × £0.25 = 6.25. That makes £17.25. Five bumper packs from Company C cost £14, and 25 × £0.10 = £2.50, making £16.50. Company C is cheapest.

10. **C: £17.40.** The sum is 20 × 0.87 = 17.40.

11. **A: 8.44 p.m.** The marking should take 224 minutes, or three hours and 44 minutes. Adding an hour for watching TV takes the time to 8.44 p.m.

12. **B: 40.9 litres.** The sum is 9 ÷ 0.22 = 40.9 (to one decimal place).

Test C: ALAN Numeracy Exam

This test is designed to be the same level as the ALAN numeracy exam. If you're preparing for this qualification, try answering the questions without a calculator because you're not allowed one in the exam; if you're studying for a different test, use a calculator as normal. This test has 20 questions and your target time without a calculator is 40 minutes, or with a calculator, 20 minutes.

The ALAN test is a multiple-choice exam; you get to choose from four options.

Test C Questions

1. Uri travels 205 miles at an average speed of 62 miles per hour. Approximately how long does his journey take?

A: 15 minutes   B: 25 minutes   C: 3 hours 20 minutes
D: 4 hours

2. Suzie knows two towns are about five kilometres apart. On her map, the distance between them is about 2.5 cm. What is the scale of the map?

A: 1:500,000   B: 1:200,000   C: 1:250,000   D: 1:50,000

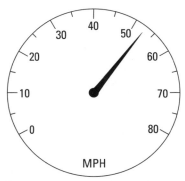

Figure 10-3: A bus's speedometer.

3. Figure 10-3 shows a speedometer on a bus. How fast is the bus travelling, to the nearest ten miles per hour?

A: 50mph   B: 53mph   C: 55mph   D: 60mph

4. A shop is open from 10 a.m. to 2 p.m. and 5 p.m. to 9 p.m. every weekday, and 10 a.m. to 4 p.m. at weekends. How many hours per week is it open?

A: 8   B: 40   C: 48   D: 52

5. A worker in the shop from question 4 earns £7 per hour on weekdays and £8.50 per hour at the weekends. If he works all the time the shop is open, which of these calculations gives his pay for the week?

A: $7 \times 5 \times 8 + 8.5 \times 2 \times 6$ B: $7 \times 5 \times 6 + 8.5 \times 2 \times 8$
C: $7 \times 8.5 \times 8 \times 6$ D: $(7 + 8.5) \times (5 \times 8 + 2 \times 6)$

6. The shop takes both euros and pounds. It works on the exchange rate that one pound is worth €1.10. A customer wants to buy £66 worth of shopping using euros. How much should she pay?

A: €60   B: €66.66   C: €70   D: €72.60

7. An artist wants to know the capacity of one of his ceramic bowls. He uses the formula $C = 2dr^2$, where C is the capacity, d is the depth and r is the radius. His bowl is 10cm deep and has a radius of 7cm. What is the capacity?

A: 98cm^3 B: 280cm^3 C: 980cm^3 D: 2800cm^3

8. Anna has an hour-long music lesson booked for 9.30 a.m. The tutor turns up ten minutes late, but still wants to give an hour's lesson. During the class, she checks the clock and sees that it's 10.15 a.m. – how much of her hour class is left?

A: 5 minutes   B: 15 minutes   C: 20 minutes   D: 25 minutes

9. Marc regularly makes the same journey by coach, and has a card that gives him a 30% discount. The normal price of a ticket is £80, and plans to make the journey 15 times next year. How much does he expect to spend on these journeys?

A: £1200   B: £360   C: £840   D: £120

10. Phil is making a recipe that calls for 300g of pasta and serves four people. If he wants to make the recipe for three people, how much pasta does he need?

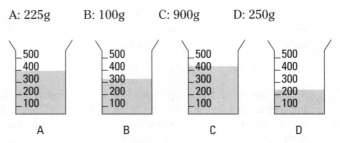

A: 225g   B: 100g   C: 900g   D: 250g

Figure 10-4: Four measuring cups.

11. Phil also needs to measure 375ml of milk for the sauce. Which of the measuring cups in Figure 10-4 is closest to 375ml?

12. Carol is packing packs of tomato sauce into a box. The packs of sauce are 8cm wide, 5cm deep and 10cm tall. The box is 40cm wide, 20cm deep and 20cm tall. How many packs can she fit in the box?

A: 400   B: 16,000   C: 40   D: 11

13. Pierre is travelling from Northampton to Birmingham, a distance of 40 miles. He knows that one mile is the same as 1.6 kilometres. How long is the journey in kilometres?

A: 25km   B: 56km   C: 40km   D: 64km

St Andrews	1315	1415	1515	1615	1715	1815
Glenrothes	1355	1455	1555	1655	1755	1855
Dunfermline	1445	1545	1645	1745	1845	1945
Edinburgh	1515	1615	1715	1815	1915	2015

Figure 10-5: A bus timetable.

14. Tessa arrives in St Andrews at 11 o'clock in the morning. She needs to be back in Edinburgh before 7 p.m. She checks the timetable in Figure 10-5 to see which bus she needs to catch. How long can she stay in St Andrews before she needs to leave?

A: 3 hours 15 minutes   B: 3 hours 45 minutes
C: 4 hours 15 minutes   D: 5 hours 15 minutes

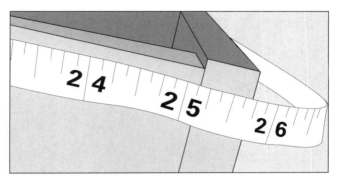

Figure 10-6: Christina's bookshelves.

15. Christina measures the width of her bookshelves with an old tape measure marked in inches, as shown in Figure 10-6. She knows that one inch (imperial) is about 2.5 centimetres (metric). Approximately how wide are her bookshelves in metric?

A: About one metre   B: About 65cm   C: About 6.5 metres
D: About 10cm

16. A box is 30 centimetres wide, 50 centimetres deep and 20 centimetres tall. What is its capacity in litres? (One litre is 1000 cubic centimetres).

A: 3 litres   B: 30 litres   C: 300 litres   D: 30,000 litres

17. Louis knows he can walk at around four miles per hour. He arranges to meet a friend for lunch at a pub ten miles from his home. They arrange to meet at 1.15 p.m. What time does Louis need to leave if he walks there?

A: 10.15 a.m.   B: 10.45 a.m.   C: 11.15 a.m.   D: 11.30 a.m.

18. Figure 10-7 shows the amount of air left in a diver's scuba tank. When full, the tank would supply enough air for two hours of diving. How long would the air in the tank last?

A: 40 minutes   B: 48 minutes   C: 60 minutes   D: 80 minutes

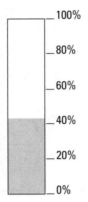

Figure 10-7: A scuba tank scale.

Apples	£1.50 per kilogram
Mushrooms	£1.60 per kilogram
Peppers	75p each
Potatoes	70p per kilogram

Figure 10-8: A grocery price list.

19. Figure 10-8 shows the price list at a farmer's market stall. Nick buys 500 grams of mushrooms, 4 kilograms of potatoes, 3 peppers and 1 kilogram of apples. How much does this cost him?

A: £7.35　　　B: £4.55　　　C: £8.15　　　D: £7.00

20. The volume of a child's toy is given by the following formula:

$$\pi\,(\,h + 2.5w)w^2 \div 12$$
h is the height of the toy
w is the width of the toy
π is approximately 3

If the toy is 10 centimetres tall and 4 centimetres wide, what is the toy's volume?

A: 20cm³　　　B: 240cm³　　　C: 320cm³　　　D: 80cm³

Worked Answers for Test C

1. **C: 3 hours 20 minutes.** Uri travels *approximately* 200 miles at about 60 miles per hour. The sum is $200 \div 60 = 20 \div 6 = 10 \div 3 = 3\,\frac{1}{3}$ hours.

2. **B: 1:200,000.** If 2.5cm represents 5km, then 10cm represents 20km, and 1cm represents 2km. Two kilometres is the same as 2,000m or 200,000cm. So 1cm represents 200,000cm, and the scale is 1:200,000.

3. **A: 50mph.** The reading is 53 miles per hour, which is closer to 50 than it is to 60.

4. **D: 52 hours.** It's open for eight hours each weekday, making $5 \times 8 = 40$ hours; it's open for six hours per day at the weekend, making $2 \times 6 = 12$ hours. Altogether, that's 52 hours.

5. **A: $7 \times 5 \times 8 + 8.5 \times 2 \times 6$.** On weekdays, he earns £7 per hour, five days a week, for eight hours, making $7 \times 5 \times 8$. On weekends, he earns £8.50 per hour, for two days, each for six hours, making $8.5 \times 2 \times 6$. To get his total, you add these up.

6. **D: €72.60.** The sum is £66 × 1.1 ÷ 1. Sixty-six times one is 66 (obviously) and 66×0.1 is 6.6 (simply divide by 10). Add these together to get €72.60.

7. **C: 980cm^3.** The formula gives $2 \times 10 \times 7^2$. Following BIDMAS (explained in Chapter 5), you do the index first, and work out $7^2 = 49$. Now you have $2 \times 10 \times 49 = 2 \times 490 = 980$cm^3.

The answer is a capacity, so the correct units are cm^3.

8. **D: 25 minutes.** The class is now due to end at 10.40 a.m., which is 25 minutes after 10.15 a.m.

9. **C: £840.** The total full-price cost of the tickets is $80 \times 15 = £1200$. The 30% discount is £360, which you take away to get £840. You could also work out 30% off of £80, which is £56, and multiply by 15 to get £840.

10. **A: 225g.** If he made the pasta for one person, he'd need 75g $(300 \div 4)$, and $75 \times 3 = 225$g.

11. **A.** This beaker shows between 350 and 400 millilitres, and is closer to 400 than to 300.

12. **C: 40.** She can fit five across, four back and two up. $5 \times 4 \times 2 = 40$.

13. **D: 64km.** You can do this with the Table of Joy; the sum works out to be $40 \times 1.6 \div 1 = 64$.

14. **D: 5 hours 15 minutes.** She needs to catch the 4.15 p.m. bus to reach Edinburgh before 7 p.m., and 4.15 p.m. is 5 hours 15 minutes after 11 a.m.

15. **B: About 65cm.** The bookshelves measure about 26 inches, which is $26 \times 2.5 = 65$cm.

16. **B: 30 litres.** The capacity is $30 \times 50 \times 20 = 30{,}000$ cubic centimetres; $30{,}000 \div 1{,}000 = 30$ litres.

17. **B: 10.45 a.m.** It will take him $10 \div 4 = 2.5$ hours to walk there. Two hours before 1.15 p.m. is 11.15 a.m., and half an hour before that is 10.45 a.m.

18. **B: 48 minutes.** The tank is 40% full, and two hours is the same as 120 minutes. 10% of two hours is 12 minutes, and 40% is 48 minutes.

19. **A: £7.35.** The mushrooms cost 80p, the peppers £2.25, the potatoes £2.80 and the apples £1.50. Adding those up gives £7.35.

20. **D: 80cm³.** The sum is $3 \times (10 + 2.5 \times 4) \times 4^2 \div 12$. Looking at the bracket (remember BIDMAS from Chapter 5!), you work out the times before the plus, and $2.5 \times 4 = 10$. That makes the bracket $10 + 10 = 20$. The sum is now $3 \times 20 \times 4^2 \div 12$. Next you work out 4^2, which is $4 \times 4 = 16$. Now work out $3 \times 20 \times 16 \div 12$ from left to right to get $60 \times 16 \div 12$, then $960 \div 12 = 80$.

Test D: General

Test D is useful for all numeracy students so give it a go. The test contains 25 questions and should take you around 25 minutes with a calculator, or about 45 minutes without.

Test D Questions

1. One ounce is about 28 grams. A recipe calls for 4 ounces of flour. How much is this in grams?

2. A shipping container is 6 metres long, 2.5 metres wide and 2 metres high. It needs to be filled with boxes which are one metre long, 50 centimetres wide and 40 centimetres tall. How many boxes will fit in the crate?

Bus Station	1035	1055	1115
Railway Station	1040	1100	1120
Hospital	1100	1120	1140
St. Mark's Church	1110	1130	1150
Superstore	1125	1145	1205

Figure 10-9: A bus timetable.

3. Figure 10-9 shows a bus timetable. How long does it take to travel from the bus station to St Mark's Church?

4. Alex builds a 1:360 scale model of a railway station. The platform is 108 metres long in real life. How long should the model platform be?

5. Anthony leaves for work at 7.20 a.m., and arrives at 9.05 a.m. after hitting traffic. How long did his journey take?

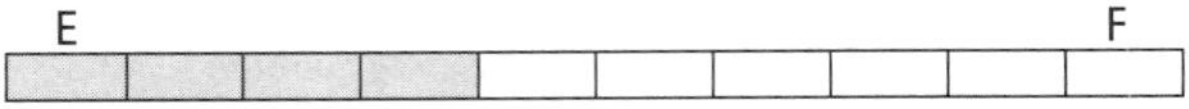

Figure 10-10: A fuel gauge.

6. The fuel gauge in Figure 10-10 is for a tank which holds 50 litres when full. How much fuel is now in the tank?

7. James is going on holiday. At the airport, he picks up two books for £14.95 each, a cup of coffee for £2.30 and a travel adapter plug for £4.95. How much does he pay altogether?

8. Richard uses the formula $5 + 2s + 4c$ to work out how many minutes a tube journey takes him, where s is the number of stations he passes through and c is the number of times he has to change train. He makes a journey that passes through eight stations and involves one change of trains. How many minutes should the journey take, according to his formula?

9. Delia has a recipe that makes 20 profiteroles and requires 80 grams of butter. She wants to make 50 profiteroles for a party – how much butter does she need?

10. Jenson drives 200 miles in one hour and 40 minutes. What is his average speed for the race?

Don't try this at home.

11. A cricket pitch is 22 yards long. One yard is about 90 centimetres. How long is a cricket pitch, to the nearest metre?

12. A shoe box is 30cm long, 15cm wide and 10cm tall. What is its volume?

Newcastle to Dublin	Dublin To Newcastle
Leaving Newcastle:	**Leaving Dublin:**
0950 (Not Saturday)	1130 (Not Saturday)
1050 (Saturday only)	1230 (Saturday only)
1230	1400
1550	1730
1940	2200
Flight time: 1 hour 10 minutes	

Figure 10-11: A plane timetable.

13. Figure 10-11 shows a timetable for flights between Newcastle and Dublin. Joey wants to leave Newcastle after 10 a.m. on Monday – what is the earliest he can arrive in Dublin?

14. A map has a scale of 1:25,000. A path on the map is 12 centimetres long. How long is the path in real life?

15. A call centre allows its employees an average of six minutes per phone call. A shift lasts four hours, but that includes a half-hour break. How many calls does an average employee make during a shift?

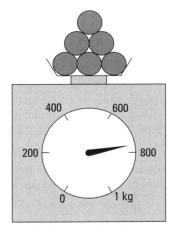

Figure 10-12: A kitchen scale.

16. Figure 10-12 shows a bag of fruit on a kitchen scale. To the nearest 100 grams, how much does the bag of fruit weigh?

17. While on holiday, Elaine bought a hat for €13.75 and ten postcards for €0.15 each. She paid with a twenty-euro note. How much change did she get?

18. The area of a complicated shape is given as $4xy + 3x^2$ / $2 + 2y^2$. If x is 4cm and y is 7cm, what is the area of the shape?

19. One week, Basil notices that he uses 12 tins of magnolia emulsion while painting for 20 hours. The following week, he plans to paint for 15 hours. How much magnolia emulsion does he need (assuming he uses it at the same rate)?

20. Leela cycles 42 miles at an average speed of 12 miles per hour. How long does it take her?

21. The exchange rate between pounds and American dollars is £1 = $1.60. Cameron finds $56 in a travel wallet that she'd forgotten about. How much is this worth in pounds?

22. An Olympic swimming pool is 50 metres long, 25 metres wide and 2 metres deep. What volume of water do you need to fill an Olympic pool?

Cardiff	1800	1900	2000	2100
Newport	1815	1915	2015	2115
Bristol	1855	1955	2055	2155
Exeter	1955	2055	2155	2255

Figure 10-13: A timetable.

23. Graham looks at the timetable in Figure 10-13. He wants to be in Bristol before 9 p.m. What time is the last train he can catch from Cardiff?

24. An atlas shows a region at a scale of 1:150,000. Two villages are 3 kilometres apart in real life. How far apart are they on the map?

25. A cricket match consists of up to five days' play. Each day is made up of two 90-minute sessions and a two-hour session. How many hours of cricket could be played altogether?

Worked Answers for Test D

1. **112 grams.** The sum is 4×28. If you're trying this without a calculator, you can break the sum up as either $4 \times 20 = 80$ and $4 \times 8 = 32$ (making 112 altogether) or $4 \times 25 = 100$ and $4 \times 3 = 12$. There are other ways as well!

2. **150.** You can fit six boxes along the length, five across the depth and five up. $6 \times 5 \times 5 = 30 \times 5 = 150$.

3. **35 minutes.** It takes 25 minutes to get to the hospital (at 11 a.m.) and another 10 to get to the church. You could also just look at the last column and say that 11.50 is 35 minutes after 11.15.

4. **30cm.** The sum is $108 \div 360$, which (if I didn't have a calculator) I would do by cancelling down fractions: $\frac{108}{360} = \frac{54}{180} = \frac{27}{90} = \frac{9}{30} = \frac{3}{10} = 0.3$ metres, or 30 centimetres.

5. **One hour and 45 minutes.** After 40 minutes, it's 8 o'clock, after another hour it's 9 a.m., and after five more minutes it's 9.05. That makes 1 hour 45 minutes all together.

6. **20 litres.** Each square is 5 litres, so four shaded squares would make 20 litres.

7. **£37.15.** The books come to £29.90; adding on the coffee takes him to £32.20, and adding on the adapter makes £37.15. As usual, there are several ways to do this – whichever works for you is fine.

8. **25 minutes.** The sum is $5 + 2 \times 8 + 4 \times 1 = 5 + 16 + 4 = 21 + 4 = 25$.

9. **200 grams.** Each profiterole requires 4 grams of butter, so 50 profiteroles would need 200 grams.

10. **120 miles per hour.** He travelled 200 miles in 100 minutes, which is two miles every minute. In 60 minutes, he'd travel 120 miles.

11. **20 metres.** The sum is $22 \times 0.9 = 19.8$ metres. To the nearest metre, that's 20 metres.

12. **4,500cm^3.** The sum is $30 \times 15 \times 10 = 450 \times 10 = 4{,}500\text{cm}^3$.

13. **13:40 (1.40 p.m).** The 10:50 plane only flies on Saturdays, so he has to catch the 12:30 plane instead.

14. **3 kilometres.** The sum is $12 \times 25{,}000$, which is 300,000cm. That's the same as 3,000 metres, or 3 kilometres. Alternatively, you can see that 1cm on the map is 25,000cm in real life, which is the same as 250m. 12×250 is 3,000m, or 3km.

15. **35 calls.** A full shift is 240 minutes long, less a 30 minute break, leaving 210 minutes of calls. $210 \div 6 = 35$ calls.

16. **800g.** The arrow is closer to 800 than it is to 700.

17. **€4.75.** The postcards cost €1.50, so the total bill was 13.75 + 1.50 = €15.25. Taking that away from €20 gives €4.75.

18. **234cm^2.** Break it down into the three parts:
$4xy = 4 \times 4 \times 7 = 16 \times 7 = 112$;
$3x2 / 2 = 3 \times 4^2 / 2 = 3 \times 16 / 2 = 48 / 2 = 24$;
$2y2 = 2 \times 7^2 = 2 \times 49 = 98$.

Adding these up gives 234cm^2.

19. **9 tins.** You can do this with the Table of Joy (refer to Chapter 5). The sum is $15 \times 12 \div 20 = 180 \div 20 = 9$. Alternatively, you can say he uses three tins in five hours, so in fifteen hours, he'd use nine.

20. **Three hours and 30 minutes.** The sum is $42 \div 12$, which you can do using long division to get 3.5. You could also cancel down fractions to get $^{42}\!/_{12} = {}^{21}\!/_6 = {}^7\!/_2 = 3.5$.

21. **£35.** The Table of Joy sum is $56 \times 1 \div 1.6$. You can start by multiplying top and bottom by 10 to get $560 \div 16$. From there, you can use long division or cancelling fractions ($^{560}\!/_{16} = {}^{280}\!/_8 = {}^{140}\!/_4 = {}^{70}\!/_2 = 35$).

22. **2,500m^3.** The sum is $50 \times 25 \times 2 = 1{,}250 \times 2 = 2{,}500$m^3. You don't have to do it in that order, though – I find it easier to do $25 \times 2 = 50$ first, then $50 \times 50 = 2{,}500$.

23. **2000.** This train gets into Bristol at 2055, or 8.55 p.m.

24. **2cm.** Three kilometres is 3,000 metres, or 300,000 centimetres. Dividing that by 150,000 gives two centimetres. Alternatively, 1cm on the map is 150,000cm in real life, or 1.5km. Three kilometres divided by 1.5km is two.

25. **25 hours.** Each day can have up to 90 + 90 + 120 = 300 minutes of play, which is five hours; multiplied by five days, which gives 25 hours.

Answers at a Glance

Test A

1. **66 miles.**

2. **675ml.**

3. **£180.**

4. **2.**

5. **6$\frac{1}{12}$ days.**

6. **1 hour, 40 minutes**

7. **$\frac{17}{30}$.**

8. **1$\frac{3}{4}$.**

9. **9.**

10. **0.75.**

11. **0.05 litres.**

12. **24.**

13. **200.**

14. **12 metres.**

15. **280.**

16. **417, 410.**

17. **8.64 × 10^4.**

18. **1.9 kilometres per hour.**

19. **84.**

20. **$x = 3$, $y = 2$.**

21. **$(x - 4)$ $(x + 2)$.**

22. **55m^2.**

23. **120°.**

24. **$s = (x - m) / z$.**

25. **−15.**

Test B

1. **£8.50.**

2. **2 hours and 5 minutes.**

3. **£69.35.**

4. **£40.**

5. **D: PrestoPress is £2.50 cheaper.**

6. **B: 5.**

7. **A: 3.10 p.m.**

8. **B: 5.**

9. **C: Company C.**

10. **C: £17.40.**

11. **A: 8.44 p.m.**

12. **B: 40.9 litres.**

Test C

1. C: **3 hours 20 minutes.**

2. B: **1:200,000.**

3. A: **50mph.**

4. D: **52 hours.**

5. A: $\mathbf{7 \times 5 \times 8 + 8.5 \times 2 \times 6.}$

6. D: **€72.60.**

7. C: **980cm^3.**

8. D: **25 minutes.**

9. C: **£840.**

10. A: **225g.**

11. A.

12. C: **40.**

13. D: **64km.**

14. D: **5 hours 15 minutes.**

15. B: **About 65cm.**

16. B: **30 litres.**

17. B: **10.45 a.m.**

18. B: **48 minutes.**

19. A: **£7.35.**

20. D: **80cm^3.**

Test D

1. **112 grams.**

2. **150.**

3. **35 minutes.**

4. **30cm.**

5. **One hour and 45 minutes.**

6. **20 litres.**

7. **£37.15.**

8. **25 minutes.**

9. **200 grams.**

10. **120 miles per hour.**

11. **20 metres.**

12. **4,500cm^3.**

13. **13:40 (1.40 p.m).**

14. **3 kilometres.**

15. **35 calls.**

16. **800g.**

17. **€4.75.**

18. **234cm^2.**

19. **9 tins.**

20. **Three hours and 30 minutes.**

21. **£35.**

22.
2,500m^3.

23. **2000.**

24. **2cm.**

25. **25 hours.**

Chapter 11

Data Handling Tests

. . . .

In This Chapter

▶ Testing yourself

▶ Checking your answers

. . . .

*T*his section contains four tests on interpreting and working with data, and is mainly based on the material in Chapter 8.

Each test is based on the handling data skills you need for a particular numeracy exam, but the level is similar for all four tests (Chapter 12 gives you more advanced data tests, which may be of use to you if you're studying for Qualified Teacher Status or the UKCAT).

Each test has a suggested target time with or without a calculator. Some of them are multiple-choice tests, some of them require you to give your own answer, and some are a mixture of the two.

Test A: Armed Forces Entrance Exam

Test A is designed to test your knowledge of data handling at about the level you need to pass entrance tests for the armed forces. It contains 12 questions and your target times are 10 minutes (with a calculator) or 20 minutes (without). The actual tests are different for each service – you can find the details of what to expect in Chapter 1.

Test A Questions

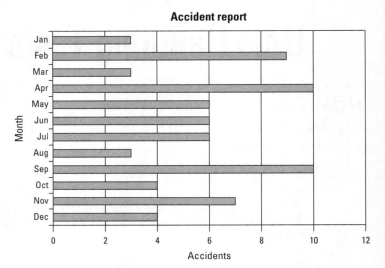

Figure 11-1: An accident report.

1. Look at the graph in Figure 11-1. How many accidents were reported in February?

2. Look at the graph in Figure 11-1. What was the range of the number of accidents reported over the year?

Town hall	08:48	09:18	09:48	10:18	10:48	11:18	11:48
High Street	09:00	09:30	10:00	10:30	11:00	11:30	12:00
Post office	09:05	09:35	10:05	10:35	11:05	11:35	12:05
Railway station	09:16	09:46	10:16	10:46	11:16	11:46	12:16
Supermarket	09:25	09:55	10:25	10:55	11:25	11:55	12:25
Football stadium	09:37	10:07	10:37	11:07	11:37	12:07	12:37

Figure 11-2: A bus timetable.

3. Figure 11-2 shows a bus timetable. How long does it take the bus to go from the railway station to the football stadium?

4. Look at the bus timetable in Figure 11-2. Karen catches the bus at the post office and wants to be at the supermarket by 11.30 a.m. What is the latest she can catch the bus?

	Initial cost	Daily charge	
		less than 1 week	more than 1 week
Small	£80.00	£45.00	£40.00
Medium	£100.00	£50.00	£45.00
Large	£110.00	£55.00	£50.00

Figure 11-3: Prices for car hire.

5. Brad wants to hire a medium-sized car for four days. He uses the table in Figure 11-3 to work out the cost. How much is the car hire?

6. Oscar wants to hire a small car for ten days. Using Figure 11-3, how much would it cost?

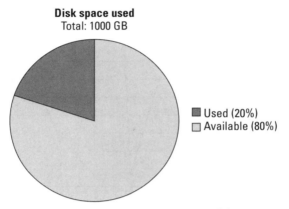

Figure 11-4: A pie chart showing available disk space.

7. Look at Figure 11-4. What fraction of the disk space has been used up?

A: ½   B: ⅓   C: ¼   D: ⅕

8. Looking at Figure 11-4, how many gigabytes of disk space are available?

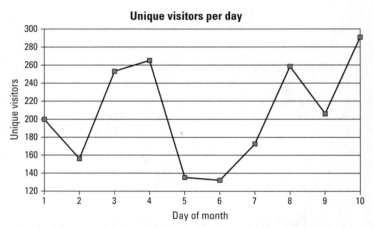

Figure 11-5: Line graph showing the number of visits to a website.

9. Look at the graph in Figure 11-5. Which day of the month had the most unique visitors to the website?

10. Look at the graph in Figure 11-5. Gavin says the number of visitors to the site on the 10th is more than double the number of visitors on the 1st. Is he correct?

	Free	Basic	Advanced
Games per month	5	20	50
Email support	Yes	Yes	Yes
Telephone support	No	Yes	Yes
In-game chat	No	No	Yes
Price per month	Free	£27.00	£35.00

Figure 11-6: Computer service feature chart.

11. Emily is picking a computer game service from the chart in Figure 11-6. She wants to play at least 15 games per month and needs only email support. Which of the three options is the best for her?

12. Look at the table in Figure 11-6. For the 'advanced' service, what is the mean cost of each game?

Worked Answers for Test A

1. **9.** The February bar is midway between the 8 and 10 lines.

2. **7.** The worst months for accidents saw 10 of them; the best month saw 3. The range is the difference between them, and $10 - 3 = 7$.

3. **21 minutes.** The first bus leaves the railway station at 09:16 and arrives at 09:37. $37 - 16 = 21$ minutes.

4. **11:05.** The last bus to arrive at the supermarket before 11.30 is the one that arrives there at 11.25. It leaves the post office at 11:05.

5. **£300.** He pays the initial charge of £100, plus four daily fees of £50. The daily fees add up to £200, so that's £300 all together.

6. **£480.** The initial fee is £80, and ten daily fees of £40 would be £400. All together, that's £480.

7. **D: ⅕.** 20% is the same as $20 \div 100 = 2 \div 10 = ⅕$.

8. **800GB.** You need 80% of 1,000GB. Ten per cent is 100GB, so 80% is 800GB.

9. **The 10th.** This is simply where the line is highest.

10. **No.** Gavin has been misled by the vertical axis not starting at zero. There were about 200 visitors on the 1st and about 290 on the 10th: nowhere near double.

11. **The Basic service.** It is the cheapest service that allows her to play more game than she needs.

12. **70p.** The sum is £35 ÷ 50 = £7 ÷ 10 = £0.70.

Test B: Emergency Services Data Handling

Test B is designed to test your data handling at the level you need to join the emergency services. It contains 15 questions and your target times are 15 minutes (with a calculator) and 25 minutes (without). The details of the real test vary from service to service – check out Chapter 1 to see what to expect when you sit the exam.

Test B Questions

1. A firefighter entered a fire at 11.15 a.m. with 60 minutes of oxygen remaining. It is now 12.05 p.m. How much oxygen does the firefighter have remaining?

A: 40 minutes   B: 30 minutes   C: 20 minutes   D: 10 minutes

2. It is 10.53 p.m., and you have 23 minutes of air remaining. At what time will you run out?

A: 10.30 p.m.   B: 11.03 p.m.   C: 11.16 p.m.   D: 11.26 p.m.

3. An oxygen tank contains 3 hours of oxygen when full. The dial says the tank is 40% full. How long will the oxygen in it last?

A: 90 minutes   B: 72 minutes   C: 120 minutes   D: 60 minutes

Questions 4 to 6 refer to Figure 11-7, which shows supplies of a home safety leaflet.

		Black and white	Colour	Glossy
Leaflet stocks (end of April)		2500	450	50
May				
	Delivered	500	50	10
	Printed	1000	500	0
June				
	Delivered	600	500	20
	Printed	0	0	0
July				
	Delivered	1000	200	30
	Printed	1500	1000	50
August				
	Delivered	1750	500	40
	Printed	1000	500	0

Figure 11-7: Supplies of a home safety leaflet.

4. How many black and white leaflets were delivered in August?

A: 500   B: 600   C: 1000   D: 1750

5. In which month were the most leaflets delivered?

A: May   B: June   C: July   D: August

6: How many glossy leaflets remained in stock at the end of August?

A: None   B: 10   C: 20   D: 50

Questions 7 to 9 refer to Figure 11-8, which shows a comparison of causes of hospital admissions in Bartonshire in the second half of 2010.

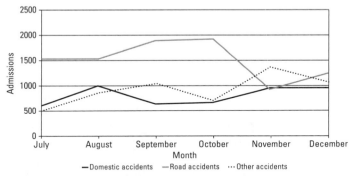

Figure 11-8: Hospital admissions in Bartonshire, July to December 2010.

7. Which month had the fewest admissions as a result of road accidents?

A: July   B: August   C: September   D: November

8. How many hospital admissions in total were there in November?

A: About 1,000   B: About 2,000   C: About 3,000
D: About 5,000

9. How many more admissions from domestic accidents were there in December than in July?

A: About 350 B: About 650   C: About 900   D: About 1,500

Questions 10 to 12 refer to the graph in Figure 11-9, which shows numbers of coastguard rescues in 2008 to 2010 in three different areas.

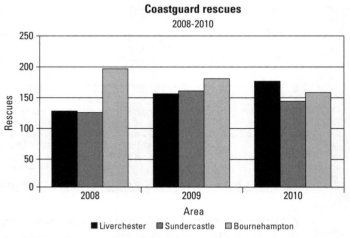

Figure 11-9: Coastguard rescues, 2008 to 2010.

10. How many rescues took place in 2009 in the Liverchester area?

A: 126   B: 156   C: 180   D: 495

11. In which area did the number of rescues consistently fall over the three years?

A: Liverchester   B: Sundercastle   C: Bournehampton
D: None of these.

12. How many more rescues were there in Liverchester than Sundercastle in 2010?

A: 2   B: 12   C: 32   D: 175

Questions 13 to 15 refer to the table in Figure 11-10, which shows 999 response times in several areas of a city.

	Mean response time	% under 15 mins	% under 30 mins
North	14:35	77	95
South	12:15	95	99
East	17:20	44	90
West	10:30	99	100
Central	19:15	38	75

Figure 11-10: 999 response times.

13. What is the mean 999 response time in the north of the city?

A: 14:35   B: 14:47   C: 17:20   D: 19:15

14. Which area of the city had the longest average 999 response times?

A: North   B: South   C: East   D: Central

15. To meet targets, at least 90% of 999 response times must be below quarter of an hour. How many of the areas of the city met their target?

A: 5   B: 4   C: 3   D: 2

Worked Answers for Test B

1. **D: 10 minutes.** The oxygen will run out at 12.15 p.m.

2. **C: 11.16 p.m.** In seven minutes, it'll be 11 p.m. and you'll have 16 minutes remaining.

3. **B: 72 minutes.** Three hours is 180 minutes, so 10% is 18 minutes and 40% is $4 \times 18 = 72$ minutes.

4. **D: 1750.**

5. **D: August.** There were at least as many leaflets delivered in every category than any other month.

6. **A: None.** There were 50 glossy leaflets to begin with and 50 more printed, making 100 altogether. Over the summer, 100 glossy leaflets were delivered, so none are left.

7. **D: November.** This is where the road accidents line is lowest.

8. **C: About 3,000.** Road accidents and domestic accidents are both at around 1,000. Other accidents are about 1,300, making a total of around 3,300 – the closest answer to that figure is 'about 3,000'.The actual number is 3,242.

9. **A: About 350.** In December, there were 960 and in June, 602, a difference of 358.

10. **B: 156.**

11. **C: Bournehampton.** Each bar is lower than the one before.

12. **C: 32.** The sum is $175 - 156$.

13. **A: 14:35.**

14. **D: Central.**

15. **D: 2.** Only the South and West regions managed this.

Test C: ALAN Level 2 Data Handling

This test is designed to test your data handling at the level you need to pass the Adult Literacy and Numeracy (ALAN) Level 2 numeracy test. It contains 25 questions and your target times are 25 minutes (with a calculator) or 45 minutes (without a calculator).

The ALAN is a non-calculator exam, so if you're studying for the ALAN, try this test without a calculator.

Questions for Test C

Mark range	Number of students
0-19	47
20-39	1568
40-59	5999
60-79	1954
80-99	432
Total	**10000**

Figure 11-11: Exam results.

1. Figure 11-11 shows the results of an exam. Students needed to get at least 80% in the exam to earn a distinction. How many students earned a distinction?

A: 47   B: 9,568   C: 2,386   D: 432

2. Students who scored less than 40% were asked to resit the exam. Looking at Figure 11-11, what percentage of the students had to resit?

A: 15.68%   B: 16.15%   C: 16.05%   D: 83.85%

3. The examiner wants to display the results from Figure 11-11 in a graph. Which type is most appropriate?

A: A line graph.   B: A scatter graph.   C: A bar graph.
D: A pictogram.

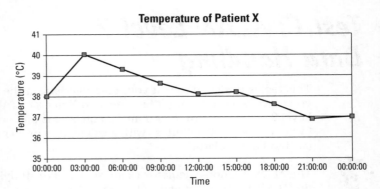

Figure 11-12: A patient's temperature.

4. Figure 11-12 shows the temperature of a patient taken every hour for 24 hours. What was the patient's maximum temperature over the day?

A: 37°C   B: 39°C   C: 40°C   D: 41°C

5. To convert Celsius into Fahrenheit, the nurses use the following recipe:

✔ Divide the temperature by 5.

✔ Multiply the result by 9.

✔ Add 32 to the answer.

Looking at Figure 11-12, what was the patient's temperature in Fahrenheit at 3 a.m.?

A: 104°F   B: 101°F   C: 98°F   D: 40°F

6. A temperature of more than 37.5°C is considered to be a fever. At roughly what time did the patient stop having a fever?

A: 6 a.m.   B: noon   C: 6 p.m.   D: midnight

	Home	Away
Adult	£15.00	£18.00
Child	£9.00	£10.80
Programmes		£2.50

Figure 11-13: Entry prices for a football match.

7. Figure 11-13 shows a list of prices for admission to a football match. How much does it cost for a family of two adults and three children to attend a match as home supporters and buy two programmes?

A: £62   B: £84.40   C: £57   D: £79.40

8. What fraction of the price of an adult home ticket is a child home ticket?

A: ⅔   B: ⅗   C: ⅖   D: ½

9. A crowd of 3,000 home supporters goes to the football match. A third of the crowd is children. How much money does the club earn from the home fans? Ignore programme sales.

A: £39,000   B: £33,000   C: £46,800   D: £45,000

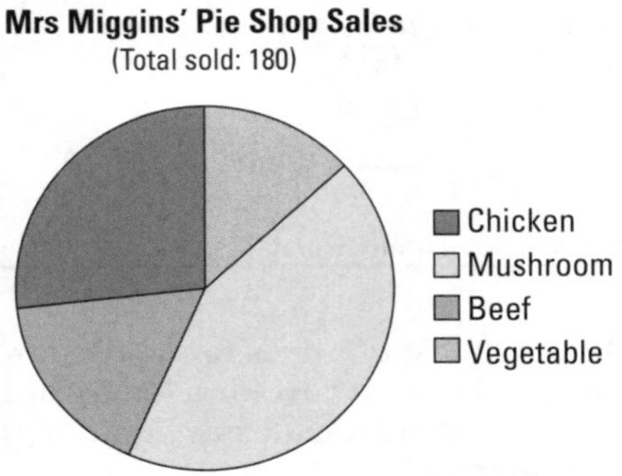

Mrs Miggins' Pie Shop Sales
(Total sold: 180)

- Chicken
- Mushroom
- Beef
- Vegetable

Figure 11-14: Sales results from Mrs Miggins' Pie Shop.

10. Mrs Miggins' Pie Shop sells several different pies. The pie chart in Figure 11-14 shows her sales for one day. The angle of the slice for mushroom pies in Figure 11-14 is 60°. How many mushroom pies did she sell?

A: 20   B: 30   C: 60   D: 120

11. If Mrs Miggins sold the same number of each type of pie the following day, what would the pie chart showing her sales for the two days look like?

A: It would look just the same.   B: The circle would be bigger.
C: The angles would get bigger.   D: The angles would get smaller.

12. If Mrs Miggins finds she has miscounted and sold ten more beef pies than she thought, what would happen to the chart in Figure 11-14?

A: Nothing would change.   B: The graph would get bigger.
C: The beef pie slice would get bigger and the others smaller.
D: The beef pie slice would get bigger and the others would stay the same.

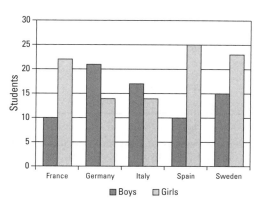

Figure 11-15: Nationalities of students on an exchange visit.

13. Figure 11-15 shows the nationalities of students on an exchange visit to London. Which country sent the most students?

A: Spain   B: Sweden   C: Spain and Germany   D: Germany

14. What is the ratio of Spanish boys to girls in Figure 11-15, in its simplest form?

A: 2:7   B: 5:7   C: 2:5   D: 5:2

15. Which two countries sent the same number of boys?

A: Spain and Germany   B: France and Spain
C: Germany and Italy   D: France and Sweden

16. Each country has to supply one adult for every eight students. How many adults does France need to send?

A: 2   B: 3   C: 4   D: 5

	Monday	Tuesday	Wednesday	Thursday	Friday
Accounts	2:00	2:30	1:30	2:00	2:00
Email	0:30	0:45	1:00	0:45	0:45
Meetings	2:30	1:00	0:30	0:00	0:45
Other	2:00	2:45	4:00	4:15	3;30
Total	**7:00**	**7:00**	**7:00**	**7:00**	**7:00**

Figure 11-16: Julia's week.

17. Julia keeps a record of how she spends her time at work for a week, as shown in Figure 11-16. How many hours did she spend in meetings?

A: 4¾ hours   B: 5 hours   C: 7½ hours   D: 10 hours

18. Roughly what percentage of Julia's time is spent answering emails?

A: 10%   B: 20%   C: 25%   D: 50%

19. Julia's company installs new software that promises to save her a quarter of the time she spends on accounting. How much time would this have saved her this week?

A: 10 hours   B: 5 hours   C: 2 hours 50 minutes
D: 2 hours 30 minutes

Edinburgh	Glasgow	London	Manchester	
05:10	04:45	02:15	01:45	**Birmingham**
	01:05	07:15	04:05	**Edinburgh**
		06:50	03:40	**Glasgow**
			03:45	**London**

Figure 11-17: Approximate driving times between UK cities.

20. Figure 11-17 shows approximate driving times between several UK cities. How long does it take to drive from Edinburgh to Manchester?

A: 5:10   B: 4:05   C: 3:45   D: 6:50

21. Which two cities are furthest apart in terms of driving time?

A: London and Edinburgh   B: London and Glasgow
C: Glasgow and Manchester   D: Manchester and Birmingham

22. The distance from Birmingham to Glasgow is about 300 miles. How fast would you need to drive if you wanted to travel from Birmingham to Glasgow in the time given by Figure 11-17? Round the time to the nearest hour.

A: 50mph   B: 60mph   C: 70mph   D: 80mph

0-60cm	++++	++++						
60-80cm	++++	++++	++++					
80-100cm	++++	++++	++++	++++	++++	++++		
100-120cm	++++	++++	++++	++++	++++	++++	++++	++++
120-160cm	++++							

Figure 11-18: Dawn's sunflower survey.

23. Dawn records the heights of her prize sunflowers in the tally chart in Figure 11-18. Which group is the modal group?

A: 60-80cm   B: 80-100cm   C: 100-120cm   D: The data has no mode.

24. In which group does the median lie?

A: 60-80cm   B: 80-100cm   C: 100-120cm   D: The data has no median.

25. Which of the following is the best estimate for the mean height of Dawn's sunflowers?

A: 80cm   B: 91.5cm   C: 100cm   D: 110cm

Worked Answers for Test C

1. **D: 432.**

2. **B: 16.15%.** A total of 1615 students didn't make the grade, out of 10,000. One percent of 10,000 is 100, so 1615 is 16.15%.

3. **C: A bar graph.** Bar graphs are good for showing how many people are in a particular group. A pictogram might be appropriate for smaller groups, but it's not much good for big numbers because it's hard to read.

4. **C: 40°C.** The maximum is the highest point on the graph.

5. **A: 104°F.** The sum is $(40 \div 5) \times 9 + 32 = 8 \times 9 + 32 = 72 + 32 = 104$.

6. **C: 6 p.m.** The line drops below 37.5°C at about 18:00, which is 6 p.m.

7. **A: ₤62.** The adults cost $2 \times ₤15 = ₤30$. The children cost $3 \times ₤9 = ₤27$. The programmes cost $2 \times ₤2.50 = ₤5$. Altogether, that's ₤62.

8. **B: ⅗.** The fraction is ⁹⁄₁₅, and if you divide top and bottom by three, you get ⅗.

9. **A: ₤39,000.** The adults bring in $2,000 \times ₤15 = ₤30,000$, and the children bring in $1,000 \times ₤9 = ₤9,000$. All together, that's ₤39,000.

10. **B: 30.** There are 360 degrees in a circle, and 180 pies – so there are two degrees for each pie. If the angle is 60°, that corresponds to 30 pies.

11. **A: It would look just the same.** A pie chart shows the *relative* sizes of the categories – and if Mrs Miggins sells pies in the same proportion the next day, the relative sizes of the categories remain the same.

12. **C: The beef pie slice would get bigger and the others smaller.** There's a higher proportion of beef pie than the original graph shows, to that slice has to be bigger; the angles of

the slices have to add up to 360°, so the other slices have to shrink to fit!

13. **B: Sweden.** Sweden sent a total of 38 students, Germany and Spain only 35.

14. **C: 2:5.** There are 10 Spanish boys and 25 Spanish girls, so the ratio is 10:25; you can divide both sides by five to get 2:5.

15. **B: France and Spain.** Both countries sent 10 boys.

16. **C: 4.** France is sending 32 students, and $32 \div 8 = 4$.

17. **A: 4¾ hours.** The sum is 2½ + 1 + ½ + ¾= 4¾.

18. **A: 10%.** She spends a total of 3¾ hours out of a total of 35 hours – 10% of 35 is 3½.

19. **D: 2 hours 30.** She spends a total of 10 hours a week on accounting. A quarter of 10 is 2½ hours, or 2 hours 30 minutes.

20. **B: 4:05.**

21. **A: London and Edinburgh.** They're 7 hours and 15 minutes apart.

22. **B: 60mph.** The time to travel from Birmingham to Glasgow is 4 hours and 45 minutes, which is five hours to the nearest hour. You can use the Table of Joy to work out the sum, which is $300 \times 1 \div 5 = 60$.

23. **C: 100-120cm.** The modal group is the one containing the biggest number of sunflowers.

When you're working with a tally chart, it's usually easier to work with numbers than with tally marks. Count up the tallies (each cluster is worth 5) and write them down next to the group so you can refer to them.

24. **B: 80-100cm.** 100 sunflowers are in the survey, so the median value is the height of the 50th- or 51st-biggest sunflower. Both of those are in the 80-100cm group.

25. **B: 91.5cm.** This is a horrid question! You need to multiply the midpoint of each group by the number of sunflowers in

the group; you then add up all of those numbers and divide by the total number of sunflowers. I show the working in Figure 11-19.

Group	Number	Midpoint	Number x midpoint
0-60cm	10	30	300
80-60cm	15	70	1050
80-100cm	30	90	2700
100-120cm	40	110	4400
120-160cm	5	140	700
Total	**100**		**9150**

Figure 11-19: Working for Question 25.

Test D: General Data Handling

Test D is a general data-handling test containing 25 questions. Your target times are 45 minutes without a calculator or 25 minutes with a calculator.

Test D Questions

Questions 1 to 5 are about Figure 11-20, which shows the age groups of people attending the Dumstock music festival.

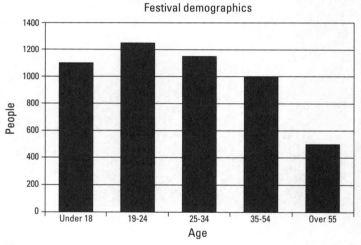

Figure 11-20: Festival demographics.

1. How many people are in the 19-24 age group?

2. What percentage of the people are under 18?

3. The Giant Acoustic Tent holds 800 people. Twenty per cent of the people at the festival want to see Rolf Harris play in the Giant Acoustic Tent. If it's big enough, how many extra people could fit in the tent; if not, how many fans will be left outside with their inflatable kangaroos and fake beards?

4. The organisers arrange to have one portable toilet for every 40 tickets sold. How many toilets do they arrange for?

5. The organiser says the range of ages at the festival is 37 years. Is she correct?

Questions 6 to 10 are about the line graph in Figure 11-21, showing the changes in value of a company's stock over a year.

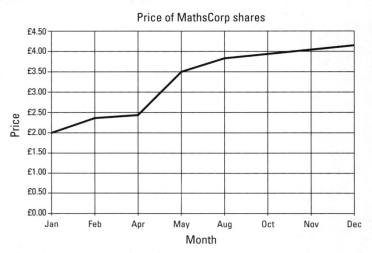

Figure 11-21: A line graph of a stock price.

6. What is wrong with this graph?

7. Which period saw the greatest increase in value?

8. Which of the following statements is certainly true?

A: The price of the company's stock rose every month.
B: The value of the stock in December was more than double the value in January.
C: The range of values was £4.15.
D: The company's stock continued to rise in value the following year.

9. Gavin bought 1,000 shares in this company for £1.20 a few years ago. He sold them in January. How much profit did he make on his investment?

10. On top of the price of the shares, a stockbroker charges a flat fee of £50 for the first 1000 shares you buy plus 1% of the value of any further shares. How much would it have cost you to buy 2,500 shares in November when they were £4 each through a stockbroker?

Questions 11 to 15 are about the pie charts in Figure 11-22, which show the punctuality record of a train company in 2005 and 2010.

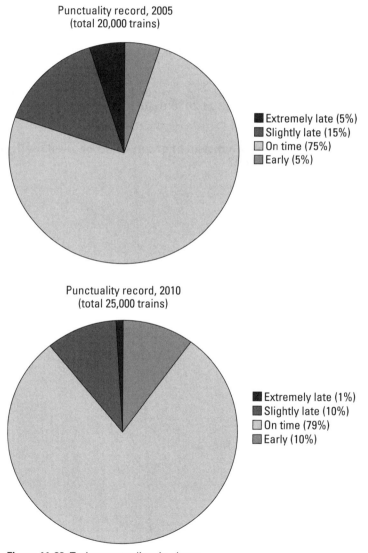

Punctuality record, 2005
(total 20,000 trains)

■ Extremely late (5%)
■ Slightly late (15%)
☐ On time (75%)
■ Early (5%)

Punctuality record, 2010
(total 25,000 trains)

■ Extremely late (1%)
■ Slightly late (10%)
☐ On time (79%)
■ Early (10%)

Figure 11-22: Train punctuality pie charts.

11. What was the percentage point difference between the number of extremely late trains in 2005 and extremely late trains in 2010?

12. What is the angle in the middle of the chart for the sector representing on-time trains in 2005?

13. How many more trains were slightly late in 2005 than in 2010?

14. The company advertises that all of its trains were more punctual in 2010 than 2005. What is wrong with this statement?

15. What other type of graph could be used to display this information?

Questions 16 to 20 are about the price table for sailing lessons in Figure 11-23.

	Intensive	Weekend	
Basic training	£350.00	£320.00	*Installment plans available*
Competent Crewman	£450.00	£400.00	*Pay 20% deposit and*
Navigation	£500.00	£450.00	*spread the remaining cost*
All in One Super Combo	£1,200.00	£1,120.00	*Into 12 easy monthly payments!*

Figure 11-23: A price table for sailing lessons.

16. Mark takes the Competent Crewman qualification as a weekend course. He has a 10% discount voucher. How much does the course cost him?

17. Ishmael wants some of his crew to take the Navigation qualification as a weekend course. He has a budget of £5,000 for training. How many of his crew can he send on the course?

18. Kerry takes the Intensive All In One Super Combo course and pays using the installment plan. How much are her monthly payments?

19. Lemuel is planning a sea voyage which will cost him £500 per day. If he trains as a navigator, it will take him 35 days, and 40 if not. How much cheaper would the journey be if he took the intensive Navigation course?

20. Darius says the intensive Navigation course is 10% more expensive than the weekend version. Is he correct?

Questions 21 to 25 are about the stacked bar graph in Figure 11-24, showing the results of an election in three different towns, each of which had 50,000 votes cast.

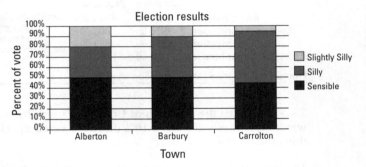

Figure 11-24: A stacked bar chart: election night special!

21. What percentage of the total votes did the Silly Party win?

22. A party must win at least 10% of the votes in a town to avoid losing its deposit. In how many of the three towns did the Slightly Silly party lose its deposit?

23. The Slightly Silly party was hoping for 10,000 votes in Carrolton. Did it do better or worse than it hoped, and by how much?

24. A party's *relative majority* is how many votes it is ahead of its nearest rival. What was the Silly Party's relative majority in Carrolton?

25. After a recount in Barbury, it was found that 500 Slightly Silly votes had been miscounted as Silly votes. What percentage of the votes should have been counted as Slightly Silly?

Worked Answers for Test D

1. **1250.** The bar is a quarter of the way between 1200 and 1400.

2. **22%.** You need to add up all the columns. There are 5,000 people all together. There are 1,100 under-18s. You can use the Table of Joy to find that the sum is $1,100 \times 100 \div 5,000 = 22$.

3. **200 people will be left outside.** Twenty per cent of 5,000 is 1,000 Rolf fans, and $1,000 - 800 = 200$.

4. **125.** $5,000 \div 40$ is the same as $500 \div 4 = 125$.

5. **No.** You can't work out the range from the data given – you don't know the age of the oldest or the youngest festival goer.

6. **The months aren't evenly spaced!** Many months are missing.

7. **April to May.** This is where the graph is steepest.

8. **B: The value of the stock in December was more than double the value in January.** You don't know what the stock's price was in several of the months, so it's not clear that it rose each month (so A is false). The value of the stock in January was £2, £4.15 in December, which is more than double, so B is true. You can't tell what the range of values was, because some of them are missing, so C is false. Finally, the graph doesn't tell you about the next year, so D is false. Some of the others *may* be true, but aren't *certainly* true.

9. **£800.** He paid $1,000 \times £1.20 = £1,200$ for the shares, and sold them for $1,000 \times £2 = £2,000$ in January. $£2000 - £1,200 = £800$.

10. **£10,110.** The shares themselves cost $2500 \times £4 = £10,000$. The stockbroker charges £50 for the first 1,000 shares, and 1% of the value of the remaining 1,500. These are worth £6,000, so the broker charges another 1% of £6,000 = £60. Altogether, the shares cost £10,110.

11. **4 percentage points.** The percentage point difference is simply the difference between the percentages.

12. **270°.** The whole circle is 360°; 75% of 360 is 270.

13. **There were 500 more slightly late trains in 2005.** In 2005, 15% of 20,000 trains were slightly late – which was 3,000. In 2010, 10% of 25,000 trains were slightly late, making 2,500.

14. Although punctuality has generally improved, the charts don't say anything about individual trains!

15. A multiple or stacked bar graph would also be a good choice for displaying this data.

16. **£360.** The original cost is £400, and a 10% reduction gives £40 off. The total cost is £360.

17. **11.** Sending ten would cost £4,500, but he would have enough left over for one more (plus £50 to spend on harpoons).

18. **£80.** The 20% deposit is £240, so she still has £960 to pay. £960 ÷ 12 = £80.

19. **£2,000.** If he doesn't train, the voyage will cost 40 × £500 = £20,000. If he does, it'll cost 35 × £500 = £17,500, plus £500 for the course, making £18,000 altogether. The difference is £20,000 – £18,000 = £2,000.

20. **No.** If it was 10% more expensive than £450, it would be £495.

21. **40%.** They took 30% in Alberton (15,000), 40% in Barbury (20,000) and 40% in Carrolton (25,000) – a total of 60,000 out of 150,000, which is 40%.

22. **Only one (Carrolton).** It won 10% in Barbury and 20% in Alberton.

23. **2,500 worse than they hoped.** They won 15% of the vote, which is 7,500.

24. **2,500.** The Silly Party polled 45% in Carrolton (22,500); the Sensible Party polled 40% (20,000).

25. **11%.** There were originally 5,000 Slightly Silly votes in Barbury (10%); after the recount, there were 5,500, which is 11% of 50,000.

Answers at a Glance

Test A

1. **9.**

2. **7.**

3. **21 minutes.**

4. **11:05.**

5. **£300.**

6. **£480.**

7. **D: ⅕.**

8. **800GB.**

9. **The 10th.**

10. **No.**

11. **The Basic service.**

12. **70p.**

Test B

1. **D: 10 minutes.**

2. **C: 11.16 p.m.**

3. **B: 72 minutes.**

4. **D: 1750.**

5. **D: August.**

6. **A: None.**

7. **D: November.**

8. **C: About 3,000.**

9. **A: About 350.**

10. **B: 156.**

11. **C: Bournehampton.**

12. **C: 32.**

13. **A: 14:35.**

14. **D: Central.**

15. **D: 2.**

Test C

1. **D: 432.**

2. **B: 16.15%.**

3. **C: A bar graph.**

4. **C: 40°C.**

5. **A: 104°F.**

6. **C: 6 p.m.**

7. **A: £62.**

8. **B: ⅗.**

9. **A: £39,000.**

10. **B: 30.**

11. **A.**

12. **C.**

13. **B: Sweden.**

14. **C: 2:5.**

15. **B: France and Spain.**

16. **C: 4.**

17. **A: 4¾ hours.**

18. **A: 10%.**

19. **D: 2 hours 30.**

20. **B: 4:05.**

21. **A: London and Edinburgh.**

22. **B: 60mph.**

23. **C: 100-120cm.**

24. **B: 80-100cm.**

25. **B: 91.5cm.**

Test D

1. **1250.**

2. **22%.**

3. **200 people will be left outside.**

4. **125.**

5. **No.**

6. **The months aren't evenly spaced!**

7. **April to May.**

8. **B.**

9. **£800.**

10. **£10,110.**

11. **4 percentage points.**

12. **270°.**

13. **There were 500 more slightly late trains in 2005.**

14. Although punctuality has generally improved, the charts don't say anything about individual trains!

15. A multiple or stacked bar graph would also be a good choice for displaying this data.

16. **£360.**

17. **11.**

18. **£80.**

19. **£2,000.**

20. **No.**

21. **40%.**

22. **Only one (Carrolton).**

23. **2,500 worse than they hoped.**

24. **2,500.**

25. **11%.**

Chapter 12

Advanced Data Handling Tests

. . . .

In This Chapter

▶ Working with percentages, ranges and areas

▶ Looking at plots, graphs and bar charts

. . . .

*S*ome numeracy tests – particularly teacher training and the UKCAT – ask you to interpret graphs and tables in slightly more detail than the other tests. Just to give you a bit more practice at this slightly more advanced level, I've put together a couple of tests for you. Aren't I nice?

Test A: Qualified Teacher Status Exam

This test contains handling data questions at the same level as you'd expect to find in the on-screen questions of the Qualified Teacher Status exam. In this version of the test, there are 25 questions and your target time is 25 minutes. In the actual exam, you're allowed to use an on-screen calculator, so feel free to use a calculator if you like.

Test A Questions

Questions 1 to 5 refer to the scatter diagram in Figure 12-1, comparing students' scores in a Maths and a Science exam.

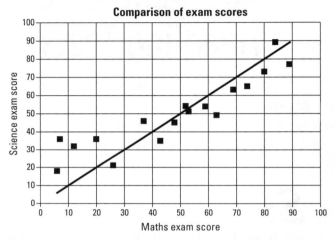

Figure 12-1: Scatter diagram comparing students' scores in a Maths and a Science exam.

1. What is the range of the Maths exam scores of these students?

2. What is the greatest difference between a student's Maths exam and Science exam scores?

3. What percentage of the students performed better in Science than in Maths? Give your answer to one decimal place.

4. The school offers a prize to any student achieving 70% or better in both exams. How many prizes does it give out?

5. True or false: the same student had the lowest score in both papers.

Questions 6 to 10 refer to the table in Figure 12-2, which shows a class's performance in three end-of-year tests, all marked out of 100.

	Range	Median	Mode
Test 1	76	56	50
Test 2	40	70	76
Test 3	50	45	55

Figure 12-2: Class performance in three end-of-year tests.

6. True or false: at least one student must have scored less than 25% in Test 1.

7. True or false: everyone must have scored at least 50% in Test 2.

8. The class had 30 students. How many scored at least 45% in Test 3?

9. True or false: no student could have scored 100% in any of the tests.

10. True or false: the marks in Test 1 must have ranged from 19 to 93.

Questions 11 to 15 refer to the box-and-whiskers plot in Figure 12-3. A sports class has run two cross-country races, one in rainy conditions and one in fine weather. The sports teacher is using the box-and-whiskers plot to compare the results.

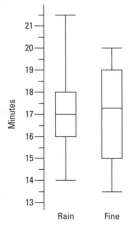

Figure 12-3: Comparing race results run in rainy and fine weather.

11. True or false: the range of times in rainy conditions is greater than the range in fine weather.

12. True or false: the median time in fine weather was about fifteen seconds faster than in the rain.

13. True or false: a quarter of the athletes completed the course in 15 minutes or faster in good weather.

14. Twenty-eight athletes ran the race in rainy conditions. How many of them completed the course in more than 18 minutes?

15. What is the interquartile range of the athletes' times in fine weather?

Questions 16 to 20 refer to the pie chart in Figure 12-4, which shows a school's inspection results for two consecutive years.

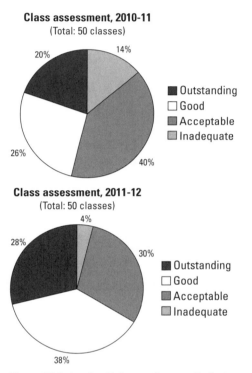

Figure 12-4: A school's inspection results for two consecutive years.

16. What is the percentage point improvement in classes rated 'outstanding'?

17. How many classes were rated 'acceptable' or better in the second year?

18. How many fewer classes were rated 'inadequate' in the second year than in the first?

19. True or false: in the first year, more than one in ten classes were rated 'inadequate'.

20. What fraction of the classes in the second year were rated 'outstanding'? Give your answer in its lowest terms.

Questions 21 to 25 refer to the bar chart in Figure 12-5, which gives a school's A-level pass rates in Geography over a ten-year period.

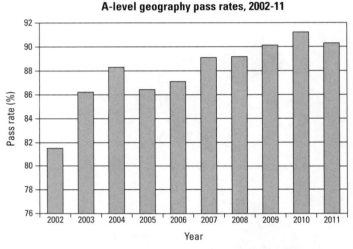

Figure 12-5: A-level pass rates in Geography over a ten-year period.

21. True or false: the A-level pass rate increased every year.

22. What was the mean pass rate over the three-year period 2009-2011?

23. True or false: the pass rate more than doubled between 2002 and 2011.

24. What was the range of the pass rates?

25. In what fraction of the years was the pass rate greater than nine out of ten?

Worked Answers for Test A

1. **83.** The range is the difference between the highest and lowest scores. The highest maths score is 89 and the lowest is 6, so the range of the maths scores is 89 – 6 = 83. (Anything between 81 and 85, inclusive, is fine.)

2. **29.** The student with the greatest difference between maths and science scores is represented by the point furthest from the line. That student scored 7 on the maths test and 36 on the science test, where the difference is 29 marks. (Any answer between 27 and 31 inclusive is acceptable).

3. **41.2%.** The students that performed better in science are the ones above the line. There are seven of those, out of 17 altogether. Using the Table of Joy (refer to Chapter 5 for an explanation of this neat time-saver), the sum to do is $7 \times 100 \div 17 = 41.2\%$ (to one decimal place).

4. **3.** Three students scored more than 70 in both tests.

5. **True.** The student who scored the lowest (6) in maths also scored 18 in science – the lowest science score.

6. **True.** The range is 76, so even if the best score was 100 marks, the worst would be 24. If the best score was any lower, the worst score would be lower than 24.

7. **False.** The highest score you know about is 76. If the range is 40, then it's possible for someone to have scored 36.

8. **15.** In Test 3, 45% is given as the median, which means the middle score. Half of the students did better than it and half did worse. Half of the 30 students (15) did better.

9. **False.** In fact, someone could have scored 100 on any one of the tests.

10. **False.** The median is not necessarily in the middle of the range.

11. **True.** In a box plot, the *range* is the difference between the ends of the 'whiskers'. For the rainy race, that's 21.5 –

14 = 7; for the fine race, it's 20 – 13.5 = 6.5 minutes. The range is larger in rainy weather.

12. **False.** The median is the line in the middle of the box. The median time for the rainy race is 17 minutes and the median for the fine race is 17 minutes 15 seconds so the difference is indeed 15 seconds; however, the rainy median is the one that's faster.

13. **True.** The ends of the box are the *quartiles* (see Chapter 8 for all you could possibly want to know about quartiles), and the lower quartile of the fine race is 15 minutes – which means a quarter of the athletes completed the race this quickly.

14. **7.** The upper quartile of the rainy race is 18 minutes, so a quarter of the 28 athletes ran more slowly. A quarter of 28 is 7.

15. **4 minutes.** The interquartile range is the difference between the ends of the box. In this case, 19 minutes – 15 minutes.

16. **8 percentage points.** The percentage point improvement is simply the difference between the percentages, and 28 – 20 = 8.

17. **48.** The easiest way to do this is to spot that only 4% of the classes were 'inadequate', and 4% of 50 is 2. The remaining classes were all 'acceptable' or better.

18. **5.** Fourteen per cent (seven classes) were 'unacceptable' in the first year and 4% (two classes) in the second.

19. **True.** One in ten is the same thing as 10%, and 14% of classes were 'inadequate' in the first year.

20. **$\frac{7}{25}$.** Twenty-eight per cent is the same thing as $\frac{28}{100}$, which cancels down to $\frac{7}{25}$.

21. **False.** Although there's a general upward trend, results fell from 2004-5 and from 2010-11.

22. **90.5%** (anywhere between 90 and 91 is okay). The actual readings are 90.1, 91.2 and 90.3, which add up to 271.6. Dividing that by three gives 90.5 (to one decimal place).

23. **False.** It looks like it, but the graph misleadingly doesn't start at zero. In fact, the pass rate rose from 81.5% to 90.3%: a much less dramatic increase.

24. **9.7%** (anything between 9 and 10 is good). The highest pass rate was 91.2%, and the lowest 81.5%. The range is the difference between them.

25. ³⁄₁₀. Nine out of ten is the same as 90%, and only the last three years had such a good pass rate.

Test B: UKCAT

This test contains data handling questions at the same level as you'd find in the quantitative reasoning section of the UKCAT exam. In this version of the test, you have 25 questions and your target time is 25 minutes. In the actual exam, you're allowed to use an on-screen calculator, so feel free to use a calculator if you like.

Test B Questions

Questions 1 to 5 refer to the table in Figure 12-6, which shows information about the share prices in euros of several companies.

	Price today (€)	% change (24h)	12-month low	12-month high
DumOil	47.54	+ 3.0%	37.64	55.13
Phones2Go	25.40	− 0.2%	10.02	33.93
KnowNews	13.42	− 1.1%	5.49	15.59

Figure 12-6: Share prices (in euros).

1. What is the cost difference, at today's prices, between buying 50 shares of DumOil and 100 shares of Phones2Go?

2. Phones2Go's share price has dropped by 20% in the last three months. What was the price three months ago?

3. How much did a share in Know News cost yesterday to the nearest cent?

4. If €1 is worth 90p, how much is a share in DumOil worth, to the nearest penny?

5. Which of the companies saw the biggest range of prices over the last year?

Questions 6 to 10 refer to the pie charts in Figure 12-7, which show how customers heard about a particular business over two years.

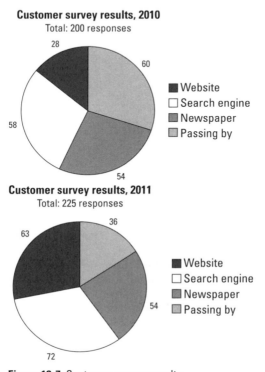

Customer survey results, 2010
Total: 200 responses

Customer survey results, 2011
Total: 225 responses

Figure 12-7: Customer survey results.

6. How many more people heard about the company through its website in 2011 than in 2010?

7. Which sector showed the smallest percentage point increase?

8. In 2010, what percentage of people heard about the company over the Internet?

9. True or false: the percentage of people who heard about the company through newspaper ads decreased from 2010 to 2011.

10. True or false: if a sector grows from one year to the next, it means that more people were in that sector.

Questions 11 to 15 refer to the table in Figure 12-8, giving population figures for the different parts of the United Kingdom.

	2010			2009		
	Total	Male	Female	Total	Male	Female
England	52,234.0	25,757.6	26,476.4	51,809.7	25,514.6	26,295.2
Scotland	5,222.1	2,530.3	2,691.8	5,194.0	2,515.3	2,678.7
Wales	3,006.4	1,470.9	1,535.5	2,999.3	1,465.5	1,533.8
N Ireland	1,799.4	884.4	915.0	1,788.9	878.6	910.3
Total	62261.9	30643.2	31618.7	61792.9	30374	31418

All figures in thousands.

This data was kindly provided by the Office of National Statistics under the Open Government License and remains under Crown Copyright

Figure 12-8: Population figures for the different parts of the United Kingdom (in thousands).

11. What percentage of the UK population lived in England in 2010 to one decimal place?

12. Which region had the highest proportion of females in 2009?

13. Which region had the largest absolute increase in population?

14. How many more people lived in Wales than in Northern Ireland in 2010?

15. Scotland has an area of 78,800km^2. Northern Ireland has an area of 13,800km^2. Which was more densely populated in 2010?

Questions 16 to 20 refer to the bar chart in Figure 12-9, which compares the regular and overtime wages of five workers.

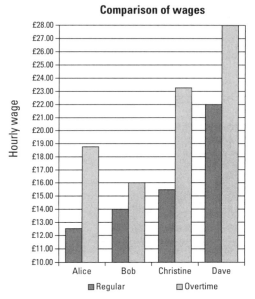

Figure 12-9: Bar chart comparing wages.

16. Christine expects to work 1,800 regular hours and 50 hours of overtime this year. How much will she earn?

17. A project has a budget of £2,000 for employee wages. It will require equal amounts of regular hours from Alice and Bob. What is the greatest number of full hours it could hire them both for?

18. A widget takes 75 minutes of Dave's time to make. If he works overtime to make 18 widgets, how much does he earn?

19. What is the ratio of Bob's regular pay to his overtime pay, in its simplest form?

20. Christine and Bob would take 12 hours each of regular time to complete a project. The same project would take 14 hours of Alice's time and 10 of Dave's – although two of Dave's hours would have to be overtime. Which pair would be cheaper?

Questions 21 to 25 refer to the line graph in Figure 12-10, which shows the monthly sunlight records for England and Scotland over a year.

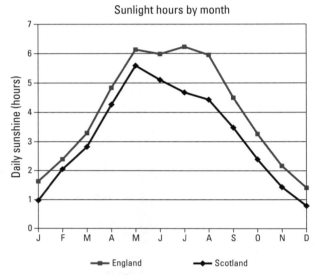

Figure 12-10: The monthly sunshine records for England and Scotland over a year.

21. True or false: in every month there were more hours of sunlight in England than in Scotland.

22. What percentage of the months had more than 3 hours of sunlight per day in Scotland?

23. What was the range of hours of sunlight in England?

24. In which month was the greatest difference between the number of hours of sunlight in England and Scotland?

25. True or false: on average, Scotland had more hours of sunlight per day in February than England did in January.

Worked Answers for Test B

1. **€163.** 50 shares of DumOil cost 50 × €47.54 = €2377. 100 shares of Phones2Go cost 100 × €25.40 = €2540. The difference is €2540 - €2377 = €163.

2. **€31.75.** The current share price is 80% of its price three months ago, so your Table of Joy sum works out to be 100 × 25.40 ÷ 80 = 31.75.

3. **€13.57.** Today's share price is 98.9% of yesterday's. Your Table of Joy sum works out to be 100 × 13.42 ÷ 98.9 = 13.57.

4. **£42.79.** You have to be careful to convert 90p into pounds, so that your Table of Joy sum is £0.90 × €47.54 ÷ €1.00 = £42.79.

5. **Phones2Go.** The range is the difference between the last two columns. Phones2Go had a range of 33.93 − 10.02 = €23.91. DumOil's range was €17.49, and Know News had a range of €10.10.

6. **35.** No trick to this one: it's simply 63 − 28 = 35.

7. **Search engine.** You can reduce your workload here by eliminating 'passing by' (which has clearly dropped) and 'newspaper' (which must also have dropped – it's the same number of people in a bigger sample). The 'website' sector has increased much more dramatically than the 'search engine' sector, so the 'search engine' sector is the smallest percentage point increase. You could also work out the percentages for each year using the Table of Joy.

8. **44%.** The Internet (website and search engine) sectors add up to 88 people out of a survey of 200. The Table of Joy tells you to do 88 × 100 ÷ 200 = 44%.

9. **True.** You can use the same argument as in answer 7, or work out that last year, 27% of customers heard about the business through the newspaper; this year, the figure is just 24%.

10. **False.** Pie charts measure proportion, not absolute numbers, so it's quite possible for a sector to grow in size but

drop in number. So if this year's survey was smaller than last year, the same number of people in a sector would translate to a bigger proportion of the total.

11. **83.9%.** The Table of Joy sum is $52,234 \times 100 \div 62,261.9$ = 83.9% (to one decimal place).

12. **Scotland.** To work out the percentage of females in (for example) England, the sum would be $24,676.4 \times 100 \div 52.234$ = 50.75. You work out the percentages for the other countries in a very similar way. The percentages are England: 50.75%; Scotland: 51.57%; Wales: 51.14%; Northern Ireland: 50.89%.

13. **England.** The difference between 2009 and 2010 populations is 424,300.

14. **1,207,000.** $3,006.4 - 1799.4$ = 1,207; however, all of the figures given are in thousands, so you need to add three zeros at the end.

15. **Northern Ireland.** Scotland's population density was $5,222,100 \div 78,800$ = 66.27 people per km^2; Northern Ireland's was $1,799,400 \div 13,800$ = 130.39 people per km^2.

16. **£29,062.50.** 1,800 hours $\times$ £15.50 = £27,900. 50 hours $\times$ £23.25 = £1,162.50. Adding up those answers gives £29,062.50. As it's tricky to read the scale, I reckon any well-worked answer between about 28,500 and 29,500 would be ok.

17. **75.** To employ both Alice and Bob for an hour would cost £26.50. The right sum is £2,000 $\div$ £26.50 = 75.47, but you're only interested in full hours, so you have to ignore the decimal part.

18. **£630.** The total time Dave needs is 75×18 = 1350 minutes, or 22.5 hours. Twenty-two and a half hours at £28 per hour gives £630.

19. **7:8.** His regular pay is £14; his overtime pay is £16, so the ratio is 14:16; you can divide both parts by two to make 7:8.

20. **Bob and Christine.** Twelve hours of Christine's regular time would cost £186. Twelve hours of Bob's time cost £168, making a total of £354. Fourteen hours of Alice's time cost £175; eight hours of Dave's regular time cost £176; two hours

of Dave's overtime cost £56. Altogether, that's £407, so Bob and Christine are cheaper.

21. **True.** The 'England' line is always above the 'Scotland' line.

22. **50%.** Easy one, this: six of the months on the 'Scotland' line are over 3 hours per day.

23. **4.8.** The maximum is 6.2 hours in June, and the minimum 1.4 hours in December. Anything between 4.6 and 5 is fine.

24. **July.** This is where the largest gap between the lines is.

25. **True.** Scotland in February has 2.1 hours of sunlight per day; England in January has only 1.6 hours.

Answers at a Glance

Test A

1. **83.**
2. **29.**
3. **41.2%.**
4. **3.**
5. **True.**
6. **True.**
7. False.
8. **15.**
9. False.

10. **False.**
11. **True.**
12. **False.**
13. **True.**
14. **7.**
15. **4 minutes.**
16. **8 percentage points.**

17. **48.**
18. **5.**
19. **True.**
20. **⁷/₂₅.**
21. **False.**
22. **90.5%.**
23. **False.**
24. **9.7%.**
25. **³/₁₀.**

Test B

1. **€163.**
2. **€31.75.**
3. **€13.57.**
4. **₤42.79.**
5. **Phones-2Go.**
6. **35.**
7. **Search engine.**
8. **44%.**
9. **True.**

10. **False.**
11. **83.9%.**
12. **Scotland.**
13. **England.**
14. **1,207,000.**
15. **Northern Ireland.**
16. **₤29,062.50.**

17. **75.**
18. **₤630.**
19. **7:8.**
20. **Bob and Christine.**
21. **True.**
22. **50%.**
23. **4.8.**
24. **July.**
25. **True.**

Chapter 13

Mixed Tests

· ·

In This Chapter

▶ Maps, forecasts and temperatures, oh my!

▶ Converting currency and figuring out volume

· ·

*T*his chapter contains three tests covering the whole of the numeracy spectrum. They're designed to follow the style of particular tests, but feel free to attempt as many or as few as you like.

 Test yourself against the clock to see how you're getting on and highlight questions you struggle with so you can revise those topics afterwards.

In this chapter I make things a little harder and give you five possible answers rather than four. Your numeracy test will almost certainly give you four or five options.

Test A: ALAN Level 2 Qualification

This test is designed to help students working towards the ALAN Level 2 qualification. It's a non-calculator test containing 25 questions and has a target time of 45 minutes. The questions are multiple choice.

Test A Questions

1. Mo is looking at a map with a scale of 1:50,000. On the map, her campsite is 10cm away. How far away is it in real life?

A: 200m   B: 500m   C: 2km   D: 50km   E: 5km

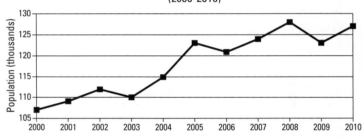

Figure 13-1: The population of Garretsborough, 2000-2010.

2. What is wrong with the graph in Figure 13-1?

A: The axis labels are wrong.   B: The scale is incorrect.
C: It's the wrong type of graph. D: The vertical axis is wrong.
E: The horizontal axis is wrong.

3. The graph in Figure 13-1 shows the population of a Garretsborough since 2000. Between 2000 and 2010, the population increased by:

A: 20,000   B: 15,000   C: 17,000   D: 25,000
E: 8,500

4. Darren is training for a marathon and runs a training race of 20 kilometres. He knows 8 kilometres is about the same as 5 miles. How many miles does he run?

A: 12.5 miles   B: 32 miles   C: 400 miles   D: 10 miles
E: 20 miles

5. A chef is preparing a risotto. The recipe is for six servings and calls for 450 grams of rice. The chef makes ten servings. What weight of rice should he use?

A: 75g   B: 750g   C: 270g   D: 900g   E: 600g

6. Nikki and Oscar divide their lottery win in the ratio of 3:4. If they win £2,800 altogether, how much does Oscar get?

A: £400   B: £700   C: £1,200   D: £1,600   E: £2,100

7. The weather forecast says the lowest temperature in Portsmouth one night will be −7°C, but will rise by 12°C by the following lunchtime. What should the temperature be by lunchtime?

A: −19°C   B: −5°C   C: 5°C   D: 19°C   E: 3°C

8. Rob records the temperature at noon each day for thirty days. On six days, the temperature is between 10°C and 15°C. He reports the information in a pie chart. What angle should he use for the slice representing 10°C to 15°C?

A: 5°   B: 20°   C: 72°   D: 90°   E: 100°

9. Paul wins 35% of his squash matches. What is 35% as a fraction?

A: $\frac{3}{5}$ B: $\frac{7}{20}$ C: $\frac{1}{3}$ D: $\frac{2}{5}$ E: $\frac{3}{10}$

10. Harriet goes to the post office. Sending a letter to the USA costs £1.65. She sends three letters to the USA and also buys some paper for £5.85. How much does she spend altogether?

A: £7.50   B: £9.90   C: £8.80   D: £4.95   E: £10.80

Figure 13-2: Weighing luggage on the scales.

11. Ashley weighs her luggage before going to the airport. The scales look like the ones in Figure 13-2. What weight is her luggage?

A: 23.2kg   B: 23kg   C: 51.1kg   D: 51kg   E: 23.5kg

12. Ian's luggage weighs 27.4kg. The airline charges a surcharge of £20 for each full kilogram over 25kg. How much extra does he have to pay?

A: £48   B: £540   C: £40   D: £50   E: £548

13. Eric works eight hours a day for twenty days in June, and wants to know what percentage of the month he spent at work. June has 30 days. Which of these calculations gives him the correct answer?

A: $30 \times 20 \times 100 \div (8 \times 24)$ B: $8 \times 30 \times 100 \div (20 \times 24)$
C: $8 \times 20 \times 24 \div (30 \times 100)$ D: $8 \times 20 \times 100 \div (30 \times 24)$
E: $8 \times 30 \times 24 \div (20 \times 100)$

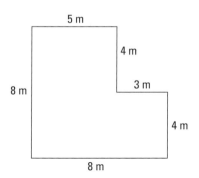

Figure 13-3: A plan of a function room.

14. Figure 13-3 shows a plan of a function room. Carpet tiles cost £2.25 per square metre. How much would it cost to carpet the function room with these tiles?

A: £52   B: £104   C: £110   D: £117   E: £135

15. The owner of the function room in Figure 13-3 needs to find the perimeter so she can buy skirting boards. What is the perimeter of the room?

A: 20m   B: 32m   C: 36m   D: 44m   E: 56m

16. Senti is running around a 5-kilometre fitness loop and passes the 1200 metre marker. What percentage of the fitness loop has she completed?

A: 22%   B: 60%   C: 12%   D: 24%   E: 41%

17. Brenda's train was due to arrive at 8.25 p.m., but is running 45 minutes late. It takes 20 minutes to get to her hotel from the station. What time can she expect to get to the hotel?

A: 8.45 p.m.   B: 9.10 p.m.   C: 8.50 p.m.   D: 10.30 p.m.
E: 9.30 p.m.

18. Every morning, Ken drinks a 0.3 litre glass of orange juice. This contains ¾ of his recommended vitamin C for the day. How much more orange juice should he drink to obtain his recommended amount of vitamin C?

A: 0.4 litres   B: 0.1 litres   C: 0.225 litres   D: 0.9 litres
E: 0.2 litres

19. The total attendance for the 2009-10 Premier league season was around 700,000. The following season, the number increased by 3%. What was the total attendance for 2010-11?

A: 703,000   B: 697,000   C: 721,000   D: 679,000
E: 700,003

20. Charlie is packing his collection of *For Dummies* books into a box. Each book is 15cm wide, 4cm tall and 25cm long. The box is 90cm wide, 40cm tall and 1 metre deep. How many books can Charlie fit in the box?

A: 20   B: 24   C: 3600   D: 240   E: 420

21. Frank takes a trip to America and buys a souvenir cuddly toy that costs him $25. One dollar is about 60p. How much did the cuddly toy cost in pounds?

A: £25   B: £12   C: £10   D: £30   E: £15

	Monday	Tuesday	Wednesday	Thursday	Friday	Saturday	Sunday
Morning	3	5	3	7	4	5	5
Afternoon	5	3	4	6	3	5	4
Evening	5	4	2	0	0	0	4
Total	13	12	9	13	7	10	13

Figure 13-4: A chiropodist's workload.

22. The table in Figure 13-4 shows the number of clients a chiropodist works with in one week. What is the mean number of clients she sees per day?

A: 6   B: 11   C: 12   D: 13   E: 3⅔

23. What was the range of the number of clients the chiropodist in Figure 13-4 saw in a day?

A: 6   B: 11   C: 12   D: 13   E: 3⅔

24. Out of all of the clients the chiropodist in Figure 13-4 saw, 30 needed their toenails clipped. The chiropodist estimates how many nail clippings she does as a percentage of all her clients. Which of these is the closest estimate?

A: 30%   B: 40%   C: 50%   D: 60%   E: 70%

25. Jon drives from Swindon to London – a distance of 120 miles – in 90 minutes. What is his average speed?

A: 1.5mph   B: 80mph   C: 45mph   D: 65mph
E: ¾mph

Worked Answers for Test A

1. **E: 5km.** Ten centimetres becomes 500,000cm in real life, which is 5,000m or 5km.

2. **D: The vertical axis is wrong.** It doesn't begin at zero. (The horizontal axis is fine – year numbers on a graph don't have to start at zero.)

3. **A: 20,000.** In 2000, there were 107,000 people, and in 2010 there were 127,000.

4. **A: 12.5 miles.** The Table of Joy sum is $20 \times 5 \div 8 = 12.5$. (See Chapter 5 for an explanation of the Table of Joy.)

5. **B: 750g.** One serving requires $450g \div 6 = 75g$, so ten servings make 750g. You can also do this with the Table of Joy – the sum is $450 \times 10 \div 6 = 750$.

6. **D: £1,600.** There are seven shares altogether (3 + 4). One share is worth £2,800 ÷ 7 = £400, and Oscar takes four of them. Four times £400 = £1,600. Again, the Table of Joy is your friend here: you could also do $2800 \times 4 \div 7 = 1600$.

7. **C: 5°C.** The temperature would rise seven degrees to 0°C, then another five degrees to 5°C.

8. **C: 72°.** The Table of Joy sum is $360 \times 6 \div 30 = 72$.

9. **B: ⁷⁄₂₀.** Start from ³⁵⁄₁₀₀ and spot that you can divide top and bottom by 5.

10. **E: £10.80.** The letters cost $3 \times £1.65 = £4.95$, and you add £5.85.

11. **A: 23.2kg.** Be careful to pick the right scale and work out how much each 'tick' is worth.

12. **C: £40.** $27.4 - 25 = 2.4$, so Ian is two full kilograms over the limit. Two times £20 is £40.

13. **D: $8 \times 20 \times 100 \div (30 \times 24)$.** Eric is at work for (8×20) hours out of a total of (30×24) hours in the month. The Table of Joy sum works out to be this monster.

14. **D: £117.** The area of the function room is 52m². I split it with a vertical line, so the left rectangle is $5 \times 8 = 40$ and the

right rectangle is $3 \times 4 = 12$, making a total of $52.52 \times £2.25 = £117$. (You can do this as $2 \times 52 = 104$, and a quarter of 52 is 13, and add them together). See Chapter 7 for how to find the area of combined rectangles.

15. **B: 32m.** It's $5 + 4 + 3 + 4 + 8 + 8$.

16. **D: 24%.** The Table of Joy sum (see Chapter 5) is $1,200 \times 100 \div 5,000 = 24$. Alternatively, you can say that 1% of 5 kilometres is 50 metres, and $1,200 \div 50 = 24$.

17. **E: 9:30 p.m.** The train should now arrive at 9.10 p.m., and she'll reach the hotel 20 minutes later than that.

18. **B: 0.1 litres.** One quarter of his quota would be 0.1 litres, so his full recommended amount is 0.4 litres.

19: **C: 721,000.** One percent of 700,000 is 7,000 (you just divide by 100), so 3% is 21,000 (three times as much). It's an increase, so you add it on. (These aren't the real figures, by the way, but they're not far off.)

You can also do this with the Table of Joy if you don't mind big numbers: the increase is $700,000 \times 3 \div 100 = 21,000$.

20. **D: 240.** On the bottom layer of books, Charlie can fit six books across the box and four books along it making $6 \times 4 = 24$ books in one layer. There's room for 10 layers, making 240 books altogether.

21. **E: £15.** The sum is $25 \times 0.60 \div 1 = £15$.

22. **B: 11.** To find the mean, you add up how many clients she sees and divide by how many days there are. She sees a total of 77 clients over seven days, and $77 \div 7 = 11$.

23. **A: 6.** Her busiest days had 13 clients, and her quietest day 7. The range is $13 - 7 = 6$.

24. **B: 40%.** 77 is very close to 80. Ten percent of 80 is 8, so 20% would be about 16 people, 30% about 24 people and 40% about 32 people, which is close to 30. You could also round the numbers off and do a Table of Joy sum: $30 \times 100 \div 80 = 37.5$, which is closest to 40%.

25. **B: 80mph.** The Table of Joy sum is $120 \times 60 \div 90 = 80$. Naughty boy!

Test B: The Army Technical Test

This test is about the same level as the British Army's technical test. It contains 25 questions and has a target time of 25 minutes (with a calculator). I've given slightly fuller answers than normal for the four questions marked with a star because I don't explain these concepts in Part II of this book.

Test B Questions

1. A coach carries 53 people. 954 people need to travel to an event – how many coaches are needed to carry them?

A: 16   B: 17   C: 18   D: 19   E: 22

2. You need to carry a bottle of water weighing 1.5kg, a tent weighing 18.4kg and a book weighing 0.094kg. Don't ask why, it's classified. What is the total weight of your load?

A: 19.94kg   B: 19.994kg   C: 20.04kg   D: 20.84kg
E: 20.94kg

3. You have £15 to buy stationery. You buy a pack of pens for 97p and a stack of paper for £4.45. How much do you have left over?

A: £5.42   B: £9.58   C: £10.12   D: £10.42
E: £10.58

4. A car travels at 68mph for 3.05 hours. To the nearest ten miles, how far does it travel?

A: 20 miles   B: 180 miles   C: 200 miles   D: 210 miles
E: 240 miles

5. $25.4 \times 7.96 \div 4.9$ is approximately:

A: 40   B: 50   C: 80   D: 100   E: 200

6. In the morning, Amal walks 3¾ miles. In the afternoon, he walks 4½ miles. How far does he walk all together?

A: 7¼ miles   B: 7⅔ miles   C: 7⅜ miles   D: 8 miles
E: 8¼ miles

7. Ian's petrol tank holds $10\frac{3}{10}$ gallons of petrol. He fills up the tank, and then makes a journey that uses $2\frac{2}{3}$ gallons of petrol. How much is left in the tank?

A: $7\frac{19}{30}$ gallons B: $7\frac{29}{30}$ gallons C: $8\frac{1}{7}$ gallons
D: $8\frac{29}{30}$ gallons E: $12\frac{29}{30}$ gallons

8. Jim has a work-day of $7\frac{1}{4}$ hours. He plans to spend half of it on a project. How much time should he allocate to the project?

A: $6\frac{3}{4}$ hours B: $3\frac{5}{8}$ hours C: $3\frac{1}{8}$ hours
D: $14\frac{1}{2}$ hours E: $7\frac{3}{4}$ hours

9. You have $3\frac{3}{4}$ litres of water to split up into $\frac{3}{4}$ litre bottles. How many bottles can you fill?

A: $\frac{1}{5}$ B: $\frac{3}{4}$ C: 2 D: 4 E: 5

10. Express $\frac{3}{8}$ as a decimal.

A: 0.3 B: 0.35 C: 0.375 D: 0.38 E: 0.4

11. Marian runs 3,600 metres. How much is that in kilometres?

A: 0.36 B: 2.5 C: 3.6 D: 36 E: 360

12. Four people have a mean height of 1.75 metres. The mean height of three of them is 1.70 metres. How tall is the other person?

A: 1.70m B: 1.725m C: 1.75m D: 1.80m
E: 1.90m

13. Paul and George divide 60 poker chips in the ratio of 5:7. How many does Paul get?

A: 300 B: 12 C: 35 D: 25 E: 30

14. A map has a scale of 1:20,000. A straight path on the map is 3cm long. How long is it in real life?

A: 60km B: 60m C: 600m D: 6km E: 6m

15. In a class of 35 students, 20% are absent one day. How many students were present?

A: 5   B: 7   C: 15   D: 25   E: 28

16. Which numbers are missing from the series 153, 144, 135, . . . , . . . , 108, 99?

A: 126 and 117   B: 124 and 115   C: 125 and 116
D: 126 and 115   E: 124 and 117

17*. Swindon has a population of around 184,000 people. In standard form, this is:

A: 0.184×10^6 B: 184×10^3 C: 1.84×10^5 D: 18.4×10^4
E: 184,000

18. Steve works out the answer to a calculation as 3.72572214. To three significant figures, this is:

A: 3.726   B: 3.725   C: 3.72   D: 3.73   E: 3.736

19. A box has internal dimensions of 20cm × 30cm × 40cm. He has nothing better to do, so Phil wants to fill it with cubes whose edges are each 5cm long. How many blocks will fit in the box?

A: 24,000   B: 4,800   C: 960   D: 192   E: 24

20*. Find the value of x that solves the simultaneous equations:

$$3x + y = 13$$
$$2x - 2y = 6.$$

A: 1   B: 2   C: 3   D: 4   E: 5

21*. Factorise $x^2 + x - 6$.

A: $(x - 3)(x + 2)$ B: $(x + 3)(x - 2)$ C: $(x + 3)(x + 2)$
D: $(x + 5)(x - 1)$ E: $(x - 5)(x + 1)$

22*. If $V = IR$, what does R equal?

A: IV B: I/V C: V/I D: $I + V$ E: $I - V$

23. A room has two walls that are 4m long, and two walls that are 5.5m long. What area of carpet is needed to cover the room?

A: $15m^2$ B: $22m^2$ C: $484m^2$ D: $9.5m^2$ E: $24m^2$

24. A triangle has two angles of 35 degrees and two sides of length 53cm. What is the size of the other angle?

A: $35°$ B: $37°$ C: $45°$ D: $60°$ E: $110°$

25. What is $22 - 3 (6 - 4)^2$?

A: 10   B: -14 C: 76   D: 1444   E: -8

Worked Answers for Test B

1. **C: 18.** An easy way to do this is to see that 20 coaches would carry 1060 people, which is 106 too many – and 106 people would fit on 2 coaches, so you only need 18 coaches.

2. **B: 19.994kg.** 18.4 + 1.5 + 0.094 = 19.994.

3. **B: £9.58.** You spend £5.42 in total, so you end up with £15.00 – £5.42 = £9.58.

4. **D: 210 miles.** Rounding off, the sum is 70 mph × 3 hours = 210 miles. (The exact answer is 207.4 miles.)

5: **A: 40.** Rounding off, the sum is 25 × 8 ÷ 5, which is 200 ÷ 5 = 40. (The exact answer is around 41.26.)

6. **E: 8¼ miles.** He walks seven full miles and five quarter-miles (one half is the same as two quarters). The five quarter-miles are the same as one and a quarter miles, so the total is 8¼.

7. **A: 7¹⁹⁄₃₀ gallons.** You want the bottoms of the fractions to be the same before you take them away. If you have 10 and 3 on the bottom to begin with, a good common denominator is 30. Ian starts with ³⁰⁄₃₀ gallons and uses ⁸⁰⁄₃₀ gallons, leaving ²²⁹⁄₃₀ gallons. One gallon is ³⁰⁄₃₀, so seven gallons is ²¹⁰⁄₃₀; of the 229 thirtieths he had, 19 are left over, so the final answer is 7 and ¹⁹⁄₃₀.

8. **B: 3⅝ hours.** Half of 7 hours is 3½ hours; half of a quarter is an eighth, which you add on. (Note: once you spot it's about 3½ hours, but a little on the high side, there's only one possible answer. Also, you can immediately dismiss answers D and E because they're longer than Jim's workday.)

9. **E: 5.** Three litres is the same as twelve quarter-litres, so altogether there are 15 quarter-litres. Each bottle contains three quarter-litres, so you can fill five bottles.

10. **C: 0.375.** You have several ways of working this out. The easiest ones are to divide three quarters (0.75) by two, or to divide three by eight. If you know that an eighth is 0.125, you could also multiply that by three. Bonus points if you can spell *eighth*. You can brush up on dividing decimals in Chapter 4!

11. **C: 3.6.** One kilometre is 1,000 metres, so she has run between three and four kilometres. Alternatively, you can divide 3,600 by 1,000 by putting a decimal point at the end and moving it three spaces to the left, giving you 3.600 – and you can ignore the zeros at the end.

12. **E: 1.90m.** The total height of the four is $4 \times 1.75 = 7$m. The total height of the three is $3 \times 1.70 = 5.10$m. The last person's height is $7.00 - 5.10 = 1.90$m.

13. **D: 25.** Paul gets five out of every twelve chips (5+7). Since sixty is five twelves, Paul gets five lots of five, making 25 chips.

14. **C: 600m.** The path is $3 \times 20,000 = 60,000$cm long. You divide this by 100 to find how many metres – knocking off two zeros gives you 600m.

15. **E: 28.** Ten per cent of 35 is 3.5, so twenty per cent is twice as many, $2 \times 3.5 = 7$. If 7 are away, 28 are still there. (You can also do this with the Table of Joy; 80% of the class is present, so the sum is $80 \times 35 \div 100 = 2,800 \div 100 = 28$.)

16. **A: 126 and 117.** The sequence is going down in nines. $135 - 9 = 126$, and $126 - 9 = 117$.

17. **C: 1.84×10^5.** A standard form number is made up of a number between 1 and 10, multiplied by a power of ten. This lets you compare large numbers easily without having to write down a load of zeros (you can just look at the power of ten to get a sense of scale).

18. **D: 3.73.** To work out significant figures, you start counting from the first digit that isn't a zero (here, the first three). You put a line after the third digit – 3.72|572214 – and decide whether the next number is high or low. Five is a high number, so you round the last digit before the line *up* to get 3.73.

19. **D: 192.** You can fit four blocks along the 20cm side, six along the 30cm side and eight along the 40cm side. Multiplying those together, you get $4 \times 6 \times 8 = 24 \times 8 = 192$.

20. **D: 4.** You can rearrange the first equation to get $y = 13 - 3x$, and the second to get $2y = 2x - 6$ (or, dividing it by two,

$y = x - 3$). That means $13 - 3x = x - 3$. Add $3x$ and 3 to both sides to get $16 = 4x$ and divide by four to get $4 = x$.

21. **B: $(x + 3)(x - 2)$.** *Factorise* means 'find things that multiply together to make the thing you're given'. To do this, you need to find a pair of numbers that multiplies to make –6 but adds to make +1. The only pair that works is +3 and –2, and these are the two that go in the bracket. You could also multiply out each set of brackets to see which one works.

22. **C: V/I.** If $V = IR$, you get R by dividing both sides of the equation by I. That gives you V/I on the left and R on the right. You can also try putting in values for V, I and R that work and check which of the answers is correct. For example, you could pick $V=6$, $I = 2$ and $R = 3$ (or any other numbers that give $V = IR$. Checking the possible answers, you want one that gives you 3. A gives you 12, B gives you ⅓, C gives you 3 (bingo!), D gives you 8 and E gives you –4.

If you're completely baffled by the algebra (or just want to brush up), you may want to check out some GCSE revision websites – the BBC Bitesize site at `www.bbc.co.uk/schools/gcsebitesize/maths` is particularly good.

23. **B: $22m^2$.** The area of a rectangle is one side multiplied by the other – here, that's 4×5.5, which is 22.

24. **E: $110°$.** The angles in a triangle add up to $180°$. You've already used up $70°$ (the two $35°$ angles), so you have $110°$ left. The lengths of the sides are irrelevant.

25. **A: 10.** To work out $22 - 3(6 - 4)^2$, you need BIDMAS (see Chapter 5). The first thing you do is the sum in the brackets, giving you two. That leaves you with $22 - 3 \times 2^2$. Next it's the index (the little number above the 2) – you square two to get four. Now you have $22 - 3 \times 4$. The next step is multiply and divide – you only have a times, so you work out $3 \times 4 = 12$. Lastly, you're left with $22 - 12$, which is 10.

Test C: General Numeracy

This test is designed to be at a level suitable for most numeracy students. It contains 25 questions and has a target time of 25 minutes (with a calculator) and 45 minutes (without).

Test C Questions

	Alex	Bob	Chris	Derek	Evan	Frank
Alex		15 Jan	22 Jan	29 Jan	5 Feb	12 Feb
Bob	15 Jan		29 Jan	12 Feb	22 Jan	5 Feb
Chris	22 Jan	29 Jan		5 Feb	12 Feb	15 Jan
Derek	29 Jan	12 Feb	5 Feb		15 Jan	22 Jan
Evan	5 Feb	22 Jan	12 Feb	15 Jan		29 Jan
Frank	12 Feb	5 Feb	15 Jan	22 Jan	29 Jan	

Figure 13-5: The squash league schedule.

1. The table in Figure 13-5 shows the schedule for a squash league. Frank wants to know who his last game will be against. Is it:

A: Alex   B: Bob   C: Chris   D: Derek   E: Evan

2. A horse race is 5½ furlongs long. One furlong is about 200 metres. How many metres is the race?

A: 550m   B: 1,000m   C: 1,050m   D: 1,100m
E: 1,200m

Figure 13-6: Two scales.

3. Figure 13-6 shows Paula's weight three months ago and her weight today. How much weight has she lost in the last three months?

A: 5kg   B: 5.5kg   C: 6kg   D: 6.5kg   E: 10kg

4. A path is 20 metres long and 1.5 metres wide. Kevin is going to pave it with square slabs that are 50cm on each side. How many slabs does he need?

A: 30   B: 60   C: 120   D: 180   E: 300

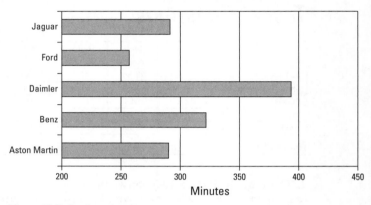

Figure 13-7: Car bar chart.

5. The bar chart in Figure 13-7 shows the time taken by five cars to complete a race. How much longer did the Daimler take than the Jaguar?

A: About 100 minutes   B: About 150 minutes
C: About 170 minutes   D: About 200 minutes
E: About 400 minutes

6. One week, a worker earns £7.50 per hour for 40 hours. Her normal weekly wage is £250. How much more than normal did she earn in that week?

A: £300   B: £1.25   C: £30   D: £50   E: £70

7. A map has a scale of 1:500,000. A road on the map is 5cm long. How long is the road in reality?

A: 25km   B: 2.5km   C: 250m   D: 10km   E: 5km

8. Steve's phone screen is 960 pixels wide and 640 pixels tall. What is the ratio of the width to the height, in its simplest terms?

A: 3:2   B: 2:3   C: 5:3   D: 3:5   E: 1:1

Martin	91	94	97	76	100	95	90
Olly	85	75	91	96	79	91	100
Patrick	78	83	78	87	85	83	89
Quinn	83	77	92	77	85	94	97
Robert	77	91	79	92	77	80	90

Figure 13-8: Golf scores.

9. Figure 13-8 shows the golf scores of several players. What is the range of Patrick's scores?

A: 15   B: 7   C: 11   D: 19   E: 89

10. Hiring a bike costs £20 plus £5 per full hour. If Boris hires a bike at 9.30 a.m. and returns it at 2.45 p.m., how much does it cost him?

A: £35   B: £40   C: £45   D: £50   E: £55

	Monday	Tuesday	Wednesday	Thursday	Friday
Morning	3.5	3	4	3	4
Afternoon	4	4.5	4	4	2.5
Evening	1	1.5	1	2	0

Figure 13-9: Stuart's timesheet.

11. Figure 13-9 shows the hours Stuart worked in one week. He is contracted to work 35 hours per week, and anything more than that is overtime. How many overtime hours did he work in this week?

A: 5   B: 7   C: 42   D: 40   E: 50.5

12. Stuart's boss asks him for the mean number of hours he works each morning. Stuart's answer should be:

A: 3 hours   B: 3.25 hours   C: 3.5 hours   D: 3.75 hours
E: 4 hours

13. In a card game, a player's score is worked out as $10H + 5C + 7A^2$, where *H* is the number of hearts a player holds, *C* is the number of clubs, and *A* the number of aces. Martin has three hearts, six clubs and two aces. What is his score?

A: 256 B: 88 C: 74 D: 55 E: 22

	Monday	Tuesday	Wednesday	Thursday	Friday
To work	20	15	20	15	30
Home	25	30	30	20	15

Figure 13-10: Kieran's journey time in minutes.

14. Kieran records his journey times in minutes to and from work for a week, and his results are shown in Figure 13-10. What is the difference between his mean journey time to work and his mean journey time home?

A: 4 minutes B: 8 minutes C: 10 minutes D: 15 minutes E: 20 minutes

15. Europe has an annual birth rate of around 10 births per 1000 inhabitants. It has a population of about 500 million people. Approximately how many births would you expect there to be in Europe in a year?

A: 5000 B: 50,000 C: 500,000 D: 5,000,000 E: 50,000,000

16. Alan sells paintings at an art fair for £245 each and sketches for £97 each. He sells 15 paintings and 25 sketches. Which of the following is a good estimate of how much money he took in?

A: $250 \times 15 + 100 \times 25$ B: $250 \times 25 + 100 \times 15$
C: $250 + 100 + 15 \times 25$ D: $250 \times 100 \times 15 \times 25$
E: $250 \div 25 \times 15 \div 100$

17. A restaurant worker earns £250 one week in salary plus £150 in tips. What fraction of his total pay came from tips?

A: $\frac{3}{8}$ B: $\frac{3}{5}$ C: $\frac{5}{8}$ D: $\frac{1}{5}$ E: $\frac{2}{3}$

18. A sandwich costs £2.00, a cookie costs 90p and a drink costs 70p. If Chris buys three sandwiches, two cookies and a drink, how much change does he get from £20?

A: £3.60   B: £5.60   C: £8.50   D: £11.50   E: £14.40

19. A sink is 20cm deep, 40cm wide and 50cm long. What is its volume in litres?

A: 40,000 litres   B: 400 litres   C: 40 litres
D: 4 litres   E: 0.4 litres

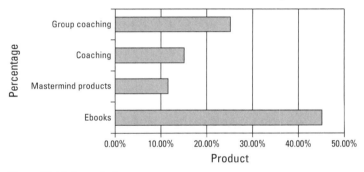

Commission rates for various products

Figure 13-11: Commission rates.

20. Figure 13-11 shows a bar chart showing commission rates for several products. What is the error in the chart?

A: The vertical scale is wrong.
B: The horizontal scale is wrong.
C: The bars shouldn't be touching.
D: The title is wrong.
E: The axis labels are the wrong way round.

21. A sales rep sells a mastermind product for £1,497. Which of the following gives a good estimate of her commission, in pounds?

A: $1,500 \times 100 \div 10$ B: $1,500 \times 10 \div 100$
C: $10 \times 100 \div 1,500$ D: $10 \times 100 \times 1,500$
E: $10 \div 100 \div 1,500$

22. Darren is a DJ. He earns £200 for a concert, but has to pay £30 in equipment hire. What percentage of his earnings does he pay out in equipment hire?

A: 6 ⅔%   B: 10%   C: 15%   D: 16 ⅔%   E: 20%

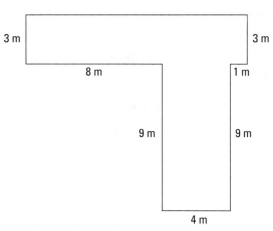

Figure 13-12: A plan of an office.

23. Figure 13-12 shows a plan of an office. What is the area of the floor?

A: 70m²   B: 75m²   C: 34m²   D: 68m²   E: 80m²

24. What is 85% as a fraction?

A: ⅝   B: ⅚   C: ⅘   D: ¹⁷⁄₂₀   E: ⁹⁄₁₀

25. One pound is worth €1.15. Emily converts £240 into euros for her holiday to Spain. How many euros does she get?

A: €276   B: €253   C: €260   D: €255   E: €209

Worked answers for Test C

1. **A: Alex.** The final round of matches is on February 12th.

2. **D: 1,100m.** Five times 200 is 1,000, and half times 200 is 100. Altogether, that's 1,100m.

3. **D: 6.5kg.** Her original weight was 65.5kg, and her current weight is 59kg.

4. **C: 120.** The path is 40 slabs long and 3 slabs wide, and you need to multiply those together to get 120.

5. **A: About 100km.** The Daimler went 394km, and the Jaguar 291km.

Note also that the horizontal axis ought to start at zero instead of 200.

6. **D: £50.** The worker earns £7.50 × 40, or £300 (the easy way to do that is 7.5 × 10 = 75 and 75 × 4 = 300). If she normally earns £250, that's £50 extra.

7. **A: 25km.** Five centimetres multiplied by 500,000 is 2,500,000cm. To get to metres, divide by 100: that's 25,000 metres, or 25 kilometres.

8. **A: 3:2.** The ratio as it stands is 960:640, which you can cancel down to 96:64, then 48:32, then 24:16, 12:8, 6:4 and finally 3:2. Phew! (You can do this quicker if you spot higher numbers to divide both numbers by.)

9. **C: 11.** His highest score is 89 and his lowest 78. The range is the difference between them, which is 11.

10. **C: £45.** From 9.30 to 2.45 is five hours and 15 minutes. This company (unlike most companies!) only charges for full hours, and Boris was only cycling for five full hours – so Boris needs to pay £20 + £5 × 5 = £45.

11. **B: 7.** Stuart worked a total of 42 hours, 7 more than the 35 he was contracted for.

12. **C: 3.5 hours.** He worked a total of 17.5 hours over five days, and 17.5 ÷ 5 = 3.5.

13. **B: 88.** This is a BIDMAS question. The first thing to do is to replace all of the letters with the correct numbers: $10 \times 3 + 5 \times 6 + 7 \times 2^2$. There aren't any brackets, so the first thing to do is the index – two squared is 4. Then you have $10 \times 3 + 5 \times 6 + 7 \times 4$. Now work out all the multiplications to get 30 + 30 + 28 this gives you 88. See Chapter 5 for more about BIDMAS.

14. **A: 4 minutes.** His mean time to get to work is 20 minutes, and his mean time to get home is 24 minutes.

15. **D: 5,000,000.** The sum to do is 500,000,000 × 10 ÷ 1,000. That's 5,000,000,000 ÷ 1,000 = 5,000,000.

16. **A: 250 × 15 + 100 × 25.** If he sells 15 paintings, that's around 250 × 15. If he sells 25 sketches, that's around 100 × 25. Altogether, that's 250 × 15 + 100 × 25.

17. **A: ⅜.** His total is £400, so the fraction is ¹⁵⁰⁄₄₀₀. You can immediately divide top and bottom by 10 to get ¹⁵⁄₄₀, and then divide top and bottom by 5 to get ⅜.

18. **D: £11.50.** Chris's sandwiches cost £6, his cookies £1.80 and his drink 70p. Altogether, that makes £8.50. If he pays with a £20 note, he gets £11.50 change.

19. **C: 40 litres.** The volume of a cuboid is the dimensions multiplied together, in this case 20 × 40 × 50 = 800 × 50 = 40,000 centimetres cubed. One litre is 1,000cm³, so the sink holds 40 litres.

20. **E: The axis labels are the wrong way round.**

21. **B: 1,500 × 10 ÷ 100.** Her commission is close to 10%, and the product price very close to £1,500. This is exactly the sum that comes out of the Table of Joy!

22. **C: 15%.** The question is asking what percentage 30 is of 200. The Table of Joy sum is 30 × 100 ÷ 200 = 3,000 ÷ 200 = 15.

23. **B: 75m².** The area of the top of the T-shape is 3 × 13 = 39; the other part has an area of 4 × 9 = 36. Altogether, that's 75m².

24. **D: ¹⁷⁄₂₀.** 85% is the same as ⁸⁵⁄₁₀₀; if you divide top and bottom by five, you get ¹⁷⁄₂₀.

A quick way to divide by five is to double and then divide by ten.

25. **A: €276.** £200 is the same as €230, and £40 is the same as €46. Altogether, that makes €276.

Answers at a Glance

Test A

1. **E: 5km.**

2. **D: The vertical axis is wrong.**

3. **A: 20,000.**

4. **A: 12.5 miles.**

5. **B: 750g.**

6. **D: £1,600.**

7. **C: 5°C.**

8. **C: 72°.**

9. **B:** $^7/_{20}$.

10. **E: £10.80.**

11. **A: 23.2kg.**

12. **C: £40.**

13. **D:** $8 \times 20 \times 100 \div (30 \times 24)$.

14. **D: £117.**

15. **B: 32m.**

16. **D: 24%.**

17. **E: 9:30 p.m.**

18. **B: 0.1 litres.**

19: **C: 721,000.**

20. **D: 240.**

21. **E: £15.**

22. **B: 11.**

23. **A: 6.**

24. **B: 40%.**

25. **B: 80mph.**

Test B

1. **C: 18.**

2. **B: 19.994kg.**

3. **B: £9.58.**

4. **D: 210 miles.**

5: **A: 40.**

6. **E: 8¼ miles.**

7. **A:** $7^{19}/_{30}$ **gallons.**

8. **B:** $3^5/_8$ **hours.**

9. **E: 5.**

10. **C: 0.375.**

11. **C: 3.6.**

12. **E: 1.90m.**

13. **D: 25.**

14. **C: 600m.**

15. **E: 28.**

16. **A: 126 and 117.**

17. **C:** 1.84×10^5.

18. **D: 3.73.**

19. **D: 192.**

20. **D: 4.**

21. **B:** $(x + 3)(x - 2)$.

22. **C:** V/I.

23. **B: 22m^2.**

24. **E: 110°.**

25. **A: 10.**

Test C

1. **A: Alex.**

2. **D: 1,100m.**

3. **D: 6.5kg.**

4. **C: 120.**

5. **A: About 100km.**

6. **D: £50.**

7. **A: 25km.**

8. **A: 3:2.**

9. **C: 11.**

10. **C: £45.**

11. **B: 7.**

12. **C: 3.5 hours.**

13. **B: 88.**

14. **A: 4 minutes.**

15. **D: 5,000,000.**

16. **A: 250 × 15 + 100 × 25.**

17. **A: ⅜.**

18. **D: £11.50.**

19. **C: 40 litres.**

20. **E: The axis labels are the wrong way round.**

21. **B: 1,500 × 10 ÷ 100.**

22. **C: 15%.**

23. **B: 75m^2.**

24. **D:** $^{17}/_{20}$.

25. **A: €276.**

Part IV
The Part of Tens

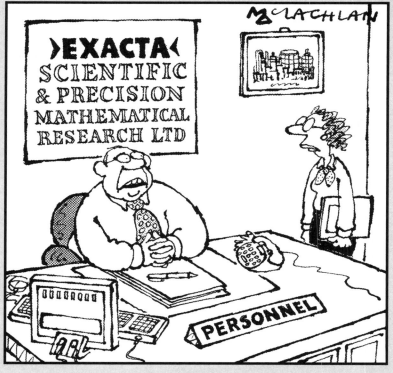

'I was very disappointed with the latest job applicants & their numeracy tests — 27% were only average & the other 76% were hopeless.'

In this part . . .

You can't have a *For Dummies* book without a Part of Tens! It would be like a calculator without an 'on' button. In this part, I share some of my best tips for calming yourself down, motivating yourself to do the work, dealing with difficult questions and for making the best of your exam.

Chapter 14

Ten Ways to Find a Sense of Calm While Studying

*W*hen you're stressed, panicky or generally distracted, it's difficult to do almost anything. You may find yourself going around in circles and not really getting anything done at all.

Studying while you're stressed is doubly hard, because your brain is extra-reluctant to soak up the information you're trying to learn.

There's only one thing for it, then: you've got to learn to relax.

This is a good life skill to have – finding ways to relax in stressful situations is good for your health and relationships. Oh, and being relaxed is much more pleasant than being stressed.

In this chapter, I give you some practical tips on how to relax and make studying for your numeracy test pleasant and easy.

Talk Yourself Up

The way you talk to yourself makes an incredible difference to how you perform. Instead of saying, 'Maths is stupid and difficult. I can't do it, I'm not a maths person and my brain doesn't work that way', or anything else that's demoralising or unhelpful, try saying, 'I'm smart, and I can figure it out. I have an amazing brain – I just need to train it a bit more.'

Best of all, try saying, 'Ah, I got that wrong. That's interesting. I wonder why?'

Sit Up Straight

Posture is incredibly important for top performance. Like positive self-talk, sitting up straight can make a big difference to how you fare in your studies.

Your brain speaks fluent body language. If you sit upright, with your shoulders back and head up, your body says 'I'm confident and capable of dealing with anything life throws at me' and your brain says 'Bring it on!' If you crunch up and cower over your desk, your body says 'Don't bother me, I don't want to interact', and your brain says 'Sorry, closed for business.'

If you start to feel a bit overwhelmed with your studies, or when you're sitting in the exam, take a few seconds to notice how you're sitting – try to adjust yourself slightly and adopt a more commanding posture.

Breathe Like a Singer

I used to suffer from panic attacks – they're horrible and I wouldn't wish them on anyone. One of the tricks I was taught for dealing with panic attacks involved diaphragmatic breathing.

The diaphragm is a muscle somewhere in your lower chest. Instead of taking shallow breaths into the top of your lungs as you do with normal breathing, with diaphragmatic breathing you take the breath as far down into your lungs as possible and then breathe out slowly. Singers use diaphragmatic breathing before they go on stage: it has the twin benefits of helping lung capacity so they can sing better, and calming them down so stage-fright doesn't hit so hard.

Here's how to do it:

1. Put one hand on the top of your chest and the other hand on your belly.

2. Breathe in as deeply as you can, trying not to move your upper hand. Your lower hand should move out as your lungs fill with air.

3. Breathe in for a count of seven, but don't hold your breath.

4. Breathe out very slowly for a count of 11. Don't worry if you can't manage all the way up to 11 – just breathe out for as long as you can and make a note to breathe more slowly next time.

5. Keep doing this for a minute or so and you'll feel your heart rate drop and your head start to clear. A clear head makes maths a lot easier.

I can't emphasise enough how helpful this type of breathing is to me when I feel panicky or stressed or even just out of sorts. Taking a few minutes to breathe deeply and get some oxygen into my body has saved more than one day from being a complete write-off for me. Coupled with positive self-talk, diaphragmatic breathing is a tremendously powerful weapon against the panic-monsters, either when you're revising or just before the test.

Put Out the Welcome Mat

A doormat with 'Welcome!' on it is so much of a cliché that it barely even registers these days, but once upon a time the idea was to make visitors feel immediately at home and to stay longer.

If you set up your learning experience to welcome new knowledge and to make maths feel comfortable, at home and wanted, you'll find that having new knowledge come and stay in your brain becomes a regular experience.

If you think 'I have to learn this' instead of 'I'd really love to know this', your mind tends to push away what you try to learn.

Try saying to yourself 'I'd like to learn about percentages' rather than 'I have to wade through this'.

Make Mistakes Merrily

When was the last time you got through a day without making a mistake of any description? Where you didn't miss a call, where you didn't have to say 'sorry' or 'I mean . . .', where you didn't have to press the delete button on your computer?

I'm betting on never.

As with anything else, you will make mistakes when you figure things out in maths. You mess up. I mess up. Stephen Hawking messes up. Making mistakes is nothing to be afraid of or ashamed of. The language you use can really help you out. Try not to mutter 'I got this wrong, so I must be rubbish at maths.' Instead, say 'I got this wrong – I wonder why? What can I learn from this?'

Mistakes are good. Celebrate them, write them down, and see how much it helps you to learn!

Work Within Limits

On occasion – when I'm studying something interesting, or watching a fascinating movie – I can concentrate like a fiend for hours on end. Other times – say, when I'm cleaning – I'm lucky if I can think straight for two minutes.

You may find that you study best in ten-minute bursts scattered throughout the day. Maybe you prefer two 25-minute sessions with a short break between. You may work better in the morning, in the evening or somewhere in between. Whichever suits you is the one to choose.

Try setting a timer and see what happens if you try to concentrate for 10 minutes, 20 minutes and 40 minutes. I do this with writing: I set a timer for 15 minutes and write furiously until it goes ping. A quarter-hour is short enough not to be intimidating, but long enough to get something useful done.

Try several permutations and see what works best for you –
then stick to those limits.

Make Studying a Habit

Remembering numeracy skills is much easier if you do a few
minutes of work each day, rather than trying to cram everything into one long session. Even just five minutes of studying
a day can make maths significantly easier to understand.

Try to get into a routine and commit to keeping to the schedule
you choose.

In Chapter 15 I introduce the calendar of crosses, a really
effective psychological ploy to convince yourself to keep at
your studies, even when you don't feel like working (*especially*
when you don't feel like working).

Fitting studying around work, family and social commitments
isn't easy, but the more regularly you study, the better your
brain will get at accepting that this is study time – and it's
better to put energy into study than into protesting about it.

Stay Well-Fuelled

If you're not physically comfortable, concentrating on what
you're trying to learn is pretty much impossible.

The key is to set yourself up before you start. Grab a snack
and a bottle of water or a cuppa. Pop to the loo. Get everything you need in one place.

Turn off your phone. Put your music on, if you study with
music in the background. Get everything as perfect as you
can, as quickly as you can.

The last thing you want is to get halfway through a difficult
problem and realise you're ravenous or parched with thirst,
so you have to stop and refresh yourself. Getting back into the
zone after that is very difficult. The more you set yourself up
so that you don't have an excuse to stop studying, the more
likely you are to study well.

Don't go hungry in the exam, either! Find out if you're allowed to take in a snack and a drink; if not, grab a bite to eat and drink just beforehand.

Jump Around

If you've ever tried to fix a computer, you know that the first thing to try when things aren't working is to turn it off and on again.

Unfortunately, the human brain doesn't have a reset button (although I know a few people who seem to have found an off button). It does have a simple way to get it working again, though: by getting your blood pumping.

If you just don't feel like getting started with studying, stand up and jump up and down for a few seconds. Try it! I'm always amazed at how much a little jumping around can wake me up. You can do whatever you like to get your heart-rate up: if you like running on the spot, or dancing, or doing push-ups, or walking up and down the stairs, fine. The important thing is to say 'I don't want to be Mr or Mrs Procrastinator-Pants any more', get the blood flowing, and get back to work.

Don't do serious exercise without a gentle warm-up. You'll hurt yourself. Don't come running to me with a torn hamstring.

Warm Up Gently

Just as you need to warm up before exercising, so the same warning applies to your studies. Trying to dive straight into the hardest thing you have to study is a one-way route to demoralisation, misery and – worst of all – having to study that bit all over again.

Instead, try to start off your study sessions with a few minutes reviewing topics you find a bit easier.

You're not going to pull a hamstring by studying too hard, too fast, but easing yourself into a session can make the prospect much less daunting.

Chapter 15

Ten Ways To Motivate Yourself To Study

S tudying to pass a numeracy test is hard work. It can be frustrating, and some days you just don't want to. It's perfectly normal not to want to put in the hard hours, thinking that one missed day won't hurt you . . .

But it does. If you want to do really well in your test, you need to get into the habit of studying regularly, even when you don't want to.

To do that, you need to be able to make your own motivation – by convincing yourself and your friends to support you in your studies, and by making them as enjoyable as possible.

Remember Why You're Studying

If you've ever watched a detective show or read a crime novel, you'll have experienced a detective saying something like, 'He couldn't have done it – he had no motive.' Sometimes they're wrong about the suspect not having a motive, but they're almost always right about the other part: if you don't have a reason for doing something, you don't do it.

'Because' is one of your mind's favourite words. If you tell yourself 'I have to study', your mind usually resists. On the other hand, if you tell yourself 'I want to study because I need to pass the test for this amazing new job', you'll most likely find your mind saying 'That sounds like a great idea, how can I help?'

Find a picture of what you want to be able to do once you've passed your numeracy exam. If you're studying to be a teacher, find a photo of someone inspiring their students; if you're working towards the armed forces, find a picture of a parachutist or someone getting over an assault course obstacle, or whatever else it is you're aiming for. Put this picture somewhere prominent, near your workspace, and take inspiration from it.

Make Your Workspace Wonderful

Few things are more depressing than working in an environment that's untidy, unwelcoming and unpleasant. Even if you *can* bring yourself to sit down and hit the books there, there's always a niggling thought that things are somehow out of order.

I know I sound like your mum, but here's a quick checklist of things you can do to make your workspace somewhere you're happy to be:

✔ **Keep it tidy.** Spend a few moments before the start or at the end of each study session getting your ducks in a row – put your loose notes in a folder, make sure your pens and pencils are arranged neatly and that your desk is clear.

✔ **Make it pretty.** I like to keep photos and postcards around my desk – it makes me feel like my friends are cheering me on as I work.

✔ **Make it comfortable.** Adjust your chair so it's the right height for you – use cushions if they help. It's hard to study with a sore back! Make sure the temperature is good and that you have enough light to read comfortably.

- ✔ **Minimise distractions.** Unless I'm researching, I turn off the Internet while I'm working at the computer. I also crank up some tunes on my nice noise-reducing headphones so I can disappear into my own little world.

- ✔ **Keep supplies handy.** Make sure you have your beverage of choice and a healthy snack available when you're studying – it really reduces the temptation to get up and fix a cup of tea or grab a sandwich if you have a glass of water and some apples on your desk.

Cross Off the Days

When Jerry Seinfeld was starting his career as a comedian, he realised that the only way he could produce quality material was by writing something every day.

He bought a calendar, and whenever he wrote something, he put a big cross over the day, so he could see how he was doing. After a while, he noticed that the crosses were forming an attractive chain on the calendar. This motivated him even more, because now he was thinking 'If I don't write today, I'll break my beautiful chain and have to start from day one again.'

It's the same kind of idea as the signs in dangerous workplaces that say '15 days since the last accident'. Breaking records is its own motivation!

Put a calendar somewhere near where you work – and every day you study for your numeracy test, cross off a day. See how many days you can manage in a row!

A calendar is also a good motivator when you put a big circle around the date of your exam. This works in two ways: it reminds you how close you're getting and encourages you to put in the work, but it also reminds you how soon you'll be finished – how soon you'll be able to celebrate your success and get on with your career or education.

Treat Yourself

When you receive a reward for doing something, you tend to carry on doing the thing that earned the reward.

So, set yourself up for small rewards along the way – I treat myself to a slice of carrot cake when I do something I'm proud of, but you might prefer a shopping trip, a night out, a massage, an evening off or a movie . . . really, anything you enjoy doing as a special treat.

If you say to yourself 'I've earned this slice of delicious carrot cake by studying extra hard', your brain begins to associate studying with the reward more quickly – and helps encourage you to do the work.

Find a Study Buddy

You're much more likely to do something fun than something boring. That's why most people watch comedy DVDs within days of them arriving, but serious documentaries sit unwatched for days, weeks (or forever).

Studying is much more fun in company. It's also much more effective, for several reasons:

- **Two heads are better than one.** If your friend understands a topic and you find it gibberish, your friend can explain it to you and vice-versa.

- **Your brain works differently.** Trying to *explain* something is a very different process than trying to *understand* – you end up making new connections and reinforcing the things you know.

- **You get some accountability.** If you know you have a study date on Thursday, you're more likely to put the work in so you don't show yourself up in front of your friend.

- **Most things are more fun with two or more people.** Humans are social animals.

If you're taking lessons, try talking to someone in your class who looks friendly – the chances are, they're just as eager to do well as you are.

Get Your Friends and Family Onside

It's hard to do anything worthwhile without support. I know I wouldn't have been able to get through my exams without knowing my parents wanted me to do my best and would do all they could to help me succeed.

It's much easier to do well when people are cheering you on, so make sure your family and friends know that doing well in maths is important to you. If your friends don't respect that, find better friends.

Here are some things you can ask your friends and family to do to help you:

- ✔ **Leave you in peace when you're studying.** It's hard enough to study when you don't have distractions, so it's a good idea to set boundaries and ask your family or flatmates not to disturb you unless the house is on fire. Whatever it is they need you for can wait until you've finished studying.

- ✔ **Nag you to study when you're not doing enough.** It doesn't have to be a nasty kind of nagging – you can just encourage your friends and family to ask you how things are going once in a while and hold you to account.

- ✔ **Help test you on the things you want to learn.** Get your friends and family to quiz you on the things you want to learn – it's a great way for them to feel involved in your studies. See Chapter 2 for tips on using flashcards.

- ✔ **Support and encourage you.** It feels a bit weird asking people to encourage you, but all the same, it's a great boost to hear people close to you saying 'I'm proud of you' or 'You're doing really well' – even if you asked them to.

Make sure your loved ones know how important it is to you to do well in the test – and what support you need from them.

Set a Timer

As I write this, I have a small kitchen timer in the shape of a tomato ticking on my desk. It's a constant reminder that I'm supposed to be working, rather than playing Angry Birds or thinking about interesting sums, or going for a nice walk in the park with a cup of coffee.

So, while it's ticking, I write. When it rings (obnoxiously loudly), I get to take a break for a few minutes before I set it going again.

It works just as well for studying as it does for writing. I've always found that splitting up an hour of study into two 25-minute sessions with a 10-minute break in between helps me focus much better than trying to work for an hour straight – but you can experiment! Try 10 minute bursts, 20 minute challenges, or longer if you have a great attention span.

Knowing that you have a pause coming up in a few minutes can really concentrate your mind.

Remember it's not Forever

Obviously, I hope that this book gives you a thirst for discovering more about maths and inspires you to go further with your mathematical studies, but I understand that you probably just want to get this qualification out of the way and get on with your career, perhaps never to look at another sum again.

If that's the case, you can motivate yourself by saying, 'If I study my socks off, I'll pass the test and I'll never have to do another maths test *ever again*!' Just think about that for a minute – freedom from the chains of maths! Getting away from the tyranny of times tables! No more furrowing your brow while you try to remember what the interquartile range is!

So, remember that it's not forever – once you've passed, you get to stop. You just need to make sure you pass.

Give Yourself a Good Name

By giving yourself a good name, I don't mean call yourself 'Thraxador The Magnificent' or anything daft like that (although that would be a *fantastic* name). Instead, giving yourself a good name is about the way you think about yourself. If you can tell yourself 'I'm the kind of student who studies for half an hour a day, no matter what', you're more likely to do the work than if you say things like 'I can never seem to find the time to study.'

I believe that you can do maths, whether you believe it or not. I get really angry when I hear that a student's teacher has told them they have no aptitude for maths or will never be good at it – for one thing, it's simply not true (I've taken many such students from failing to excelling) and for another, I can't think of anything more discouraging to hear.

So, even if some idiot has told you you'll never be any good at maths, ignore them. They're wrong. Listen to me, instead, and tell yourself 'I might not know all I need to yet, but if I keep up the good work, I'll get there in the end.' Give yourself a good reputation to live up to and you'll find it much easier to keep on track.

If you find yourself thinking discouraging thoughts, tell yourself off and put it right by saying, 'Hang on – that's not true. I *do* make time to study. In fact, I'll make time today. That'll show me!'

Think of the Outcome

Every summer, every newspaper in the country carries at least one picture of excited students with their exam results. Smiling faces, jumping for joy because they've got the grades they wanted, these shiny happy people can go on and pursue the course or career they wanted to.

If you drive, you probably remember passing your driving test. Maybe you cut up, threw away or burned your L-plates in happiness. Remember how good it felt to get over that hurdle?

Take a moment to stop and think about what you'll be able to do after you've passed your numeracy exam. How will you react? What will you do to treat yourself? Daydream away, and make the thought as vivid as you can – then, whenever you feel your motivation slipping away, remind yourself of the dream. You'll feel like it's worthwhile straight away.

I'd be very upset if you throw this book away or set fire to it after you pass your numeracy test, even if it would lead to more sales.

Chapter 16

Ten Tips For Tackling Tough Test Questions

*T*he four things you need to do if you want to do well in an exam are:

✔ Prepare properly

✔ Stay calm

✔ Manage your time

✔ Answer the questions

They're all important, but the fourth item is the one that everything depends on: if you can correctly answer the questions you're asked, you'll do well.

The trouble is, if you're anything like me, you sometimes look at a question and just sigh: it looks too difficult or too complicated or just plain unfamiliar. Over the years, I've picked up a lot of ideas about how to tackle questions that look impossible at first glance – and in this chapter, I share some of these ideas with you.

Examiners aren't going to ask you anything impossible. Use these strategies and tactics in this chapter and you should find yourself starting to make headway on questions you didn't think you could do.

Read the Question

Here's a brutal fact: if you don't understand what the question is asking for or what information you've been given, you can think as hard as you like and still not end up with the right answer.

Making sure you read the question *carefully* is the antidote to this. Rushing through the question and getting cracking on your work as quickly as possible is really tempting, especially when you don't have much time to play with. However, the proverb 'more haste, less speed' applies here – you may save yourself a few seconds by rushing, but it makes it much more likely that you'll drop the mark. And that may be the difference between passing and having to retake the test.

If you're doing an exam where you have a physical paper rather than a computer screen, read the question and underline all of the information you think is relevant and all of the words that tell you what you're looking for. Take your time – it's very easy to miss the word 'not' that completely changes the meaning of the question if you try to read too fast.

If you're working on a computer, you'll probably get kicked out if you try to underline things on the screen, and it's unlikely to help much. Instead, just write down the details you think are most important. Sometimes simply doing this makes the answer obvious and saves you a huge amount of head-scratching.

Eliminate Wrong Answers

One of the most useful phrases in maths is 'It can't *possibly* be that!' This is a phrase you can use in many multiple-choice exams to reduce the number of possible answers to a question.

Getting rid of wrong answers isn't necessarily easy – you do need to read the question carefully and understand roughly what's going on – but it can dramatically improve your chances of getting the right answer.

For example, if your question involves scaling a recipe to serve more people and asks how much of an ingredient you need for the new recipe, you know straight away that you're looking for a bigger number than you had to begin with – you can throw out any numbers that are smaller straight away.

You can dramatically improve your chances of picking the right answer by just taking a few seconds to think about what the right answer has to look like so you can out any answers that are definitely wrong.

Think of Similar Problems

One of the beautiful things about maths is that you can often apply the same approach to questions that seem completely unrelated – if you didn't know better, would you have thought you could use the same sums to convert miles to kilometres that you use to work out percentages? (See Chapter 5 to find out how.)

Knowing that seemingly different kinds of problems often have similar solutions gives you a chance to draw analogies between questions when you feel stuck. You may be comfortable working out percentage increases but see a question with a fractional increase that you don't remember doing – rather than say 'I don't know how to do that', you could say, 'I wonder if it works the same way as the per cent problem?' . . . and you'd be right!

When you're faced with a question you don't recognise, think about what it reminds you of. More often than not, you can use the same maths for it – and it's always better to do something plausible than to guess.

Try the Answers

In a multiple-choice exam, working backwards from the answers you're given is sometimes easier than doing the sum 'properly'. It's a slightly sneaky trick, but that's okay – the important thing in an exam is to get the right answer whatever way you can.

This is particularly effective if you've already thrown out some answers that are obviously wrong so, rather than having to check five answers to see if they make sense, you may only have to consider two or three.

With some sums, you can get the right answer by doing the opposite – imagine the question asks you to work out 546 ÷ 7 and suggests the answers 68, 74, 78 and 83. If you prefer multiplying to dividing, you might try multiplying each answer by 7 to see which one gives 546.

With some kinds of questions (particularly the 'true/false' type), working backwards from the answer is the only way you can get the right answer.

If it's not stated so obviously, the question you have to ask is, 'Does this answer fully satisfy what the question wanted?' Only one option should answer the question completely.

Explain the Question to Yourself

You can't really talk aloud in an exam, even to yourself, but you can talk through the question in your head.

Think things that start with:

- ✔ I'm trying to find out . . .
- ✔ I know . . .
- ✔ I could figure this out if I knew . . .
- ✔ Another way to say this is . . .
- ✔ I can work out . . .

Imagine you're explaining your problem to a friend who doesn't know anything about maths. What's the simplest way you can state the question? What questions would they ask you?

Use a Smart Estimate

The words 'estimate' and 'guess' are sometimes used interchangeably, but they're actually two different things: a guess is an answer you pick out of the air, while an estimate is a very rough answer you work out. You guess which numbers are going to come up in the lottery, but you estimate how big the jackpot might be.

In an exam context, guessing an answer is usually saying 'eeny meeny miney mo' and writing down the answer you land on. An estimate involves reading the question, and instead of doing all of the calculations exactly, doing them very roughly – perhaps rounding all of the numbers to one significant figure – to get a rough idea of what the answer ought to be.

If you had to work out 693 ÷ 11, you could find a good estimate by working out 700 ÷ 10, giving you 70. (The actual answer is 63, so the estimate is pretty close). If you'd worked out the real answer to be, say, 6 or 600, you'd have a pretty good idea that something had gone wrong.

The more you can come up with ways to estimate your work, the more confident you'll be in your answers.

Come Back to it Later

Probably the greatest time management tip I can give you is 'don't spend too long on a question you find really hard to answer'. There's nothing (much) worse in an exam than finding that the last few questions look fairly easy, but you don't have time to answer them because you spent five minutes longer than you should have on an earlier question.

I know: it's hard to abandon a question after you've put time into it. The thing to do is to tell yourself, 'I'll come back to it later if I have time.' That way, you get the best of both worlds: you make sure you have time for all the easy questions, and – if you have time at the end – you get to attack the tricky, time-consuming question again, and hopefully get it right.

Break it Down into Smaller Parts

The way to eat an elephant (apparently) is one bite at a time.

A similar strategy works when you're attacking an intimidatingly long exam question: rather than trying to tackle the whole thing at once, break it down into smaller, more manageable parts. This kind of thinking can break a big, difficult question into three or four smaller, easier questions that you can sail through.

The trick is to figure out what information you need for the last part of the question – if you have to compare the means of two sets of data, you're probably going to need to work at least one of them out. Once you know what you need to find, think about what information you need to work that out – with the mean example, you need the total and how many items there are.

Keep working backwards until you get to information you know or can work out easily, and you'll end up with a plan for working through the question.

Guess Wildly

If time's running out and you've got a minute to answer the last five multiple-choice questions, you don't really have time to read the questions, let alone work out the answers. In this situation you have two possible approaches:

- ✓ Miss out the questions and get a guaranteed zero for those questions.
- ✓ Guess the answers and maybe pick up a few points.

Guess which of these two approaches I recommend? The clue's in the heading. Numeracy tests usually aren't negatively marked, so you don't lose points for giving a wrong answer. If you guess when you don't have time or are genuinely stuck, the worst that can happen is that you score no marks for that question.

Make guessing a last resort – and check first to see whether you can eliminate any of the answers. Always check at the start that you won't be negatively marked for incorrect answers.

Chapter 17

Ten Ways To Make Your Exam Easier

*A*lmost nobody likes exams. They're stressful situations where you can feel like your entire career is on the line – and it all comes down to whether you can jump through the hoops set for you.

However, you can take steps to prepare yourself thoroughly to reduce the stress and tackle your exam with confidence. All you need to do is know what you're up against and have a plan for dealing with it.

Knowing Your Enemy

When things are unfamiliar, they're frightening. The best way to stop exams from intimidating you is to get familiar with what the papers look like, what kinds of questions they ask and how your particular test tends to word them.

The sample tests in Chapters 9–13 are a good starting point, but you can also check out the website for the test you're taking – the more knowledge you have of what's ahead, the easier you'll find it.

Working through past papers also helps you identify your strengths and weaknesses and lets you know how well you're doing.

Practising the Hard Parts

Sometimes, when I'm working with a student, the lightbulb suddenly goes on. Their eyes open wide, they say 'Oh! This is *easy*!' and we both feel fantastic.

It can happen at any time, often when you're not directly working on maths – I've had flashes of inspiration come to me in my sleep, in the shower and even in an exam (that one was just a few hours too late for me to do anything about it, though). It's as if some invisible elves show up, whisper a clear explanation and it all makes sense.

The thing is, this kind of inspiration only comes when you've been working on something difficult and haven't come up with an answer. If you make a habit of spending a few minutes of each study session looking at something you don't quite get, you make it much more likely that the inspiration elves will pay you a visit.

Practising the Easy Parts

I can't think of many things more frustrating than sitting in an exam, looking at a question and thinking 'I used to know this, but I can't quite remember it.'

The only way to avoid it – and there's no cast-iron guarantee, even here – is to make sure you practise the things you already know. I recommend doing this at the start of a study session, like a warm-up, to give you a chance to ease in gently and give you a nice confidence boost as well! A good way to practise the easy parts is to make and work through flash cards, as I describe in Chapter 3.

Keeping Your Energy Up

Maths is hard enough when you're feeling 100 per cent. Don't make it any harder than it needs to be by being the all-nighter zombie who falls asleep as soon as your head hits the desk. When you're studying, and particularly in the exam, you want to make sure you're comfortable and well rested.

Here are some things to concentrate on:

- ✓ **Sleep well.** Make sure you get a good night's sleep before the exam. Chill out the night before, watch a movie or do something else relaxing, and get to bed at a reasonable time.

- ✓ **Eat properly.** Get up in plenty of time to have a proper breakfast. Your body needs to be fuelled to work well. (It's also really distracting, for you and everyone else, if your stomach is rumbling through the exam!)

- ✓ **Dress appropriately.** Some people think you should dress smartly for an exam, as if you're going for an interview. (It may be that your numeracy test is part of an interview . . . in which case, definitely scrub up.) Personally, I'm firmly in the 'dress comfortably' camp – the more at home you feel in the exam hall, the more relaxed you'll be and the better you'll do. If you have a lucky hat or lucky socks, wear them, too!

Accentuating the Positive

Think about the people you like; the people you respond to the best. When they see you, do they say 'You're looking well!' or do they say 'Look what the cat dragged in?'

Speaking for myself, when someone is nice to me, I tend to be more inclined to do what they ask. This also translates to the way I talk to myself: when I tell myself 'I'm a hard–working problem–solving *machine!*' I get a lot more done than when I call myself a lazy good-for-nothing.

Give yourself a good inner reputation to live up to and you'll find it much easier to motivate yourself to study – and to feel confident when you're sitting the paper.

Be kind to yourself when you make mistakes or don't understand something. It sounds daft, but if you look at a problem and say 'I don't see how to do this yet, but let me think about it', you're much more likely to solve it than if you say 'I don't understand this, I must be stupid.'

You're not stupid. I think you're smart and your hard work is going to pay off! So there.

Using the Last Few Minutes

Most people spend the last few minutes before an exam biting their nails and worrying about whether they've done enough revision. This a desperately unproductive way to use the time. Instead of worrying, here are a few things you can do instead:

- **Talk yourself up.** Remind yourself how hard you've worked and how good you'll feel when you do well.

- **Try to relax.** Roll your shoulders to try to release some tension, then spend a few moments making sure you're standing or sitting up straight and breathing deeply (see Chapter 14 for some deep breathing exercises).

- **Jump up and down.** Getting your blood pumping is a great way to burn some of that nervous energy and help your brain to work a bit better.

Having a Ritual

If you've ever watched an All Blacks rugby match, you'll have seen the team performing the haka before the game. The haka is a traditional Maori war dance that lays down a challenge to their opponents. It also sets up the players nicely for the game – they know that the natural order of things is that you do the haka and then you play great rugby.

I'm not suggesting you do the haka before you start your exam – unless you don't mind some *very* odd looks – but having some sort of ritual that you go through at the start of an exam can really take some of the worry away.

For example, you might decide that when you sit down, the first thing you'll do is stretch out your arms, take a deep breath and quietly recite your seven times table. The choice is yours – pick something that helps get you in the frame of mind to ace the exam.

Read the Paper First

If you possibly can, take a few minutes at the start of the exam to flick through the questions to get an idea of what's coming up.

Take particular note if you think any questions might be a struggle – this gives your brain a chance to work on them in the background while you're focussed on other problems.

It also stops you from worrying about what might come up later in the paper – if you've skimmed through and not seen any monsters, you know you're on track; and if there are monsters, you're prepared for them!

Managing Your Time

It's very easy to lose track of time in an exam, especially if you have a question you're *sure* you can do but is taking forever. That's dangerous, because time is the one thing you don't have very much of in a numeracy test.

You need to know how long you have to spend on each question – depending on the exam, it's usually about a minute. Once you know that, you can keep track of how you're doing – if you're running behind, it's time to pick up the pace a bit.

It takes some discipline to say 'This question is taking too long, I'll come back to it at the end if I have the time,' but you don't want to find that you've missed three easy questions because you were so focussed on one tricky one!

In paper tests, put a big star next to the question you want to come back to. On a computer test, you can normally click a button to 'flag' any questions you'd like to revisit.

If you get to the end of the exam early, that's great! Don't just sit there counting the ceiling tiles, though – use the minutes you have at the end to go back and check your work. Do your answers all make sense? Was there a question you weren't sure about? Take another look at your answers.

Checking Your Work and Putting it Right

Everyone makes mistakes under pressure. If you have a little (or a lot of) time left at the end of the exam, you can use it to go back and see if you have any glaring errors.

Find any answers you're not confident about and see if you can decide whether they're correct. If they're not, see if you can come up with a better answer.

Giving your work even a cursory check can save you a few marks – which may be the difference between getting the job and not!

Index

Notes

Notes

Notes

Notes